Financial Innovation and Monetary Policy

Financial Innovation and Monetary Policy: Asia and the West

Proceedings of the Second International Conference
held by the Institute for Monetary and Economic Studies
of the Bank of Japan

edited by Yoshio Suzuki and Hiroshi Yomo

UNIVERSITY OF TOKYO PRESS

Printed in Japan

ISBN 4–13–047029–9/UTP 47298
ISBN 0–86008–389–6

Contents

Foreword

This book is the final outcome of the Second International Conference organized and sponsored by the Institute for Monetary and Economic Studies of the Bank of Japan. The Conference was titled "Financial Innovation and Monetary Policy: Asia and the West," and was held on 29–31 May, 1985. We were very much honored by the presence of the numerous distinguished economists who assembled at our conference: many were from our counterpart central banks, others from international organizations or from academic communities around the world. We feel particularly indebted to the Honorary Advisors of the Institute, Professors Milton Friedman and James Tobin, who have guided its activities since its establishment in 1982, and who presented valuable keynote speeches at the Conference.

The financial systems of a number of countries have been undergoing dramatic changes over the past decade. The changes have been so significant and unprecedented that they might be labeled truly historic.

The speed and magnitude of the changes and the particular forms that innovations have taken vary from country to country, reflecting their social and economic conditions. Some of the innovations are the result of the marked progress in computer and communications technology in recent years. However, in many cases innovations have been interpreted as market reactions to the constraints posed by obsolescent regulations. There is no doubt that the traditional financial system, a product of the bitter experiences of the interwar years and the subsequent postwar reconstruction period, contributed to maintaining financial stability and growth under the circumstances during those years. However, many market participants argue—and to a certain extent I agree—that it has increasingly become a straitjacket that has prevented financial markets from becoming more efficient and equitable. The factors that have often been cited as background to innovative developments include the high and volatile interest rates, the flare-ups of inflation after the two oil shocks, and growing government deficits. Another important factor is the enormous increase in capital movements beyond national boundaries under the flexible exchange rate system.

We now see a number of old regulations and restrictions being eroded by market realities, and in many countries the authorities have either endorsed such developments or promoted them by taking accommodating steps. Most notable among these accommodations are the deregulation of interest rates on deposits and the relaxation of restrictions on the scope of operations of banks and other financial institutions.

Innovation in itself has no doubt been an engine of growth and prosperity for mankind; and financial innovation is certainly no exception. The efficiency not only of the financial sector but also of the economy as a whole can be increased when competition among economic agents is enhanced. However, the benefits of financial innovation have to be weighed against its costs. It is commonly thought that financial innovation has added to the uncertainty in the relationship between monetary variables and economic activity. One question that has often been raised concerns the desirability and the methodology of controlling monetary aggregates as an intermediate target when the demarcation between traditional money and other financial instruments becomes increasingly blurred. Another question concerns the variety of risks associated with the financial innovation process, not only for the management of a financial institution but also for the financial system as a whole. Changes in the set of risks may call for a re-examination of the role and responsibilities of bank supervisors, and of the adequacy of the existing regulatory framework, in order to prevent financial disorder.

The phenomena of innovation and the accompanying problems are certainly not limited to countries with developed financial markets. In this highly integrated world economy, the impact of any development in one country is quickly transmitted to others, and no country, however shielded, can escape from that influence. Most countries in Asia, now in the process of rapid industrialization, have a special incentive of their own for undertaking financial innovations which would help mobilize domestic resources and make full use of foreign capital inflows.

Encouraging efficiency and at the same time maintaining financial order and strengthening the effectiveness of monetary control is by no means an easy task. It is here that closer collaboration between policy-makers and academic economists is essential. I believe that this meeting succeeded in stimulating research on issues concerning financial innovation and monetary policy, and I hope that the exchange of views that took place here among all the participants contributed to a more clear-cut perspective on the financial system in the future, and thus to progress in attaining our common goal—maintaining price stability along with sustainable economic growth.

SATOSHI SUMITA
Governor
Bank of Japan

Financial Innovation and Monetary Policy

Financial Innovation and Monetary Policy in Asia and the West: An Introductory Note

Yoshio Suzuki

The Institute for Monetary and Economic Studies of the Bank of Japan arranges an international conference once every two years with a view to promoting mutual understanding between economists in the academic profession and those in central banks and international organizations. The second of these conferences was held in Tokyo on May 29–31, 1985, and was entitled "Financial Innovation and Monetary Policy: Asia and the West."[1] Economists affiliated with academic institutions, central banks, and international organizations came from Asia, Oceania, Europe, and North America to attend the meeting.[2]

It was the strong desire of the organizers of this conference to foster an exchange of views and experience between academics and policymakers on this important topic. As the subtitle reveals, we thought that Tokyo, as a geographical crossroads between Asia and the West, would provide an excellent forum for participants from these two parts of the world to learn more about and from each other.

The conference consisted of five sessions. The first session started with opening remarks by Governor Sumita of the Bank of Japan. This was followed by the two keynote addresses of the Honorary Advisors of the Institute, Professors Friedman (Hoover Institution) and Tobin

[1] In planning and organizing the present conference, we benefited from the advice of many individuals. In particular, I am greatly indebted to Professors Milton Friedman and James Tobin, Honorary Advisors of the Institute, for their suggestions about the organization of the conference, their stimulating keynote speeches, and the leadership they provided during the conference. My special thanks go to all participants who presented insightful papers or made valuable remarks, and also to Professor Jao, who was not able to attend the meeting but has kindly submitted his comments. Finally, I have to thank the staff members of the Bank of Japan, particularly those in the Institute, for their devoted efforts in organizing this conference.

[2] See the list of participants at the end of this volume.

(Yale University). Session Two examined the background and causes of the ongoing process of financial innovation, in both developed countries and Asian developing countries. The third session dealt with more normative aspects of the problem, such as the desirability of different processes of deregulation and the adequacy of measures to preserve financial stability in a changing environment. Session Four was devoted to discussions on the implications of financial innovation for monetary policy. The final, and summary, session focused on those issues which had emerged as most important in the preceding sessions.

The organizers did not seek a firm and general consensus. Rather, it was hoped that this conference would serve to crystallize differences of views. Nevertheless, I came out of the meeting with the following impressions.

First, and most important, the tempo and the predictability of the process of financial innovation seems to be very dependent on the success of macroeconomic policy. As long as stable economic growth can be maintained without a surge of inflation, the process of financial innovation will tend to be gradual. In this case, the problems of the stability of the financial system and the implementation of monetary policy will remain manageable for the monetary authorities. The other side of the coin is equally obvious. If policy fails to maintain economic stability and to curb inflation, the pace of financial innovation will increase and become less predictable, making it extremely difficult for policymakers to manage.

Second, the discussion succeeded to a certain extent in distinguishing those factors which were common to financial innovation in many countries from those which were more specific to individual economies. Prominent examples of common catalysts of financial innovation were (i) technical progress, particularly in the computer and telecommunication fields and (ii) inflation in the United States, which not only caused financial innovation at home but also triggered innovation and deregulation internationally through the indirect impact of high and volatile U.S. dollar interest and exchange rates in the disinflationary phase. Despite these common forces, the process of financial innovation and deregulation differed among countries, depending in particular on (i) the maturity of the financial markets, (ii) the previous regulatory framework, and (iii) the openness of the economy.

Third, there was no simple recipe for maintaining stability in the financial system during a phase of financial innovation. We may have to cope with this problem by establishing a combination of various safety networks. It did, however, seem clear that market discipline should play an even more important role in the new system, and that no avenue that may foster this discipline should be left unexamined.

Last, my sense of the need for, and the difficulty involved in, intensive dialogue between academics and policymakers from different parts of the world was strongly reinforced. The notable differences in the experiences of the various participants underline the need for greater common knowledge. This is made imperative by our common tasks of maintaining economic stability and promoting efficiency, both of which can only be fulfilled by learning from the successes and failures of others and making full use of ideas developed elsewhere.

Since the various topics considered in the conference were interrelated, similar issues arose in various sessions. In what follows, I have tried to survey the exchange of views according to topic, and not necessarily by session.

Background and Causes of Financial Innovation

Two of the papers presented at the Conference dealt with the background of financial innovation; one focused on developed countries, the other on developing Asian economies.

Financial Innovation in Major Developed Countries

Yumoto et al. (Bank of Japan) in their paper classified the various financial innovations in major industrial countries into two broad groups, according to their common characteristics. The first group encompassed innovations which resulted from, or sought to reduce, the shadow cost of regulatory constraints (Type 1). The other category referred to innovations which, independent of regulatory constraints, sought to reduce physical transactions costs or to improve allocation of risk (Type 2). The authors then reviewed recent studies of the impact of financial innovation on the management of banks and the banking system. Their conclusion was that the negative impact on safety and soundness of bank management of financial innovation may not be very large. However, so-called systemic risk may increase, calling for a more important role for the central bank as a monitor of bank management and interbank markets, and also as a lender of last resort.

There was a lively discussion on the adequacy of the classification employed in the Yumoto paper, and many alternative criteria were proposed. In Hall's (Stanford University) view, financial deregulation was more important than deregulation in other industries, only because it may affect the demand for money and therefore the aggregate price level. He therefore insisted that a more useful taxonomy would classify a particular financial innovation according to the extent to which it affected the demand for money—or, more precisely, the monetary base. Milton Friedman agreed with Hall that the impact on the demand for money was the most important aspect, but he thought that this was not sufficient. For example, the creation of a futures market may or may not affect the demand for money, but would improve the allocation of risk. He encouraged exploring arrangements which would minimize the adverse effect of unanticipated monetary shocks.

Crockett (International Monetary Fund) suggested that Type 1 innovations, or innovations which were responses to regulation, should be divided further into two groups: desirable ones which provide a second-best solution where The optimal solution was hindered by regulation, and undesirable ones which would only provoke a re-regulatory reaction by the authorities.

In a related vein, Lambert (National Bank of Belgium) observed that it might be useful to distinguish regulations which were market-oriented (for example, gearing ratio controls and balance sheet consolidation requirements) from those that were non-market-oriented. She believed that the former type of regulation would not necessarily become obsolete in the process of financial innovation.

Regarding the causes of financial innovation, there seemed to be a broad consensus that (i) progress in technology in general and in information technology in particular, (ii) rapid inflation with consequent high and volatile interest rates, and (iii) growing international financial integration were the main driving forces of financial innovation. However, there were differences of view about the relative importance of these factors. Korteweg (Bank of the Netherlands), citing the experience of his own country, commented that if the rate of inflation was kept reasonably low, and if regulations on bank activities were not too rigid, innovations would be kept within bounds that would neither harm the stability of the financial system nor seriously reduce the effectiveness of monetary policy. Cargill (University of Nevada at Reno), however, believed that inflation, although definitely important, should not be overemphasized as a catalyst of innovation. In the U.S. case, the complexity of the regulatory framework played an important role. It should also be noted that financial innovation in Japan made significant progress despite the fact that the rate of inflation has been kept very low since 1975.

Where opinions differed was about the role of the government. Yumoto et al. argued in their paper that even where it looked as if innovation had been induced by changes in government rules, in most cases it was merely a reflection of market forces and should therefore be understood as a result of private motives. This view was supported by Cargill. McClam (Bank for International Settlements), however, called attention to the coincidence of the structural change in financial flows and growing government deficits that had been observed in many countries. He was inclined to stress the important causal role of government deficits in financial innovation for several reasons: governments were themselves innovators in their own right and developed novel instruments; the huge government borrowing needs promoted the role of open markets; and government deficits contributed to inflation and thus to high interest rates, which in turn triggered financial innovation.

During the discussion, Friedman underscored the view he presented in his keynote speech, namely that governments played an important role in a negative sense: the failure of governments, evidenced particularly in the pattern of inflation, was a fundamental cause of the current process of financial innovation. Rōyama (Osaka University) compared the rigidity of the U.S. authorities, who changed the ceiling rate of Regulation Q only once during the 1970s in spite of two oil shocks and the surge in inflation, with the rather flexible attitude of their Japanese counterparts, who revised interest rate ceilings and the content of administration guidance quite frequently during the same period. He wondered whether this remarkable difference in policy attitudes should not have had a significant impact on the difference in the process of financial innovation in these two countries. Raymond (Bank of France), citing recent French experience with capital gains taxation, pointed out that changes in tax regulations had often been an important source of innovation and that the role of governments should not be understated.

Financial Deregulation in Asian Developing Countries

In his survey of financial deregulation in seven Asian developing countries, Greenwood (G. T. Management) tried to sort out recent events by means of a pair of two-fold criteria: first, whether the source of influence was domestic or foreign; and second, whether the deregulation affected the pricing of financial activity (interest rate) or other conditions of competitiveness. The main conclusions of Greenwood's study were as follows. First, the most decisive influence came from outside the economy in question. In particular, increased interest rate volatility abroad played an important role in promoting financial innovation in many of the countries considered in his paper. Second, governments were generally quite reluctant to remove administrative obstacles to free financial markets, mainly because they favored a particular pattern of resource allocation. However, where governments tried to use the financial structure for allocative goals, the efficiency of the economy was jeopardized. Third, foreign exchange control still represented the most important impediment to the process of financial innovation in many countries.

Several participants from Asia reacted to Greenwood's analysis by explaining the situation in their own countries.

According to Ganjarerndee (Bank of Thailand), the Thai monetary authorities recently increased the frequency with which regulatory ceilings on both deposit and lending rates are changed. This was in reaction to the growing share of non-bank financial companies and to the fluctuation of dollar interest rates. The strength of the dollar had also encouraged more flexible adjustment of the Baht exchange rate, which had been linked to the U.S. dollar in a rather rigid way. Kim (Bank of Korea) agreed in principle with the survey, but would have preferred a greater emphasis on the institutional structure of Korea. One major obstacle to deregulation in Korea was the large difference between organized and unorganized markets, especially the wide gap in the interest rates prevailing in these two markets. Interest rates in the organized market were kept low in order to support the development of the fragile Korean industry. As a radical deregulation involves the risk of raising interest rates rapidly in the organized market, a gradual deregulation has been pursued by introducing several new financial instruments such as CPs and CDs that bear interest rates higher than the existing assets in the organized market. Kim added that the decline in the inflation rate in recent years, which resulted in positive real interest rates in the organized market, helped to reduce the gap, thus providing a more favorable environment for further deregulation. Sabirin (Bank of Indonesia) explained that the process of financial innovation had accelerated in his country in the last few years due to a fall in oil revenues. Deregulation had already been initiated in 1966, but the real need to promote this trend was not fully recognized as long as oil revenue was increasing and a sufficient inflow of funds was secured. As oil revenue plummeted in 1982, the necessity of mobilizing domestic resources led to the introduction of a drastic liberalization program.

Although his country was not directly discussed in Greenwood's paper, Zhou Lin (People's Bank of China) stated that his bank had recently begun functioning as a real central bank, which he considered a major financial innovation. As this indicated, the problems facing the Chinese monetary authorities were rather different from those of other countries represented at the Conference: the most important question for them concerned what shape a financial market should take in a Socialist planning economy which was promoting modernization and rapidly opening its doors to the rest of the world.

Impact of Financial Innovation on the Stability of the Financial System, and Optimal Reactions

A second set of issues concerned the prudential and normative aspects of financial innovation and deregulation. How seriously does the ongoing process of financial innovation affect the stability of the system? What could and should be done to face these problems? Two papers dealt with this problem, one from a domestic angle and the other from an international perspective.

100 Percent Backing on Transaction Balance by Low Risk Liquid Assets

According to Pierce (University of California at Berkeley), the salient features of the recent U.S. financial market were the fading of differences between the activities of banks and other financial institutions, and the integration of financial and real sectors. He argued in his paper that such phenomena suggested a central role in the financial system of the future for large financial conglomerates. In spite of this, he claimed that what has been called a "revolution" in the regulatory structure had, in reality, not gone beyond the overdue elimination of interest rate ceilings; the particular emphasis on banks has not been changed much since the 1930s, despite the fact that market forces have fundamentally changed the role of banks in the U.S. Pierce emphasized that the regulatory structure cannot be separated from the realities. His prescription, which was very similar to one suggested by Tobin in his keynote speech, was that the distinction between banks and non-banks, which had already been blurred, should be replaced by a separation of the monetary and non-monetary functions of financial institutions. In his view, any institution that offers payment function should be operated through separately-capitalized corporations subject to tight regulation, including restrictions on the assets they acquired. The transaction balances should also be 100 percent guaranteed, irrespective of the size of the balance. Other functions should be operated out of separate institutions, whose liabilities would be neither insured nor guaranteed. They would not be more regulated than a firm in other industries, and the principle of *caveat emptor* should be applied to the financial instruments they offered.

Many central bankers were skeptical about the proposal to isolate the transaction function of financial institutions. Mallyon (Reserve Bank of Australia) pointed out the difficulty of defining "transaction function." In particular, the progress of electronic funds transfer (EFT) will make it extremely difficult to identify institutions which are involved in the payment system since the balance sheet of an institution at the end of a day may not have much to do with its actual function. Mallyon also refuted the idea of segmented supervision of separate functions; on the contrary, he suggested, the increased integration of different financial activities would rather call for looking more at the institutions as a whole. Bisignano (Federal Reserve Bank of California) wondered whether it was sufficient just to maintain the stability of the payment system when it was obvious that the potential collapse of the financial intermediary function would have grave impact on the real economy.

Opinions seemed to be more divided among the academics. Hester (University of Wisconsin) agreed with Pierce's proposal and stressed that the clearing balances should be perfectly protected against frauds and bank failures. But he believed that, to achieve this, the introduction of a new set of regulations would be unavoidable. Hall sympathized with Pierce's idea of providing a very safe deposit to one class of depositors, while deregulating banks and eliminating bail-outs for other types of liabilities. However, he also shared the view of the central bankers that distinguishing between transaction balances and other types of assets would be very difficult at best. Citing as an analogy the notices of caution printed on cigarette packets, he instead proposed restricting advertising so that only those deposits backed 100 percent by government paper would be permitted to be labelled "safe." For other instruments, the public should be warned that they might lose money in some cases. Hall, and also Tobin, further argued that if interest were paid on these safe accounts, most individuals—the class of depositors that really had to do with bank runs—would hold most of their transaction balances and even saving balances in these deposits. This idea was questioned by Crockett. If 100 percent reserves were supplied as just one of the various liabilities on the menu of instruments banks offered, most people would in reality use unregulated assets with higher return for transaction motives. The failure of the latter, however, would affect seriously not only the holders of such accounts but the stability of the whole financial system; taking one step further Hall's cigarette analogy, the warning on the packet would not eliminate the damage to the secondary smokers.

Friedman criticized the idea of 100 percent reserve deposits from a rather different viewpoint. A very similar scheme, the so-called 1934 Chicago Plan, had been proposed by Henry Simons and supported by Irving Fisher and others. This plan, however, was never realized—not because it was a *bad* one, but because it was in the interest of neither banks, nor politicians, nor regulatory authorities. Friedman felt that an important question raised by neither Pierce nor Hall in their papers was the assessment of political and economic interests which would promote a particular system. Hall responded that he believed economists should engage themselves with normative questions of how a system should be organized, and not be confined to positive matters such as how the system can be realized under a set of given initial conditions.

Thygesen (University of Copenhagen) warned of the danger of generalizing too much from the U.S. experience. He underscored the peculiarities of the U.S. financial system such as the existence of an excessive number of deposit-taking institutions, geographical constraints on their activities, and severe restrictions on bank mergers. He wondered if many of the current U.S. problems arose not from too much, but rather from too little and too timid doses of deregulation. He thought that in most other countries banks felt (and indeed were) less vulnerable, and depositors had far fewer reasons to worry about the risk of their transaction balances. Bisignano felt that both Pierce and Bryant were overemphasizing the potential for instability resulting from financial innovation and internationalization. He argued rather that much of the "potential for instability" came from increased government protection via explicit and tacit deposit insurance.

Cooperative Supervision and Regulation of Financial Activity

Bryant's (Brookings Institution) paper dealt with international aspects of the problem. In Bryant's view, international cooperation in regulation and supervision of financial activities had the nature of a collective good, and that as with other collective goods, there existed the danger of insufficient supply. Bryant was especially worried about the general tendency that had been observed in the regulatory frameworks of industrial countries toward "competition in laxity," or discrimination in favor of *international* financial activities in general, and by *non-residents* in particular. He stressed that this tendency was not sustainable in the long run, that sooner or later one of the following two scenarios was bound to occur. First, disintegration of financial markets, either disorderly by capital restrictions of particular nations, or by cooperative measures like the "uniform transfer tax" proposed by Tobin. Although he had some sympathy for this idea, he felt that it was very difficult at best to "push the toothpaste back into the tube." The alternative—and more desirable—scenario would be what he called "enhanced multilateral decision-making" in the field of regulation and supervision of financial activity.

Potter (Organisation for Economic Cooperation and Development) maintained that the internationalization of banking and the increased flow of capital had weakened the pressures to adjust for current account imbalances. However, the recent Latin American experience had clearly illustrated that adjustment pressures could suddenly become very acute once the "creditworthiness limit," which was not clear in advance, was reached. He therefore strongly felt that, to preserve the stability in the international financial system, it was essential that the moves on regulation and taxation proposed by Bryant should be supplemented by "multilateral surveillance" of macroeconomic policies, which should definitely include consultation on the monetary-fiscal policy mix. Bryant basically agreed with this idea but was not certain, even if the political difficulties were assumed away, whether the state of knowledge about the interaction of national policies was sufficient to assure the success of such actions.

An interesting contrast of views was observed on the issue of the separability of the two functions of monetary authorities in an international context: lender of last resort on one hand and supervisor and regulator on the other. While Bryant argued strongly that these two functions were logically inseparable, Pecchioli (Organisation for Economic Cooperation and Development) and McClam pointed out that in many countries these two functions were indeed borne by separate authorities. More importantly, while both functions had to serve the financial order, they were quite different in nature. Whereas the nature of supervision and regulation was to preserve the soundness and safety of banks, the lender-of-last-resort function came into play only after something went wrong. Bryant, on the other hand, stressed that logically the arguments for supervision and regulation on banking stemmed from the moral hazard problem, which in turn was created by the provision of the lender-of-last-resort function and deposit insurance. He understood that the existing international forums that now dealt with this important issue, notably the Cooke committee, were trying for diplomatic reasons to separate the two functions and focus on the supervision part. It seemed inevitable to him that the mandate of these forums would be expanded to include the lender-of-last-resort issue.

Implications for Monetary Policy

The third major topic concerned the implications of financial innovation for monetary policy: whether and how financial innovation affected the conduct of monetary policy; what were the feasible and desirable reactions of the central bank to these impacts. Hall and Hester delivered papers on this topic.

Hall analyzed with the help of an IS-LM model the impact of three types of shocks: (i) financial shocks, (ii) spending shocks, and (iii) price shocks on the economy. He focused on the implications of two hypotheses: first, if interest is paid on reserve assets as a result of financial innovation, the interest rate elasticity of the demand for money will decline. Second, the progress of international financial integration will increase the interest rate elasticity of demand for real expenditure. As a combined result of these two phenomena, Hall argued, spending and price shocks will have little impact on nominal GNP, which would become the most realistic policy target. Financial shocks would still be of serious concern for monetary policy, but would be difficult to predict. If, however, central banks paid near-market yields on reserves, the impact of such financial shocks would be largely absorbed by the excess reserves which financial institutions would hold voluntarily. As a result, a policy of stable growth of monetary base could assure a reasonably stable nominal GNP path.

Hester emphasized in his paper that the progress of financial innovation will pose additional difficulties for the conduct of monetary policy. First, the introduction of new financial instruments will change policy multipliers and may make reliance on accurate models describing the effects of policy actions quite impractical. Second, the widening of financial markets, especially internationally, will require greater policy intervention to achieve a certain policy objective, for example controlling the short-term interest rate. Third, an inevitable outcome of innovations will be a squeeze on interest rate margins of financial intermediaries. The decline in profits of marginal financial institutions, however, may in practice pose an important obstacle for monetary policy, especially if restrictive policies threaten bank soundness and clash with lender-of-last-resort responsibilities. To foster the linkage between the base money and economic activity, Hester proposed the prohibition of overdraft on reserves with the central bank during the day, and advocated real-time reserve requirements. In addition, Hester thought that, in order to keep innovations in rein, it was important for the monetary authorities to maintain real interest rates within a reasonable range, non-negative but not too high.

Predictability of Financial Innovation

In his paper, Hall treated financial innovations as "financial shocks." Cargill, however, thought that this conception was misleading, since shocks referred to unpredictable phenomena. When NOW accounts were introduced in the New England states, it was not very difficult to forecast the nationwide use of such accounts; the process of financial deregulation and innovation in Japan was even less difficult to foresee. Crockett endorsed this view and also pointed out that this would in any case be a transitional problem, since he found no reason to believe that the pace at which innovation had progressed in the last decade would continue. Hall replied that even in cases where the occurrence of innovations was predictable, their implications, for example to changes in base money velocity, were not.

Impacts of Financial Innovation on Monetary Control

Uzawa (University of Tokyo) stressed that innovation in economic theory meant saving production inputs of a good or service. In the case of financial services, innovation may save the input of labor, equipment, etc., but the most important input to be saved was clearly base money. Thus, financial innovation almost by definition reduces the demand for base money and increases velocity. Moreover, if the electronic clearing system becomes widespread, velocity may become nearly infinite, making life very difficult for central bankers. Friedman, however, argued that what was important for monetary stability was not the size of the multiplier but its stability. Financial innovations such as the introduction of NOW accounts and EFT systems may indeed cause a once-and-for-all change in the size of the multiplier or velocity, but this did not mean that the monetary base would be less predictably linked with the volume of total transactions. Uzawa agreed that the rise in velocity would not affect the stability of monetary policy as long as the central bank was able to pursue precisely the right policy. But it could not be denied that increased velocity inevitably meant that the disruptive consequences of any central bank error would be amplified much larger than before. His conclusion was, therefore, that in assessing financial innovation, this destabilizing effect of financial innovation should be weighed against its potential benefits. Tsiang (Cornell University) thought that it was wrong to consider financial innovation as a once-and-for-all phenomenon. On the contrary, innovations occur continually in a rather unpredictable manner and will thus harm monetary control. He felt that the kind of innovation that directly hampered monetary control, such as the evasion of reserve requirements, should at least be discouraged.

These comments provoked a heated debate on the desirability of financial innovation and deregulation, but I shall focus on that topic later in this overview.

Interest Payment on Reserves

Hall agreed with Tobin's comment that it would be sufficient to pay interest on excess reserves in order to have banks hold larger reserves voluntarily. Flemming (Bank of England), however, argued that if that were the case, it would not be different from the present situation in the U.K. where banks hold for prudential reasons substantial amounts of liquid interest-bearing reserve assets. But he did not find that this brought added stability to the financial system in the U.K., and saw no particular reason why this should happen in the U.S. case. Wenninger (Federal Reserve Bank of New York) commented that the larger monetary base would not necessarily be sufficient to absorb financial shocks during a financial crisis, since there was no mechanism that would ensure that the additional excess reserves would end up where they would be needed.

Raymond wondered whether the monetary base would not become endogenous if interest—close to market rate—was paid on reserves. He expressed sympathy for Hall's proposal of raising the level of bank reserves, and would not object in that case to an interest being paid to banks in order to compensate for the additional financial burden incurred by them and thus avoid a subsequent rise of the lending rate. In response to this, Hall explained his view on how monetary base could be kept exogenous with near-market yields paid on reserves. In the transitional period, the central bank would supply additional reserves in a one-time auction. The interest rate would most likely be slightly below the yield on government paper, since reserves have transaction balance features. After the auction, the central bank would simply pay market rates minus that fixed margin on the reserves. Once additional reserves were supplied in this way, the amount of reserves could, except for cash transactions, be changed, as before, only by central bank operations. As a policy variable, reserves would be considered more like M1. However, since demand for reserves would be nearly interest-inelastic, the link between the level of reserves and nominal GNP would be much more stable. Regarding Hester's proposal to inhibit reserve overdrafts during the day, Béguelin (National Bank of Switzerland) mentioned that his country was preparing such a measure in order to cope with an expected decline in reserve demand following the planned introduction of an electronic clearing system next year.

Internationalization and Monetary Control

There was a similar debate on the effect of the integration of inter-national financial markets on monetary control. Bryant stressed in his paper that the growth in international transactions and markets tended to weaken the effectiveness of monetary policy for individual nations. In stark contrast to this view, Hall argued that most of the recent developments on the international financial scene did not di-rectly affect the demand for domestic base money, and therefore had almost no influence on the effectiveness of monetary policy. Bryant strongly disputed this idea, contending that there are indirect effects of international transactions on domestic base money demand. Fur-thermore, even if this is neglected, the link between base money and ultimate policy targets can be loosened in other ways. Moreover, the increase in financial interdependence tends to increase the variance and covariance of policy multipliers and thus may undermine the autonomy of policy actions for any single country acting unilaterally. Béguelin said that Swiss residents had initiated huge shifts between Swiss franc assets and assets denominated in other currencies. But these kinds of shifts did not cause serious problems for monetary pol-icy, since the Swiss National Bank followed a medium-run target in-stead of trying to conduct a "fine-tuning" policy. He believed that the internationalization of finance in general would force central banks to give up the idea of "fine-tuning" and move towards a more stable policy.

Central Bankers' Views

On balance, most central bankers seemed to be optimistic about the overall impact of financial innovation on the conduct of monetary policy. In reply to a question raised by Friedman whether central bankers felt that financial innovation had impeded their monetary policy, Morris (Federal Reserve Bank of Boston) mentioned that it could not be denied that it took much larger movements in interest rates to have the same impact on real activities. Morris, and also Burger (Federal Reserve Bank of St. Louis), however, were strongly opposed to Hester's suggestion that, for the purpose of slowing down the pro-cess of financial innovation, the real interest rate should not be pushed too high. They maintained that a central bank could not assume the responsibility of targeting the real interest rate, since there were clearly situations where it had to permit high real interest rates. If this trig-gered financial innovation and made the relationship between money and economic activity unstable, Morris added, central bankers should just pay more attention to real economic activity. In a similar vein, Thiessen (Bank of Canada) thought that there existed a considerable gap between academic economists and central bankers. While the former emphasized the problems caused by the effect of financial innovation on the demand for monetary base, those problems were not very important from the practicing central banker's view; the impacts of financial innovation on the stability of policy multipliers might be inconvenient for central bankers, but not disastrous. They had only to observe more closely the ultimate targets in operating the short-term money market interest rate which was their primary policy tool.

Crockett argued that many types of financial innovation tended to weaken the impact of monetary policy actions on policy targets in the short run but worked in the opposite direction in the long run. Innovations brought discontinuities in the effect of policy tools that relied on imperfections of financial markets. However, since financial innovations generally worked in the direction of removing these imperfections, it reduced the discontinuities and increased the reliability of general financial indicators, making it easier for central banks to gauge the effects of their policy actions. He further pointed out that any attempt to suppress innovation would also lead to a change in the preexisting relationship between the monetary base and economic activity. Bub (Deutsche Bundesbank) commented that, in contrast to many other countries and to the U.S. in particular, Germany had experienced no serious problem in employing central bank money as the key target since its adoption in 1975. He thought that this owed much to the character of universal banking in his country and to the fact that interest rates had already been liberalized in the 1960s. While there were shifts of funds into instruments with market-related interest rates, there was no significant migration of funds out of banking channels, and the validity of the broadly defined target was not endangered.

Mallyon and Knight (Reserve Bank of New Zealand) called attention to a very different and positive aspect of financial innovation and deregulation: that these developments made central banks more immune from political pressures on the choice of the fiscal-monetary policy mix since policy implementation through market forces is less vulnerable to these pressures than implementation through regulations.

Desirability of Innovation and Deregulation

One fundamental issue which was not a central theme in the presented papers emerged during the free discussion. Was financial innovation and deregulation desirable in the first place? Tobin warned against the general view that financial innovations were necessarily welfare-increasing. In contrast to the world of general equilibrium theory which assumed markets for a fixed set of commodities, financial competition typically took the form of creation of new commodities and markets trivially different from already existing ones. If one took into account, in addition, that large fixed costs were involved in supplying these financial commodities, it was obvious that there was no theoretical reason why free competition should increase welfare. He believed that many newly created markets were redundant and wasted resources; was not a futures market for the cost of living index five years from now nothing more than a new type of casino? Against this, Friedman stressed that, given inept government policy, it was desirable that people had a wide opportunity to protect themselves from its consequences. To have these new markets was clearly a second-best solution; he agreed with Tobin that the best solution would be to have a policy which kept prices stable and made these markets unnecessary. Patrick (Columbia University) called attention to the fact that, in the case of the Asian countries, there was still a long way to go before Tobin's dilemma of redundant markets became acute.

According to Raymond, one merit of Regulation Q-type rules was that they would enhance the development of capital markets; the greater use of bonds in financial transaction was desirable to some extent for central banks since it allows intervention in these securities as a useful policy instrument.

Potter expressed concern that increasing financial liberalism was going hand-in-hand with increasingly less liberal trade practices. Although it would be simplistic to suggest a close casual link between the two, it was nevertheless difficult to avoid the conclusion, he said, that the worrying rise in protectionist pressures in the United States was in part attributable to the high dollar, and that the high dollar was in part attributable to the now extremely high elasticity of U.S. capital movements. Teh (Monetary Authority of Singapore) pointed to the negative consequence for developing countries of the combination of highly volatile interest and exchange rates and financial innovation in developed countries. Developing countries now had to compete more severely with developed countries for savings, since the investment in financial instruments offered in the latter had become more attractive. He argued that for many less developed countries liberalization of financial markets and capital flows would result in a loss of their scarce savings. According to Teh, the success of Japan during the 1950s and 1960s in mobilizing domestic savings for investment under tight financial regulation suggested that the lack of financial liberalization might not necessarily be harmful to economic growth, as far as developing countries were concerned. Fry (University of California at Irvine) reacted to this by noting that the negative impact of disintermediation was much more severe in developing countries than in developed ones. In the latter group of countries, disintermediation would mean only a leakage of funds away from the banking system into capital markets, which would leave total savings and investment levels almost unchanged. In developing countries, however, disintermediation would mean a shift in investment away from financial assets to tangible assets, which would seriously damage economic growth. Fry called attention to the much higher investment/income ratio in Singapore compared with that in Hong Kong, despite similar rates of growth in these two countries, and reasoned that this might have to do with the greater government involvement in the financial intermediation process of the former.

As I mentioned previously, this conference did not aim at reaching general conclusions. I believe, however, that we can legitimately claim that, thanks to the commendable contribution of the participants, it succeeded in shedding some light on these difficult issues. It is my hope that the publication of this book will contribute to making the ideas developed during the conference a common asset of those interested in the topic of financial innovation and deregulation.

1

Monetary Policy in a Fiat World

Milton Friedman

In the past decade or so, there has been a burst of scholarly interest in various aspects of monetary reform—not the conduct of current monetary policy, which for decades has been the object of active scholarly work, but the institutional structure of the monetary system. During the same period, there has been a burst of innovation in the marketplace that has produced new financial instruments and institutions, as well as pressure in country after country for the deregulation of the banking system.

Both bursts of activity have been partly fostered by internal forces. In the academy, the internal forces have included the emergence of the theory of public choice, the development of the rational expectations approach to the analysis of monetary matters, and renewed interest in so-called Austrian economics with its emphasis on invisible hand interpretations of the origin and development of economic institutions and its interpretation of the business cycle as largely reflecting the effect of non-neutral money. In the financial marketplace, the internal developments have primarily centered about the information revolution sparked by the computer and associated improvements in communications, especially the greatly expanded capacity for record keeping on a detailed and near instantaneous basis.

These internal developments, however, seem to me far less important in explaining the simultaneous bursts of activity than one key external development—the ultimate consequences of which are shrouded in uncertainty. That development is the emergence of a world monetary system that, I believe, is unprecedented: a system in which essentially every currency in the world is, directly or indirectly, on an irredeemable paper money standard—directly, if the exchange rate of the currency is flexible though possibly manipulated; indirectly, if the exchange rate is effectively fixed in terms of another fiat-based currency (e.g., since 1983, the Hong Kong dollar).

This system has emerged gradually since World War I. From then until 1971, much of the world was effectively on a dollar standard, while the United States, though ostensibly on a gold standard (except for a brief interval in 1933–34), was actually on a fiat standard combined with a government program for pegging the price of gold. The Bretton Woods agreement in the main simply ratified that situation, despite the lip service paid to the role of gold, and the provisions for changes in exchange rates.

In the United States, the gradual change in the monetary role of gold was marked by two major milestones: the prohibition of the private ownership of gold in 1933 and the elimination of gold reserve requirements for Federal Reserve deposits in 1965 and Federal Reserve notes in 1968. The end of Bretton Woods in 1971, which removed both the formal links to the dollar and the pretense that the U.S. was on a gold standard, simply set the seal on an ongoing process. The stocks of gold listed on the books of central banks are a relic of a bygone era, though a slim possibility remains that they will again become more than that at some future date. The removal by the U.S. in 1974 of the prohibition of private ownership of gold was, somewhat paradoxically, a tribute to the end of gold's monetary role.

The formal end of Bretton Woods was precipitated by an inflationary surge in the United States in the 1960s. In turn, the end of Bretton Woods helped to produce a continuation and acceleration of inflation in the 1970s and its spread to much of the rest of the world. Inflation and subsequent economic instability were the proximate stimuli for the burst of interest in monetary reform although the more fundamental reason for these developments was the momentous change in the world's monetary system of which the inflation was both a cause and a manifestation.

The irregular and highly variable inflation stimulated interest in monetary reform in several ways. In the first place, it brought into sharp focus the poor performance of the monetary authorities—reinforcing and giving greater credence to the conclusions about prior policy that various scholars had reached, including Anna Schwartz and myself in our *Monetary History*.[1]

In the second place, the inflation produced a rise in nominal interest

[1] *A Monetary History of the United States, 1867–1960* (Milton Friedman and Anna J. Schwartz). U.S. National Bureau of Economic Research, 1963.

rates that converted government control of interest rates in the United States via Regulation Q from a minor to a serious impediment to the effective clearing of credit markets. One response was the invention of money market mutual funds as a way to enable small savers to benefit from high market interest rates. The money market funds proved an entering wedge to financial innovation that forced the prompt relaxation and subsequent abandonment of control over the interest rates that banks could pay, as well as the loosening of other regulations that restricted the activities of banks and other financial institutions. Such deregulation as has occurred came too late and has been too limited to prevent a sharp reduction in the role of banks, as traditionally defined, in the U.S. financial system as a whole. Such banks now account for a far smaller share of the credit market than they did earlier. Their place has been taken by such "non-banks" as Sears Roebuck, American Express, Merill Lynch, and so on.

The irregular inflation and high and variable interest rates produced similar developments in other countries. As a result, there is pressure for deregulation everywhere throughout the world.

It is worth stressing how little precedent there is for the present situation. Throughout recorded history, commodity money has been the rule. Money, in the sense of a medium of exchange and unit of account, has commonly consisted of a claim on a specified physical quantity of a designated commodity. We are accustomed to thinking of gold and silver as the predominant money metals, but in fact an enormous variety of commodities—from cowrie shells to feathers to large stones to tobacco to iron, as in Japan—have at one time or another in one place or another served as the monetary medium.

The use of a particular commodity as money developed through its gradual acceptance in private transactions as the medium of exchange. Though the particular commodity used as money was not imposed by government, governments have invariably assumed a major role in the monetary system. Initially they simply engaged in coinage or its equivalent in order to profit from the associated seignorage. However, sovereigns have seldom been able to resist going beyond simple seignorage by debasing the currency, introducing base metal alloys in place of precious metals. Such episodes, though common and sometimes important, as in the Roman era, never prevented private individuals from continuing to use specie evaluated by weight rather than by count in their transactions.

In any event, so long as money was predominantly coin or bullion, very rapid inflation was simply not physically feasible, the extent of debasement being limited by the ratio of the value of a given physical quantity of the precious metal to the base metal used as alloy. As Forrest Capie points out in a fascinating recent paper, "Conditions in Which Hyperinflation Has Appeared,"[2] the notorious Roman inflation went "from a base of 100 in 200 A.D. to 5000 by the end of the century—in other words a rate of between 3 and 4 percent per annum compound."[3] It took the invention and widespread use of paper money to make the kind of rapid inflations that have occurred in more recent times technically feasible.

Even so, as Forrest Capie notes, "from medieval times to the present day the examples of accelerating and very rapid inflation are few." Each of those examples is associated with departure from a specie standard: the paper money inflation of the U.S. Revolution, the French episode, the suspension of specie payments by Great Britain during the Napoleonic wars and by the U.S. during the Civil War greenback period, and the much wider and more extensive departures during World War I and World War II.

In evaluating past experience with such episodes, Irving Fisher wrote in 1911: "Irredeemable paper money has almost invariably proved a curse to the country employing it."[4] Experience since Fisher wrote certainly conforms to his generalization. That period has seen the most extensive series of paper money disasters in history: the hyperinflations that followed World War I and World War II; the rapid inflations, if not hyperinflations, of many South American and other countries around the world, particularly many of the lesser developed countries; and most recently, of course, the inflationary experience of the 1970s.

The end of specie standards and the emergence of a world monetary system in which every country, in Fisher's terms, has an "irredeemable paper money" has produced two very different streams of literature: one, scientific; the other, popular. The scientific literature is that already referred to, dealing with monetary reform and the government's role in providing outside money. The popular literature is alarmist, and "hard money," essentially all of it based on the proposition that Fisher's generalization will continue to hold and that the world is inevitably condemned to runaway inflation unless and until the leading nations once again adopt commodity standards.

Interestingly enough, there has been little intersection between these

[2] Paper prepared for Carnegie-Rochester Conference, April 1985.

[3] *Ibid.*, p. 4. The implication is that the silver-copper price ratio was of the order of 50 to 1, roughly the market ratio in 1960. Since then, silver has risen sharply in price relative to copper so the ratio is now much higher.

[4] *Purchasing Power of Money*, new ed. (New York: Macmillan, 1929), p. 131.

two streams. In my opinion, the scientific literature has largely evaded the question raised by the popular literature. Have the conditions that have produced the current unprecedented monetary system been accompanied by developments that change the likelihood that it will go the way of earlier paper standards? The rest of this paper offers some tentative and preliminary observations on this question.

In the paper already mentioned, Forrest Capie offers the hypothesis that "severe civil disorder, or perhaps very weak government, has been the critical element. Grave social unrest or actual disorder provokes large-scale spending on the part of the established authority in an attempt either to suppress or placate the rebellious element. At the same time the division in society results in a sharp fall in revenue. In order to gain the resources required, the only tax available is the inflation tax, and so the printing press is brought into action."

The key element in this explanation is the inability of governments to raise by explicit taxation the revenues needed for the expenditures they undertake. Inflation has always been a very attractive alternative source of revenue since it enables governments in effect to impose taxation without voting for it and, in John Maynard Keynes's words, "in a manner which not one man in a million is able to diagnose."[5] However, the existence of a commodity standard widely supported by the public served as a check. Certainly the primary reason why hyperinflations, and even very rapid inflations, have been so rare in more advanced countries in periods of peace and the absence of widespread civil disturbance is because of the pressure imposed by public opinion on the government to keep its money convertible or, if convertibility has been suspended, to return to a situation in which it is once again convertible.

They key challenge that faces us currently in reforming our monetary and fiscal institutions is to find a substitute for convertibility into specie that will serve the same function of inhibiting resort to inflation as a source of government revenue.

I believe that it is not possible to give a confident and unambiguous answer to the question whether Fisher's 1911 generalization that "irredeemable paper money has almost invariably proved a curse to the country employing it" will hold true for the current situation. The experiences of such countries as Argentina, Brazil, Chile, Mexico, and Israel are contemporary examples of Fisher's generalization. However, they are all less developed countries that, except for dating, may have

[5] *The Economic Consequences of the Peace* (New York: Harcourt, Brace & Howe, 1920), p. 236.

more in common with the countries that Fisher had in mind than with the more advanced Western countries. The experience of those more advanced countries—Japan, the United States, and the members of the Common Market—gives grounds for greater optimism. The pressures on governments to obtain resources for government use without levying explicit taxes are as strong today in these countries as they were earlier. However, counter-pressures have developed that reduce the political attractiveness of paper money inflation. The most important such developments, I believe, arise from the greater sensitivity and sophistication of both the public at large and the financial markets with respect to inflation thanks to the information revolution, which has greatly reduced the cost of acquiring information and which has enabled expectations to respond more promptly and accurately to economic disturbances, including changes in government policy.

Inflation has added to government resources in three ways: first, the government money issues have constituted an implicit inflation tax on outside money holdings; second, inflation has produced an unvoted increase in explicit taxes as a result of bracket creep; third, inflation has reduced the real value of outstanding debt issued at interest rates that did not include sufficient allowance for future inflation. Recent economic, political, and financial developments have greatly eroded the potency of all three sources of revenue.

With respect to the first, the figures for the United States suggest the trend. Outside (or high-powered) money remained remarkably constant at about 10 percent of national income from the middle of the nineteenth century to the Great Depression. It then rose sharply to a peak of about 25 percent in 1946. Since then the ratio of outside money to national income has been declining and currently is about 7 percent. For a modern society, in which government taxes and spending have mounted to 30 to 50 percent or occasionally even more of the national income, this component is perhaps the least important of the three. Even if inflation did not reduce the ratio of outside money to national income, which it unquestionably would do, a 10 percent per year increase in outside money would currently yield as revenue to the U.S. government only about seven-tenths of 1 percent of national income. Further financial innovation is likely to reduce still further the ratio of outside money to national income even aside from the effect of inflation, making this source of revenue even less potent. Though I have not investigated the subject in detail, I am under the impression that the same tendencies have been present in many other countries as well, so that there too this source of revenue has become less important.

The second component of revenue—bracket creep—has very likely been far more important than the first. That has almost certainly been true in the United States in recent decades. Inflation has subjected low- and moderate-income persons to levels of personal income tax that could never have been voted explicitly.

Speaking again of the United States, one result of bracket creep has been political pressure that has led to the indexation of the personal income tax schedule for inflation, which largely eliminates this source of revenue. Here again, I do not know what the situation is in other countries, but I suspect that wherever there has been substantial inflation there has also been substantial indexation of the personal tax structure.

The third component has also been extremely important. Speaking for the United States again, at the end of World War II, the funded federal debt amounted to 6 percent more than a year's national income. By 1967 it was down to about 32 percent of national income despite repeated "deficits" in the official federal budget. Since then it has risen as deficits have continued and increased but, even so, to only about 36 percent currently. Real growth partly accounts for the decline in the deficit ratio, but inflation was the major explanation. Inflation converted the positive nominal interest rates at which the debt had been issued into negative real rates *ex post*.

Developments in the financial markets have sharply eroded the potency of this source of revenue. Market pressures have made it difficult for governments to issue long-term debt at low nominal rates. In the United States, one result has been a sharp reduction in the average term to maturity of the federal debt—from 9 years 1 month for the marketable interest-bearing public debt in 1946 to 4 years 1 month in 1983. Except under wartime conditions, it is far more difficult to convert positive nominal interest rates on short-term debt into *ex post* negative real rates by unanticipated inflation than it is to do so for long-term debt. Moreover, it is less profitable to do so for short-term than for long-term debt. For both short- and long-term debt, several decades of historically high and variable inflation have made it far more difficult to produce unanticipated inflation of any magnitude for any substantial period than it was even a decade or so ago, when the public's perceptions still reflected the effect of a relatively stable price level over long periods.

In the United Kingdom, the government now issues bonds adjusted for inflation. For such bonds, there is no way that the government can benefit from *ex post* negative real interest rates. There has long been support in the U.S. for the Treasury to issue similar securities, but so far the Treasury has been unwilling to do so. However, pressure to issue purchasing-power securities would undoubtedly intensify if inflation in the U.S. again became high and variable.

Perhaps several decades of a relatively stable long-run price level would again lull asset holders into regarding nominal interest rates as equivalent to real interest rates. But that is certainly not the case today.

To summarize, inflation has become far less attractive as a political option. Given a voting public very sensitive to inflation, it may currently be politically profitable to establish monetary arrangements that will make the present irredeemable paper standard an exception to Fisher's generalization.

Recent experience provides some support for that view. The inflation of the 1970s was severe by the standards that had become accepted in the United States, the United Kingdom, Japan, and other advanced countries during the nineteenth and most of the twentieth century, though it was mild by comparison with the experience of many other countries of the world. But it was sufficiently severe to establish political pressure that has led to policies of disinflation throughout the Western world, policies of restraining monetary growth and of accepting substantial unemployment in order to avoid continued inflation.

Japan offers perhaps the most impressive example. In the early 1970s, inflation in Japan reached levels well over 20 percent. The government and the Bank of Japan reacted promptly and effectively, bringing down sharply the rate of monetary growth. They have continued to maintain a relatively steady and gradually declining rate of monetary growth. As a result, not only has inflation been brought down to low levels but Japan has escaped the sharp ups and downs in inflation that have plagued many other countries.

Germany offers an example of a rather different kind, an example of how experience can alter the political attractiveness of the inflation option. Throughout the post-World War II period, Germany has tended to have lower inflation than the U.K., the U.S., and most other Western countries. The reason seems clearly to be the long-term effects of the post-World War I hyperinflation reinforced by the post-World War II experience of suppressed inflation which incapacitated the monetary system and forced a resort to barter.

Similarly, the U.K. and the U.S. have succeeded in sharply reducing inflation after the two countries had experienced double-digit inflation and despite the accompanying rise in unemployment, particularly sharp and long-lasting in the U.K.

The apparent decline in the political profitability of inflation is a source of promise, but it is far from a guarantee that Fisher's generalization is obsolete. Governments often act under short-run pressures in ways that have strongly adverse long-run consequences. Israel today offers a conspicuous example. It continues to resort to inflation under conditions that make inflation a poor source of revenue, if, indeed, in the particular circumstances of Israel, inflation is not itself a drain on government resources, at least in the long run.

These remarks are directly related to the basic theme of this conference: financial innovation and monetary policy. The unprecedented character of the world monetary system and its initial effects are major sources of the financial innovation that has occurred, and of the pressures for deregulation of financial markets. They also raise the primary questions for monetary policy. Will the temptation to use fiat money as a source of revenue lead to a situation that will ultimately force a return to a commodity standard, a gold standard of one kind or another, or shall we be successful in the course of the coming decades in developing monetary and fiscal institutions and arrangements that will provide an effective check on the propensity to inflate and that will again give us a relatively stable price level over long periods of time?

The final answer to these questions will come only as history unfolds over the coming decades. But what that answer will be depends critically on the contribution that conferences such as this can make in defining the issues, devising alternative solutions, and examining their merits and demerits. That learning process is already underway, and in one sense has been for centuries, ever since the appearance of systematic analyses of money and monetary institutions. But in another sense, the learning process is still in its infancy, because in important respects we are venturing into unexplored terrain.

2

Financial Innovation and Deregulation in Perspective

James Tobin

Deregulation of financial industries is popular these days for the same reasons that recommend it elsewhere: the perceived gains in microeconomic efficiency from unfettered competition. However, banks and other depository institutions are not just like other industries. They supply the exchange media used in the bulk of transactions in the economy. They are the institutions through which central bank operations of monetary control are transmitted to the economy at large. We need to consider how much regulation and what kinds of regulation are needed to protect and foster the payments system and to maintain the effectiveness of monetary control.

These questions arise at a time when technological and institutional innovations are changing costs, opportunities, and competitive relations in financial industries. Some of the regulations of the past are being abandoned simply because they are no longer enforceable, or because they stand in the way of new opportunities of obvious merit.

The important trends are these:

(1) Transactions, whether for financial assets or for commodities, are less and less expensive of time and resources. Electronic payments networks are making possible instantaneous payments via computer from one account to another.

(2) The issuance of obligations payable on demand and transferable to third parties by check or wire is not confined to commercial banks and other depository institutions regulated by government.

(3) Legal ceilings on interest rates payable on deposits are vanishing.

(4) Financial supermarkets and conglomerates are blurring or erasing distinctions between banks, other depositories, mutual funds, brokers, insurance companies, investment bankers, securities dealers, and other financial agencies.

The Future Trade-offs: Preview of This Paper

In this industry the benefits of competition sought by deregulation are (a) provision to the public of the services of a payments system, financial intermediation, and market access at low private and social cost, and (b) availability of products that meet the diverse tastes, needs, and circumstances of lenders and borrowers. With respect to the second goal, the menu of assets and liabilities available should accommodate different attitudes towards risk, allocate unavoidable social risks efficiently, and avoid adding avoidable risks. Here, as in other industries, product variety is desirable, but trivial differentiation of standard products is costly and wasteful. As the volume of financial advertising indicates, Chamberlinian "wastes of monopolistic competition" are endemic to financial industries, where product differentiation is very inexpensive.

The use of a common monetary unit of account and the adoption of generally acceptable media of exchange in this numeraire carry important positive externalities. Free market competition by itself cannot achieve and protect these social benefits. The advantages of competition and deregulation must be sought in ways that do not impair the payments system or subject it to interruptions and breakdowns. The regulations we have, however misguided or obsolete many of them may be, were imposed for good reasons born of bad experience. It does not make sense to ignore the lessons of the past and to have to relearn them the hard way.

The basic dilemma is this: Our monetary and banking institutions have evolved in a way that entangles competition among financial intermediary firms with the provision of transactions media. The entanglement is the source of risks of default and breakdown. Protection against those risks has brought the government interventions now seen to have inefficient by-products: bureaucratic surveillance, deposit insurance, lender-of-last-resort guarantees by central banks. There is no possible complete resolution of this dilemma, but we may hope to limit its scope.

My suggestions will be these: Create several categories of intermediaries' deposit liabilities backed by specific earmarked assets. One or more of these would be payable on demand and transferable to third parties on order. Others might be savings and time deposits particularly designed for small and unsophisticated savers. The purpose is to immunize these liabilities from risks of default due to other activities of the issuing financial firms. The segregation and earmarking would make it unnecessary to safeguard these liabilities by deposit insurance.

Deposit insurance would be limited to certain other liabilities, and would be limited to small amounts per depositor. Other liabilities issued in market competition among intermediaries would not be insured, and would be subject only to the general regulations governing securities markets. In that realm *caveat emptor* would rule, firms would be allowed to fail, and their creditors would be allowed to suffer from defaults.

The Mirage of Private Money

Contemporary literature applying general free market principles to monetary theory suggests that competitive private enterprise could supply the economy's "money." I must say that I was not surprised by this development. I had wondered about the marriage of monetarism and "invisible hand" doctrine, and I had figured that some day the exception which assigns government the responsibility to limit the supply of money would be challenged. I doubt that my fellow keynoter is any happier about the challenge than I am.

Currency is the physical embodiment of the monetary unit of account defined by the sovereign. Currency is the sure and perfectly liquid store of value in units of account. It is legal tender, for the payment of taxes and for the discharge of private obligations enforceable in courts of law for payments in units of account. Consequently it is generally acceptable in payments.

I find it difficult to imagine a system in which there is no governmentally issued store of value in the unit of account. Some discussions of "private money" in the literature seem to suggest that the government can define the "dollar" as the unit of account without printing and issuing any dollars. Private agents could issue promises to pay dollars, and these would circulate. But what are they promising to pay? Of course, if the government sanctified the issues of a particular bank or private firm or individual by agreeing to accept them in payment of taxes and by granting them legal tender status, those issues would be currency. The sovereign would be delegating its *fiat* to the favored private institution. History suggests that such an institution would eventually be nationalized and made politically responsible, like the Bank of England. The idea of a disembodied fiat unit of account, with embodiments of it freely and competitively supplied by private agents, seems to me to be a fairy tale.

Private monetary issue makes more sense for commodity money. The government can define a dollar in terms of gold or silver, or plywood or wheat, or some combination of goods. The commodity itself can circulate, especially if coinage by the state or by any other credible government or agency puts it in a form of readily ascertainable weight and quality.

Experience suggests that societies will also find it convenient to handle transactions with promises to pay the numeraire commodity. Whose promises? Just those of competing private agents? Of unregulated private agents? Once again, the government cannot escape the question what IOUs it will accept from citizens in payment of taxes and other obligations, or avoid deciding whose IOUs will be regarded as discharging private debts. Neither can the government take a *laisserfaire* attitude toward the ability of private issuers of such IOUs to redeem their promises, especially if the government gives them the cachets of acceptability and legal tender.

Free market enthusiasts may say that the judgments of private agents will price, i.e., discount, issuers' IOUs in proper relationship to their quality and their backing. Rational market pricing may not be feasible, even conceptually, because self-fulfilling prophecies are involved. Reserve ratios that suffice when there is "confidence" will not avail when there is not. In any case, a payments system, like any other communications network, derives efficiency from universality, standardization, and predictability. It is not efficient to have competing currencies with varying rates of exchange between them.

Some writers have envisaged commodity moneys without stocks of the commodities held to back the currencies, whether private or governmental. They appeal to an analogy of the unit of account to a unit of measurement: as a yard is the length of a certain stick at the Bureau of Standards, so the dollar was by definition a certain weight of gold or silver or both. It could be similarly defined in commodities again. This is not a good analogy. Those agents, private or public, who promise to pay on demand "dollars" so defined must have stocks on hand to enable them to fulfill their promises. That is the only way to assure the defined equivalence.

I conclude that there must be store-of-value embodiments of a monetary unit of account, and that basically these will be and should be designated and supplied by the central government. Once this is done, private initiatives will generate all kinds of promises to pay basic currency, on demand and at future dates. The question is how much and how those initiatives should be regulated by the state. I have an uneasy suspicion that in the general enthusiasm for deregulation we are in danger of re-establishing the conditions and problems which generated financial regulations in the first place.

Bank Deposits as Inside Money

Paper currency and coin are not very convenient media of exchange, except for small items of consumption, vending machines, and certain transactions among total strangers. Where they are useful in large payments, it is for discreditable reasons: tax avoidance or crime. Currency is too bulky for large legitimate transactions, awkward because it comes in only a few denominations, vulnerable to loss or theft, unsuitable for remittance by mail. It is in fact used for a very small fraction of transactions weighted by value. This is true whether currency and coin are fiat money or governmental promises to pay on demand commodities in which the monetary unit is defined.

Some writers complain of the government's monopoly in currency supply. Whatever inefficiencies there may be in payments systems, they surely would be mitigated very little by allowing private issue of currency and coin. Maybe some banks would put out notes in more, and more convenient, denominations than the government does. Against that gain would be the difficulty of handling and sorting different kinds of notes and coins.

Demand deposits, banks' promises to pay currency on demand or on order to third parties, are more convenient than currency itself. Historically commercial banks exploited this opportunity to obtain funds to meet business borrowers' demands for commercial loans. The banks' incentive was the interest gap between deposits, which were competing with zero-interest currency, and loans. Many of the deposits come from the same businesses to whom the banks on occasion lend. Commercial banks serve as intermediaries for businesses with temporary surpluses, seasonal or cyclical, to lend to businesses with temporary deficits. The lending depositors and borrowers change roles frequently. Commercial banks administer this circulation of deposits and credit. In addition, they transfer some saving—not very much in the United States—from household depositors to the business and public sectors.

Obtaining loanable funds via demand deposits, banks borrow very short to lend longer, and borrow liquid to lend illiquid. The risks in such intermediation do not fall solely on the managers and shareholders of the banks; their leverage is immense. Even if bank managers act with normal perspicacity in the interests of their stockholders, even if all temptations of personal gain are resisted, sheer chance will bring some failures—insolvency because of borrowers' defaults or other capital losses on assets, or inability to meet withdrawals of deposits even though the bank would be solvent if assets' present values could be immediately realized. The probability is multiplied by the essential instability of depositor confidence. News of withdrawals triggers more withdrawals (*sauve qui peut*) at the same bank or, by contagion, at others. For these reasons the banking business has not been left to free market competition but has been significantly regulated:

(1) Minimum reserves of currency or other liquid assets held against deposits have been legally specified. The original purpose was to protect depositors, in particular to prevent imprudent erosion of reserve ratios by competition among banks. Paradoxically, once fractional reserves are required, they are not available to be paid out on depositors' demand. Required reserves have turned into an instrument of central bank monetary control.

(2) The function of protecting banks and depositors against illiquidity falls to the central bank as "lender of last resort." By lending $7 billion to one troubled bank, Continental Illinois, the U.S. Federal Reserve showed how seriously it takes this responsibility. To put this number in perspective, recall that normal lending by the Fed to the U.S. whole banking system rarely exceeds $1 billion. Thus the "lender of last resort" function can seriously distort the customary use of central bank instruments for purposes of monetary control. In the instance cited, the Fed offset its extra lending by open market sales of similar magnitude. They offset it arithmetically; whether the net effect was economically neutral depended also on the psychologies of banks and public, difficult even for central bankers to assess.

(3) Regulations govern the capitalizations, accounting, asset portfolios, types of liabilities, deposit interest rates, ownership, and other business activities and interests of banking firms. They are enforced by periodic reports, inspections, and audits. New firms can enter the industry only with government charters. It is mainly these regulations that critics advocate relaxing or repealing in the name of competition and efficiency.

(4) Governmental deposit insurance has been by far the most effective measure to prevent bank failures. In the U.S. it virtually eliminated the unstable run, the contagious panic. However, it has not been altogether successful, especially during recent years of heightened competition, international in scope, among banks and other financial enterprises. These years were also characterized by severe gyrations of economic activity, prices, interest rates, and foreign exchange rates. The United States authorities found it necessary to extend the insurance guarantees to all deposits of large banks, even though the statutory protection covered only the first $100,000 of each account.

Deposit insurance, like other regulations, has been criticized on grounds of efficiency. It diminishes the incentives of the insured institutions themselves to assess and limit risks, throwing more of a burden on bureaucratic surveillance by regulators, reinforced by the insurance agency itself. It also diminishes whatever incentive depositors themselves might have for assessing the riskiness of banks where they might deposit funds. Deposit insurance, moreover, is a massive extension and delegation of the government's monetary fiat—a blank check, so to speak, which might be an enormous obligation in certain contingencies. The federal deposit insurance agencies have as reserves less than 1% of the deposits they have guaranteed. Any big bank failure would wipe them out and require Congress to appropriate additional funds.

It *is* important to provide economic agents a convenient substitute for currency, usable in payments and riskless as a store of value in the unit of account. It *is* important to protect the society's payments system from interruptions and breakdowns due to bank failures. The problem is that this provision and this protection cannot be accomplished by unregulated competition for checkable demand deposits and loans. Bank deposits are *inside* money, which has the macroeconomic advantage that no net national saving is tied up in its accumulation. However, the accident of history that made inside money the principal medium of exchange also made it vulnerable to events that impair the value and liquidity of the assets backing the money. Striking a balance between competitive efficiency and the protection of depositors seems to be increasingly difficult and costly. That is why some other ways of meeting the problem deserve consideration.

Deposited Currency

Perhaps we need means of payment like currency but without its disadvantages. *Deposited currency*—100%-reserve deposits—payable in notes or coin on demand, transferable by order to third parties, secure against loss or theft, would be a perfect store of value in the unit of account. One way to provide it would be to allow individuals to hold deposit accounts in the central bank, or in branches of it established for the purpose and perhaps located in post offices.

A more likely alternative, given current sentiment for privatization, is this: Any bank or depository institution entitled to hold deposits in the central bank could offer deposited-currency accounts to customers. One question, of course, would be how to pay the costs of managing such accounts. The government could subsidize them by paying some interest on the 100% reserves. The argument would be that the payments system is a public good which taxpayers at large should provide.

Or user charges could be levied; after all, individuals bear most of the costs of the use of ordinary currency in transactions and can afford to pay something for the greater convenience of checkable deposits.

It might be argued that no interest should be paid on these deposits, just as none is paid on ordinary currency. Banks and other depositories could compete for these deposits in terms of their charges and services. On the other hand, the government could pay the banks a low interest rate, indexed perhaps to the Treasury bill rate. The banks could then compete for the business in interest payable to depositors as well as in services and service charges. Since interest-bearing deposits would be more popular, the Treasury might save taxpayers money by making them possible. In any case, no institution would be licensed to retail currency in deposit form without meeting certain standards of service and convenience, and without participation in a common national clearing network.

Banks and Segregated Funds

Present deposit insurance in the U.S. protects not only means-of-payment deposits but all other deposits in eligible institutions, including non-checkable savings accounts and time deposits. Similar obligations of mutual funds and other debtors not covered by deposit insurance are not guaranteed. It is not clear why all kinds of liabilities of covered institutions should be insured, except that the assets are so commingled that withdrawals of non-insured deposit liabilities would imperil the insured deposits. That indeed is why the insurance guarantee was *de facto* extended beyond the statutory limit.

This problem could be avoided by segregating and earmarking assets corresponding to particular classes of liabilities, permitting a depositor in effect to purchase a fund which could not be impaired by difficulties elsewhere in the institution's balance sheet. In this way, a bank would become more like a company offering a variety of mutual funds, just as those companies—which are not insured—are becoming more like banks.

The 100% reserve deposit proposed above would be one such fund, but there could be others. For example, many households of modest means and little financial sophistication want savings accounts that are safe stores of value in the unit of account. These can be provided in various maturities without risk by a fund invested in Treasury securities. They can be provided as demand obligations either by letting their redemption value fluctuate with net asset value or by crediting a floating interest rate to a fixed value.

These options need not displace, but could supplement, standard insured savings deposits and time certificates. The total amount of these, wherever deposited, insured to a particular person (identified by social security or tax identification number) would be strictly limited to the $100,000 in current legislation.

Perhaps an even more important addition to the menu of assets, especially for small and unsophisticated savers, would be savings accounts or certificates indexed to the cost of living. The index should be purged of terms-of-trade effects and indirect taxes, contingencies against which the nation as a whole cannot be insured. (This reform in the index should apply to all public or publicly sanctioned indexations, including those in collective bargaining contracts protected by statute.) To enable financial intermediaries to offer indexed liabilities in safe, convenient, and flexible form, the government would have to issue some indexed securities.

The advantage of the "segregated funds" approach is to limit the scope of intermediaries' liabilities that need to be protected by deposit insurance, and by the same token the scope of intermediaries' assets that need to be continuously scrutinized and regulated. If there were a clear and clean line between the two kinds of intermediary activity, *caveat emptor* could apply to the uninsured and less regulated business, where banks and depository institutions would be vigorously competing with each other and with other market participants. If some of them fail from time to time in the process, that would not impair the value or even the liquidity of the segregated funds they were administering. We could expect the business of managing liabilities, certificates of deposit and the like, and of seeking profitable lending opportunities, to continue to occupy the managerial and entrepreneurial skills of banks and other financial firms. But we would not have to undergo a monetary crisis every time big depositors became suspicious of a large bank, or save either those depositors or the bank from the consequences of mistakes or misfortunes.

New Transactions Technology and Monetary Policy

Withdrawals and payments to third parties can easily be made from any demand account, and there is no good reason to restrict this convenience. Some demand accounts will be *deposited currency* or other segregated funds. Some will not be. Of these, some will be insured and others not. Some will have fixed unit-of-account values; others will not. In the brave new world of electronic payments, all can be linked in a computerized payments network.

On the initiative of the payor, payments will be made at time of purchase or settlement, or scheduled to be executed at a designated future time. They will be made from stations connected to banks and to the central bank, located at banks themselves but also in stores, offices, and homes. I suppose plastic cards will be used, as at interactive teller stations today. When the payment is executed, the accounts of payor and payee at their banks or other intermediaries will be debited and credited, and so will their banks' accounts at the central bank. There will be no float, either for depositors or for banks, and no opportunities for adventurous check-kiting cash management as recently practiced by E. F. Hutton. The immense volume of socially wasteful transactions now induced in the United States by efforts to profit from float would be eliminated. The new technology permits a greatly accelerated version of the European giro system, a more efficient flow of information than the check system.

In this payments system, it will be natural and almost inevitable that banks allow overdrafts up to established credit lines like those now defined by bank credit cards. Extensive use of overdrafts may be the principal monetary innovation of the new system for the United States. A transaction will be completed if and only if it would not result in an overdrawn balance beyond the pre-arranged limit. Likewise the central bank, on whose computerized "books" the clearings between banks and other institutions takes place, would need some tough rules about overdrafts, including those that arise and are supposedly reversed during one business day.

The likely extensive use of overdrafts would make it necessary to revise the present base for calculation of bank reserve requirements. Evidently it will not be practical to stick solely to reserve requirements against liabilities. If *deposited currency* accounts are set up, there would be of course 100% reserve requirements against them. But other types of deposits will also be transferable through the network, and overdrafts will be allowed in those accounts. I propose gearing reserve requirements to the corresponding bank assets, including overdraft advances. Assets covered by capital liabilities would be exempt from required reserves, as would be assets covered by liabilities which are neither insured nor eligible for transfer through the network. Any financial institution or firm which wants to use the network for transfer of ownership of its liabilities or equities would have to become a "bank" subject to reserve tests and associated regulations.

The central bank will still have effective monetary control in the new system. In the United States, and in many other monetary systems, the fulcrum of monetary control is the reserve test. Monetary control via reserve tests is effective if and only if the government, via the central bank, monopolizes and controls the aggregate supply of eligible reserve assets, the monetary base. This the central bank does by open market operations and by setting the rates and other terms on which it will lend reserves to the banks. I am assuming also, of course, that the "banks" subject to reserve tests are in aggregate weighty enough participants in financial and capital markets so that central bank operations affect the quantities, prices, and interest rates determined in those markets.

So far as I can see, nothing in the system of the future that I have sketched vitiates the conditions for effective control via reserve tests. Monetary aggregates will not be very interesting statistics, for the same reasons that deposits will not be entirely suitable as the base for reserve requirements. They will not be useful targets either. But variation of the Fed's instruments, open market operations and discount rates, will still affect the monetary base and will be transmitted to macroeconomic variables of importance.

Interest-bearing Money

Payment of market-determined interest rates on deposits, as I have argued elsewhere, diminishes the sensitivity of demand for money to the level of nominal market rates. In old-fashioned textbook terms, it makes the "LM" curve steeper. If the rates the central bank charges on its loans and pays on reserves deposited with it are also indexed to market rates, the "money multiplier" too is made less sensitive to interest rates. Consequently, variations of central bank instruments will have bigger effects on national income than in previous regimes where these nominal interest rates are fixed by legislation or administrative decision. So will shocks in the demands for deposits by the public and for reserves by banks. I think, moreover, that those demands will be more volatile in the new regime; when there is little to gain from sharp-pencil cash management, people will accept without prompt correction large swings in their cash balances.

The lesson I draw for the conduct of monetary policy is that it should be more accommodative in the new regime; that is, the supply of reserve should be more responsive to interest rates. Thus accommodation by the central bank would replace the accommodation now built in to the system by the control of deposit interest rates and of rates on reserves and central bank lending. This replacement is appropriate for macroeconomic reasons, while the abandonment of the interest rate controls is justified on grounds of microeconomic efficiency.

The subject of this Second International Conference is timely and important. It invites pragmatic and ingenious economic architecture. The well rehearsed differences of view about macroeconomic theory and monetary policy probably do not apply to the problems of concern to us at this meeting. I have set forth some preliminary thoughts, and I expect to learn a great deal from the papers and discussions to follow.

Background and Causes of Financial Innovation: An International Comparison

3

Financial Innovation in Major Industrial Countries

Masashi Yumoto, Kinzo Shima, Hajime Koike, and Hiroo Taguchi

I. Introduction

Innovation refers to several phenomena. It includes new financial instruments which are the objects of transaction, new financial markets which are the fields of transaction, and new media to effect transfers. While financial innovation could occur at any time in any economic system, it has become one of the most significant economic phenomena of the last decade in particular. It has exerted a considerable influence on the workings of the financial system and the conduct of monetary policy in a number of countries.

In this paper, we first provide in section II a classification of major financial innovations according to their common characteristics. In our view financial innovations may be broadly classified into two types: innovations which directly reduce the shadow cost of regulatory constraints (which we propose to call Type 1 innovations), and innovations which reduce physical transaction costs or improve allocation of risk (Type 2 innovations). Then, in section III, we apply this classification to financial innovations in selected countries. This section may be of particular interest to readers who seek general information about the chronology and the geographical location of recent innovations. Following this over-all review, we pick one particular case, that of Japan, and discuss recent developments, providing information on the progress of liberalization and descriptions of some of the newly created financial assets and services. In stark contrast to the U.S. case, the process of Type I innovation in Japan was a relatively gradual one, because the major driving force of innovations was the gradual structural change in the flow of funds that occurred after the first oil crisis in the mid-1970s; the high inflation rate did not play a very important role, since it was brought under control in a relatively short period of time by strict application of monetary policy measures.

In the fourth section, we describe the impact of financial innovation on the management of banks and the banking system. Financial innovation is not without its own costs. Its impact on the profitability of the suppliers of financial services is one of the most critical issues of the process of financial innovation. A survey of empirical studies on this subject suggests that the negative effects of financial innovation and deregulation on the safety and soundness of bank management may not be very significant. However, certain types of financial innovation, such as changes in the payments mechanism, may increase what is generally called a system risk. It is thus emphasized that as the process of financial innovation develops, central banks should continue to play an increasingly important role as monitors of bank management and interbank market transactions, and also as providers of last resort. We have deliberately excluded from our discussion the problems of financial innovation's impact on monetary control, not because we perceive this topic as unimportant, but because we wanted to leave this issue to the other papers in this volume. It was our intention to restrict ourselves to describing the background and process of innovation and thus to facilitate the following discussions on more specific topics, including the monetary policy issues.

II. Classification and Causes of Financial Innovation

In this section, we first identify two types of financial innovation. Then we discuss the process by which financial innovation occurs. We also briefly consider the role of the authorities in this process.

The term "financial innovation" has been used by many people to mean many things. A close study of the catalogue of financial innovations that have occurred in various countries suggests to us that financial innovations may be broadly classified, according to their common characteristics, into two groups:

1) innovations which result from, and seek to reduce, the shadow cost of regulatory constraints (Type 1 innovations), and

2) innovations which, independent of regulatory constraints, seek to reduce physical transaction costs or to improve allocation of risk (Type 2 innovations).

Table 3.1 shows some typical examples of these two types of innovation. We by no means want to pretend that this taxonomy is a perfect one; on the contrary, we are quite aware of its major problem, namely that the demarcation between Type 1 and Type 2 is not necessarily one hundred percent clear-cut. A case in point is the "NOW account,"

Table 3.1   Types of Financial Innovations

Type	Characteristics	Typical examples
(1) Innovations that develop new means of transaction not subject to prevailing regulations	Circumvention of deposit rate ceilings and/or reserve requirements	CD, MMMF, MMC, MMDA, etc. Euro currency markets
	Circumvention of restrictions on the scope-of-operations	CMA, Discount brokerage by banks, Non-bank banks
(2) Innovations that reduce the cost or the risk of existing means of transaction	Reduction of transaction costs	EFT system, NOW accounts, Allkonto, Daily Interest Checking Accounts
	Reallocation of risk	Floating rate contracts, Financial future markets

which appears as a Type 2 innovation in Table 3.1. It cannot be denied that a "NOW account" has elements of Type 1 innovations since it virtually circumvents the restriction on interest rates on demand deposits. However, we classified it as a Type 2 innovation because we believe that the most important characteristic of this innovation is the reduction of the transaction cost of shifting funds between a savings account and a demand account, since the interest rate paid remained subject to Regulation Q until 1983. Type 2 innovations are basically independent of restrictions and may take place as long as costs and risks are involved in financial transactions. While we do not wish to argue that the demarcation between Type 1 and Type 2 is perfectly clear-cut, we do find this classification useful, because it facilitates our effort to generalize as far as feasible the relationship between the characteristics of financial innovation in each country and the institutional features of its financial system.

In some countries, financial innovations initiated in the private market have to be approved by the authorities to become fully effective. In these cases, financial innovations appear to be initiated by the regulatory authorities themselves rather than by market forces, and it may seem inappropriate to call Type 1 innovations regulation-circumventing. In a country where market participants are so anemic that they lack the dynamism to exploit profit opportunities, the regulators could be regarded as initiators of financial innovation. In most countries with developed financial markets, however, the approval of the authorities is in fact the consequence of continuing pressure from the private financial sector which is seeking to free itself from existing regulatory constraints. In our view, therefore, the Type 1 innovations as we described them above and authority-led innovations which some call deregulation are not mutually exclusive.

Why and how are innovations initiated? Whether a particular financial innovation is initiated at all depends upon the relationship between the cost that consumers of financial services have to bear because of the existence of financial constraints, and the cost to competing financial institutions of providing new innovations. If the former exceeds the latter, there always are profit opportunities to be exploited by introducing innovations. This relationship varies depending on such exogenous factors as various social and economic conditions and technological developments. Specifically, Silber (1983), for instance, cites 1) inflation, 2) interest rate variability, 3) internationalization, 4) technological innovation, and 5) legislative initiatives. Similarly, Suzuki (1984a, 1984b) identifies 1) high and volatile interest rates, 2) innovation in computers and communications technology, 3) increasing international capital mobility, and 4) development of open financial markets as the common factors behind financial innovation in major industrial countries. They are, in our view, the kinds of exogenous factors which affect the above relationship, through either increasing the cost of constraints or reducing costs of providing means of transaction.

According to the "constraint-induced innovation hypothesis" which Silber applied to financial innovation in the United States for the period 1970–82 (Silber 1983), financial innovation would be triggered by the disequilibrium associated with changes in exogenous variables and realized through the efforts of financial institutions trying to exploit profit opportunities created by the disequilibrium. In Silber's words, the "rising costs of adhering to constraints stimulate financial innovation."

On the other hand, there is an alternative view that financial innovation derives from competition among the financial authorities, not among financial institutions. Kane (1977, 1981), for instance, argues that the financial authority aims at maximizing the welfare of financial institutions under its jurisdiction (clients) while at the same time protecting its own interests (turf) which are vested in enforcing regulations and maintaining clientele. Because the financial authorities wish their *own* clients, as opposed to other financial institutions, to exploit existing profit opportunities, they relax regulations that have been suppressing innovation, or introduce new regulations which are less burdensome than the earlier ones. The financial authorities thus compete among themselves, seeking to promote and maintain their loyal constituencies. (Kane calls this the regulatory dialectic hypothesis.)

While it is interesting and suggestive, it seems that this theory accounts for only part of the reality. First, it does not explain Type 2 innovations which are not directly related to the regulatory structure. Second, it does not seem applicable to most countries where regulatory power is highly centralized; the United States, where regulatory power is diverse and competition among the regulatory authorities is the order of the day, is the exceptional case rather than the rule. Third, Kane's hypothesis that the authorities act to maximize the welfare of the coalition of the regulators themselves and their clients is rather debatable. While it may sound self-serving for us to say this, it could reasonably be argued that the authorities act as providers of public goods, aiming at promoting public interest.

III. Financial Innovation in Major Industrial Countries

In this section, we describe the process of financial innovation in selected countries during the years since the 1960s.[1] We pay special attention to the concentration of particular types of innovation and the regulatory framework in which such innovation occurred.

1. Developments in the 1960s and Early 1970s

Financial innovation is by no means a recent phenomenon. For example, the evolution of money from commodities to deposits is itself a process of financial innovation; the cost and the risk of transactions have been reduced by increasing the homogeneity and divisibility of the medium of exchange and by reducing the costs of storage and transfer.

However, specific types of financial innovations are closely related to particular types of institutional frameworks. Table 3.2 displays chronologically the two types of financial innovations mentioned earlier, as they have occurred in selected countries. Certain financial innovations bear the characteristics of both Type 1 and 2, in which

---

[1] For financial innovations outside Japan, we relied heavily on works by Boreham (1984), Frazer and Vittas (1982), Kaufman (1984), and various papers recorded in "Financial Innovations and Monetary Policy," BIS (1984). In regard to the developments in Japan, Suzuki (1984b), Uejo (1983), Mitsui Bank EB Kenkyūkai (1983), and Cargill (forthcoming) were especially useful.

Table 3.2   Major Financial Innovations in the United States, Japan and

Type 1. Regulation-circumventing innovations	
Group A—U.S., Japan, France	Group B—U.K., Canada
1960s Euro-dollar markets ⎫ RP ⎬ (U) Bank-related CP ⎭ Investment trusts (J, F) Gensaki transactions (J)	Hire-purchase finance companies (B) Parallel markets (B) CD, BA (C)
1970s Large-lot CD with unregulated⎫ interest rates MMMF ⎬(U) CMA 6-month MMC ⎭ CD with unregulated interest rates (J) Entry of commercial banks into mortgage loans, securities broker- age, and trust services (F)	Euro-pound markets ⎫ Entry of clearing banks ⎬(B) into loan services secured⎭ by real estate Entry of chartered banks ⎫ into mortgage loan serv-⎬(C) ices ⎭
1980s SSC, Sweep accounts ⎫ 7–31-day money marke accounts 91-day MMC MMDA, Super-NOW ⎬(U) Growth of nonbank banks Entry of commercial banks into discount brokerage services ⎭ Medium-term government bond⎫ funds Foreign currency deposits Sweep services between medium- term government bond funds and ordinary deposit accounts⎬(J) MMC Over-the-counter sales and dealings of government bonds by banks Government bond time deposit accounts ⎭ Euro-yen markets SICAV, CD ⎫ Increase in bank ⎬(F) debenture issues ⎭	Entry of clearing banks into securities brokerage services (B) Entry of chartered banks ⎫ into securities brokerage⎬ service ⎬(C) Entry of large trust compan-⎬ ies into securities business⎭

European Countries

Type 2. Cost-reducing and risk-reallocating innovations	
Group C—Germany, Switzerland, Netherlands	
Bond trading with repur- chase agreements (G)	Direct credit of payrolls to deposit accounts (A) Preauthorized direct debit system for public utility charges (J and others) Expansion of consumer financial services by banks (A)
Euro-mark markets (G)	EFT system for interbank transactions (U, J) Introduction of ATM Mutual use of ATM networks by banks }(A) NOW accounts (U) Allkonto (S) Deposit combined accounts (J) Daily interest savings accounts (C) Floating-rate loans and debts (U, B, F, C) Financial futures markets (U) Options markets (U)
Increase in bank debenture issues (G)	CMS, Home banking (U and others) EFT system for interbank tranasactions (B, F, G) Daily interest checkable savings accounts (C) Save and borrow accounts High interest checking accounts }(B) New loan trusts ("Big") Bank debentures with compound interest }(J) rates ("Wide") Financial futures market (U, B)

A = All Countries   G = Germany
B = U.K.   J = Japan
C = Canada   S = Sweden
F = France   U = U.S.

Table 3.3   Financial Regulations in Major Countries since the 1960s

Countries		Regulations on Deposit Interest Rates	Effective Rate of Reserve Requirements (as percent of broadly-defined money supply)
Group A	United States	Virtually abolished in 1983	9.7 → 7.5 → 3.5 (1960) (1970) (1983)
	Japan	Regulated except for CDs and foreign currency deposits	2.2 → 2.0 → 2.2 (1960) (1970) (1983)
Group B	France	Regulated except for long term deposits	1.9 → 2.6 → 1.5 (1960) (1970) (1983)
	Sweden	Abolished in 1980	1.2 → 1.3 → 1.2 (1960) (1970) (1983)
	United Kingdom	Abolished in 1971	8.5 → 8.7 → 2.4 (1965) (1970) (1983
	Canada	Abolished in 1967	7.5 → 4.8 → 3.2 (1960) (1970) (1983)
Group C	Germany	Abolished in 1967	12.8 → 9.3 → 7.4 (1960) (1970) (1983)
	Switzerland	No regulation	No required reserves
	Netherlands	No regulation	3.9 → 1.2 → 0.6 (1960) (1970) (1983)

Regulations on the Scope of Financial Businesses	Restrictions on Bank Lendings	Exchange Controls
Legal separation between banking and securities businesses	No regulation	Free in principle except for the period of 1963–74 when capital outflows were restricted
Legal separation between banking and securities businesses, banking and trust businesses, and also long- and short-term financing	Window guidance (credit ceilings on bank lendings) if and when necessary	Substantially relaxed in 1980, Euro-yen transactions considerably liberalized in 1984
De facto separation between banks and specialized banks (i.e. Crédit Agricole)	Reserve requirements on bank lendings	Under control
De facto separation between commercial banks and savings banks	Occasionally in effect from 1970s	Under control
De facto separation between clearing banks, merchant banks, and building societies	Abolished in 1971	Free in principle (abolished in 1979)
Legal separation between banking and securities business, and also banking and trust business	No regulation	Free in principle
No regulation	No regulation	Free in principle except for the period 1970–75 when capital inflows were restricted
No regulation	Abolished in 1975	Free in principle
No regulation	Virtually ineffective since 1970s	Under control

case they are classified according to whichever characteristic we consider dominant. There could be reasonable disagreement with respect to particular assignations, but we do not think that such disagreement is serious.

The evolution of regulation-circumventing (Type 1) financial innovation depends on the regulatory framework of the countries concerned. We classify countries into three groups according to the degree of restriction on deposit interest rates and scope-of-operations (see Table 3.3), and examine the process of innovation in each group. Group A includes the United States, Japan, France, and Sweden—countries that have (or had until recently) regulations on deposit interest rates and strict restrictions on scope-of-operations. Group B includes Canada and the United Kingdom—countries that relaxed or abolished regulations on deposit interest rates in the 1960s or 1970s but still maintain some scope-of-operations restrictions. Finally, Group C includes Germany, Switzerland, and the Netherlands, where deposit interest rates and scope-of-operations have long been unrestricted. The table is obviously not comprehensive, and only of an illustrative nature since we did not have enough information on other important countries in Europe. Still, the difference in degree of concentration of Type 1 innovations—particularly between Group A and Group C—is quite impressive: things have been very quiet in Group C countries. The table also contains examples of Type 2 innovations that have been developing in most countries.

Major Type 1 financial innovations during the late 1960s and early 1970s were growth of the Euro-dollar and Euro-DM markets, expansion of the parallel market (United Kingdom) and *Gensaki* transactions (Japan), establishment of investment trusts (France and Japan), and installment of credit companies (United Kingdom and Sweden). Major Type 2 financial innovations included direct credit of payrolls to bank accounts and automatic payment of public utility charges.

Of the Type 1 financial innovations that took place during this period, expansion of the Euro-currency markets was most prominent, induced mainly by the effort on the part of market participants to bypass reserve requirements (United States) and restrictions on deposit interest rates (Regulation Q in the United States) and on foreign capital transaction (United States, Germany).

Financial innovation in the 1970s differed significantly from that of the earlier period. First, within the Type 1 classification, concentration of innovations differed. Our interpretation is that in the 1960s the shadow costs of constraints were highest in the areas of deposit interest rates, foreign capital transaction, and guidance on the amount of bank lending. The regulatory constraints on deposit interest rates continued to impose great cost in the succeeding period; however, the importance of the latter two factors declined, while the costs that accrued from the reserve requirements and constraints on the scope-of-operations became much more strongly felt. Type 2 financial innovations developed rapidly in many countries beginning around 1975. A closer look at Type 2 financial innovation reveals that in the United States, the United Kingdom, France, and Canada significant progress was made in both cost reduction and risk reallocation, while changes in Germany and Japan mainly aimed at reducing transaction costs. In the latter two countries no significant innovation was seen which aimed at improving the allocation of interest rate volatility risk.

During the 1970s, the scope of financial innovation became broader. We interpret this as a further decline in the efficiency of the existing financial framework due to changes in underlying conditions. Among the social, economic, and technological factors that contributed to financial innovation in the 1970s, the following five seem to be most important:

(a) High nominal interest rates.

(b) Increases in the volatility of market interest rates, and in the accompanying risk.

(c) Progress in international economic integration, especially growing international capital flows.

(d) The persistence of large public deficits and the need for efficient means of financing such deficits.

(e) Innovations in computers and communications technology, which increase the speed, and reduce the cost, of funds transfer.

Factors (a), (c), and (d) brought an increase in the shadow cost of regulation on deposit interest rates. While (a) directly raised the opportunity cost of non- or low-interest-bearing demand and saving deposits, (c) and (d) resulted in a wider supply of alternative opportunities for financial investments in the form of government bonds and foreign assets, which made regulated deposits less attractive. The increase in profit opportunity that was brought about by (d) also meant higher shadow cost of restriction on scope-of-operations for banks. It is obvious that (b) has raised interest rate risk for banks. Factor (e) has directly reduced the cost of introducing financial innovation, and (c) and (d) have widened the potential for innovation from the viewpoint of financial institutions.

While changes in such exogenous factors as listed above have occurred in most countries at one time or another, the response of the authorities has differed from country to country. Most countries have

taken measures to relax quantitative controls on bank loans and restrictions on foreign exchange transactions, so that the shadow cost
of such restrictions has declined or been eliminated. In Group A countries, where regulations on deposit interest rates and scope-of-operations remained strict, the introduction of financial innovations that
aim at bypassing such restrictions has been profitable. On the other
hand, in Group C countries where such regulations were non-existent,
innovation that reduces physical transaction costs has been more
significant.

2. Developments in the Last Decade

(1) *Regulation-circumventing financial innovations.* We first review the
development of regulation-circumventing financial innovations in
Group A and B countries in recent years. Major characteristics during
this period may be summarized as follows.

Financial development in the United States and France has now
reached a level that permits small savers to earn market yields. In the
United States, large-denomination CDs[2] with market-determined yields
were introduced in 1969. In 1971, MMMFs were introduced by securities companies for smaller investors. MMMFs are free from interest
rate regulations, restrictions on interstate banking, and reserve requirements. The surge in the interest rates in 1979 caused large shifts of
funds from deposits to MMMFs, and forced banks and savings and
loans associations to respond by offering time deposits with interest
rates tied to market rates (MMCs, SSCs, ASCs) and checkable time
deposits bearing freely-determined interest rates (MMDA, Super-NOW
accounts).

In France, regulations on short-term deposit rates led to a continuous shift from deposits to securities in the second half of the 1970s.
In response, banks began offering short-term securities investment
trust (SICAV de tresorerie) through their subsidiary trust companies
in 1981. Like MMMFs in the United States, they are not subject to
interest rate regulations or reserve requirements.

In Japan, since the late 1970s the ceilings on deposit interest rates
have been a serious constraint for large-scale depositors. The authorities have taken gradual steps toward liberalization by granting official
recognition to several market initiatives, notably the introduction of
large-denomination CDs and MMCs, foreign-currency deposits, and
medium-term government bond funds (investment trusts comparable
to U.S. MMMFs). Moreover, the ceilings on large deposit rates are

---

[2] A list of abbreviations used in this paper is provided as an appendix (see p. 75).

now scheduled to be removed in the next two or three years.

In Group B and C countries where restrictions on deposit interest rates do not exist, financial innovations have aimed mainly at bypassing reserve requirements. Typical examples of such innovation can be found in the United Kingdom and Germany. In the United Kingdom, the corset system substantially raised the effective reserve requirement burdens on sterling-denominated domestic bank liabilities. This promoted domestic expansion of dollar-denominated transactions (Euro-dollar markets) and transfer of sterling-denominated transactions abroad (Euro-sterling markets).

In Germany, high interest rates have also raised the opportunity cost of reserve holdings. Banks now prefer to acquire funds by issuing short-term bank debentures rather than through time deposits which are subject to reserve requirements. This partly explains why the volume of bank debentures issued has increased by 11 % annually since 1980, while bank deposits have risen only 5 % per year.

Financial innovations that aim at bypassing scope-of-operations restrictions have been especially significant in the United States, Canada, and Japan. First, CMAs and sweep accounts were introduced in the United States in the late 1970s. They are provided jointly by commercial banks and securities companies and have functioned as both payment and investment instruments. Since the beginning of the 1980s, financial institutions have taken advantage of the loopholes in the Glass-Steagall Act and the Bank Holding Company Act: commercial banks have entered into the field of discount brokerage services and insurance, while securities companies, insurance companies, and retailers of consumer goods have penetrated into the banking business by setting up so-called "nonbank banks."

Innovation of this type has also been actively taking place in Canada. The demand of chartered banks for relaxation of scope-of-operations regulations in the Banking Law that had been met in 1967 was further accommodated in 1980: banks began offering mortgage loans in the 1970s and more recently have added brokerage services. Restrictions on scope-of-operations have increasingly been blurred in other areas as well. For example, trust companies are now entering the securities business.

In Japan, banks and securities companies have accelerated entry into each other's domains in the 1980s. Banks have started dealing in government bonds and provide for automatic deposit facilities of bond coupons to help reduce transaction costs. Securities companies for their part have introduced loans secured against government bonds, and provide sweep services between medium-term government bond funds and ordinary deposits jointly with several smaller banks.

In France and the United Kingdom, where the division of various financial functions among specialized financial institutions is more a matter of customary business practice than of government regulation, commerical banks have been expanding their operations into long-term business and housing loans since the 1970s. Recently many banks in the United Kingdom have started securities brokerage services.

(2) *Financial innovations that promote efficiency of the existing means of transaction.* The progress of Type 2 financial innovation has accelerated remarkably since the mid-1970s in most countries with the development of various electronic fund transfer (EFT) systems. EFT systems can be classified into those that link financial institutions together and those that link financial institutions with their customers (ATM, POS, CBCT, etc.). All these innovations provide payment services at lower cost than the existing means of payment such as cash, drawing of checks, and mail transfers.

An advanced EFT system that links financial institutions electronically through the central bank developed relatively early in the United States (Fed Wire ⟨1970⟩), and there is now a plan to link the national system with the international SWIFT network. The United Kingdom introduced an EFT system (CHAPS) in 1984, and Japan, France, and Germany are also planning introduction of similar systems.

Since the mid-1970s, ATMs that link financial institutions with their customers were introduced in the mid-1970s in most industrial countries, and, in some cases, a nationwide network has developed. With the introduction of CBCT systems, cash management services for business firms (firm banking) and households (home banking) are expected to develop rapidly in the future.

At present, the response of banks in most countries to such technological developments differs somewhat from that of U.S. banks. In 1981, about 80% of all the commercial banks in the United States with asset size exceeding $5 billion provided on-line cash management services to business firms by setting up CBCT systems. Home banking started in 1982 and is expected to serve 12–15 million households by 1990 (Mitsui Bank 1983). In other countries, however, cash management services have remained relatively insignificant, and home banking has just entered the experimental stage in the United Kingdom, France, and Japan. This may reflect differences in the degree of competition between banks and securities companies, the capacity and availability of communication circuits, and the existence of private-sector value added networks (VAN).

Financial innovations that aim at increasing the liquidity of savings deposits have also been introduced in most countries. They include reducing penalties for early withdrawal, providing checking services, and allowing low-cost borrowing against savings deposit balances. Examples are NOW accounts in the United States (established in 1972), "Allkonto" in Sweden (1979), "Daily interest checking accounts" in Canada (1981), "Sōgō kōza" in Japan (1972), and "Save and borrow accounts" in the United Kingdom (1982).

In some countries innovation in the form of more frequent compounding of interest rate receipts has led to higher deposit yields. Examples include "Daily interest savings accounts" in Canada (1979) and loan trusts ("Big") and bank debentures ("Wide") in Japan (1981).

In the United States, the United Kingdom, France, and Canada, the need for hedging interest rate risk has led to several innovations. Typical examples are variable rate loans and floating rate bonds (the U.S., the U.K., France, and Canada) and the establishment of financial futures markets in the U.S. (1975) and the U.K. (1982). The numerous options markets in the United States and elsewhere have also reduced the transaction cost of reallocating financial risks in a fashion preferred by market agents.

3. The Japanese Experience

Having described the major developments of financial innovation in selected countries, we now focus in this section on the process of financial innovation in Japan.

Until the mid-1970s, financial markets were rigidly controlled. Regulations on scope-of-operations, comprehensive controls on international financial transactions, and interest rate controls were strictly enforced. In addition, non-financial firms depended heavily on bank finance. Because of credit availability constraints, firms were more concerned with securing adequate quantities of financial resources than with the costs of credit per se.

Under such circumstances, major financial innovations were unlikely to occur. Since deposit rates were regulated and no significant differences existed among individual banks with respect to their loan rates, differences in their margins were minimal. Thus banks concentrated on expanding their deposit volume, but through means other than interest rates. For example, they sought to attract deposits by making new payments technology available to customers free or at nominal charges (Type 2 innovations). Early examples of such efforts included direct debit of public service fees (from 1955), direct credit of payrolls (from 1969), and settlement of payments made by credit card. On-line systems with cash dispensers were made available in 1969. Banks started in

1972 a new financial service called "Sōgō kōza," a combination of a low-yielding ordinary deposit and a higher-yielding time deposit with overdraft facilities. ATMs were introduced towards the end of the 1970s.

The impact of such Type 2 financial innovations was, however, minor and did not appreciably affect the financial market as a whole: banks were able to maintain their dominant position over securities houses until the mid-1970s. It is only since that time that innovation has taken on a far-reaching character.

The major exogenous factors that increased the shadow cost of existing regulatory constraints and triggered Type 1 innovations were those related to the structural change in the flow-of-funds since the first oil crisis. Technological progress meanwhile drastically reduced the cost of providing such innovations.

The changing flow-of-funds pattern shown in percentages in Table 3.4 suggests a drastic change in the situation described above. In the earlier period, the share of deposit banks' asset-earning deposits remained above 60%. Investments in securities by the non-financial sector remained below 10%, with the exception of a temporary boom in 1970 and 1971. This pattern began to change in 1974. In 1983, the share of deposit banks dropped to 42%, while that of securities reached nearly 19% of the total. The share of public financial intermediaries that collect funds from postal savings rose from under 20% to 27%.

The most important factor underlying such structural changes was the slow down in the rate of growth after the first oil crisis. The decline in the growth rate of private investment led to a surplus of funds in the private sector. Reflecting this, net financial assets held by the private non-financial sector grew rapidly. At the end of 1983, the ratio of such assets to GNP exceeded 80%, as compared with only 31% at the end of 1973. With large accumulation of financial assets in an inflationary environment of the early 1970s, businesses and households became more interest conscious and unsatisfied with regulated deposit rates.

With tax revenues stagnating on the one hand and an expansionary fiscal policy being followed on the other, the deficit in the public sector grew rapidly, and so did issues of government bonds. The ratio of outstanding government bonds to GNP reached 42% at the end of fiscal 1984, compared with 11% in 1974. This rapid growth, in turn, made it impossible for the authority to maintain its policy of asking the banks to refrain from selling in the market the bonds they acquired through syndicates. This guidance was relaxed in the late 1970s, and as a result, transactions of bonds in the unregulated secondary market increased substantially. The deepening of this market opened the way

Table 3.4 Main Channels of Financial Flows in Japan (%)

Calendar Year	Private Financial Inter- mediaries	Deposit Banks	Trust Banks, Insurance Companies	Public Financial Inter- mediaries	Securities Markets	Bonds	Domestic Stocks	Domestic Investment Trusts	Overseas	Total
1965	78.6	63.2	11.3	15.5	5.9	3.5	5.1	-3.0	-0.3	100.0
1966	78.4	69.6	10.0	19.3	2.3	2.6	2.2	-1.7	-0.8	100.0
1967	77.4	66.1	12.0	16.2	6.4	3.1	1.0	-1.1	3.4	100.0
1968	72.5	58.3	13.0	18.4	9.1	2.5	2.7	0.2	3.7	100.0
1969	73.3	60.3	11.7	16.9	9.8	2.3	2.9	1.1	3.5	100.0
1970	71.0	60.3	12.8	16.7	12.3	3.0	4.8	0.6	3.9	100.0
1971	70.2	57.8	11.7	16.2	13.6	3.4	2.8	1.0	6.4	100.0
1972	77.5	66.2	10.5	16.1	6.4	1.3	2.0	1.4	1.7	100.0
1973	74.6	64.1	10.9	18.6	6.8	3.1	3.6	0.6	-0.5	100.0
1974	69.0	58.0	10.7	21.1	9.9	1.7	2.3	0.3	5.6	100.0
1975	69.8	58.8	10.4	23.3	6.9	3.5	2.0	1.6	-0.2	100.0
1976	67.4	56.0	10.2	23.7	8.9	3.9	1.8	1.0	2.2	100.0
1977	60.5	49.6	9.5	29.2	10.3	6.6	2.4	0.9	0.4	100.0
1978	62.4	54.2	6.7	25.4	12.2	6.4	1.4	0.7	3.7	100.0
1979	59.3	48.0	9.6	28.6	12.1	6.3	2.2	0.4	3.2	100.0
1980	54.9	41.9	11.6	31.2	13.9	7.6	1.6	-0.6	5.3	100.0
1981	61.4	49.8	9.9	25.5	13.1	7.3	2.4	1.9	1.5	100.0
1982	56.1	42.4	12.7	29.2	14.7	5.5	2.9	3.0	3.3	100.0
1983	54.5	41.6	10.0	26.6	18.9	8.5	1.2	5.8	3.4	100.0

Source: Flow of Funds Accounts, Bank of Japan.

Table 3.5   Major Characteristics of Selected New Financial Instruments in Japan

	CDs	MMCs	Medium-term Government Bond Funds
Introduction date	May 1979	March 1985	January 1980
Authorized issuers	All depository institutions (including Sōgō, Shinkin, and foreign banks).	Same as CDs	Securities companies
Authorized secondary market brokers	The above institutions, call money brokers and securities companies (from June 1985)	None	None
Secondary market trading	Relatively small volume (¥8 trillion in call money broker trading).	None	None
Restriction on issuer's portfolio	100 percent of net worth	75 percent of net worth	None
Maturity restrictions	One to six months	Same as CDs	Minimum one month
Minimum unit restrictions	¥100 million	¥50 million	¥100 thousand
Interest rate determination	Set by bilateral negotiation between financial institution and customer. No restrictions or consultations with authorities.	Upper limit is 0.75 percent lower than the weekly average rate of CDs.	Set in consultation with the Ministry of Finance, below the one-year time deposit yield.

Tax characteristics	Not subject to securities transaction tax (on *Gensaki*).	—	Suitable for tax-free personal savings up to ¥3 million
Main investors	Corporations, pension funds, and local government authorities.	Medium and small-sized business firms and local government authorities	Households and small business firms
Annual growth rate in volume in last 3 years	40 percent	n.a.	100 percent
Current volume	¥8.5 trillion (Jan. 1985) (2.5 percent of total bank liabilities).	n.a.	¥5.0 trillion (Mar. 1985)
Closest substitutes	Gensaki, large-sized time deposits, and bills traded in interbank market (correlation with Gensaki rate = 0.996, May 1979–Feb. 1985, monthly data)	Large-sized time deposits and medium-term government bond funds.	Time deposits with maturities less than one year and MMCs.

for the private non-financial sector to obtain yields higher than restricted deposit rates. Thus, funds naturally shifted from bank deposits to government bonds and other related long-term market instruments.

There also was a shift from bank deposits into postal savings. Since postal savings accounts, though short-term (six months with regulated rates), have characteristics similar to long-term financial assets (funds can be left in the account up to ten years with the rate of interest unchanged from the time of initial deposit), they attracted funds away from bank deposits during tight money conditions. This partly explains the increased share of public financial intermediaries shown in Table 3.4.

Developments in the secondary market for long-term bonds were further promoted by the growth of "Gensaki" transactions, which are similar to RPs in the United States and are initiated by securities companies. For small savers, securities companies in 1980 introduced medium-term government bond funds ("Chūki-Kokusai fund")— short-term small-denomination investment trusts which resemble U.S. money-market mutual funds (Table 3.5). The yield on such funds is set higher than that on bank liabilities with similar maturities. They have doubled in size annually for the last three years and now are equivalent to 2% of bank deposits, or 50% larger than the Gensaki market.

Banks for their part started issuing CDs in 1979 with a minimum unit of ¥500 million. The volume was first restricted to 10% of bank net worth. Since then, the minimum unit has been lowered, to ¥300 million in 1984 and to ¥100 million in April 1985, and the quantitative ceiling has gradually been raised to 100% of bank net worth. CDs have been growing by 40% annually in the last three years; currently they are 2.5 times larger than outstanding Gensaki balances and account for 3% of bank liabilities. The yields are market-determined, and are competitive with those on Gensaki transactions. Securities companies will be permitted to trade in bank CDs beginning this June [1985], and are expected to increase the negotiability of such instruments. Interest rates on time deposits are still regulated, but in March 1985 banks started issuing MMCs; these are not negotiable, but their terms are closely related to those of CDs.

These movements are forerunners of the complete liberalization of large-scale deposit rates, which is scheduled for the next few years. It should also be mentioned that in Japan one is free to establish foreign currency deposits at any domestic bank, without being subject to any interest rate restrictions. These deposits, if combined with forward cover, offer an efficient means to circumvent interest rate restrictions on yen deposits without involving any exchange risk.

A more difficult question is how to deal with interest rates on small-scale deposits. Even if the traditional conflict of interest between banks and the postal saving system is left aside there is a technical question of how and to what extent small savers can enjoy market-related interest rates. It appears that in those countries where deposit rate restrictions have long been lifted, rates on small savings have been rather stable irrespective of market rate developments, suggesting that small savers are not fully enjoying the opportunity to earn more.

A strict statutory division of functions among specialized financial institutions still exists in Japan, but this also is being challenged. One such restriction is the separation of short-term commercial banking business from long-term financing. Only long-term credit banks are allowed to issue debentures to raise medium- and long-term funds. However, commercial banks have been extending long-term credit which is not legally prohibited, and have created maturity mismatching problems. This has led to growing pressure for commercial banks to be permitted to raise medium- and long-term funds. A division between trust banks and other financial institutions is also being challenged, for similar reasons.

The third distinction that has become increasingly controversial is that between commercial banks and securities companies. Article 65 of the Securities and Exchange Law, the counterpart of the U.S. Glass-Steagall Act, prohibits financial institutions from engaging in both banking and securities transactions simultaneously. This distinction, however, has also become increasingly blurred.

Since 1983, banks have been selling newly issued long-term government bonds over the counter. In June 1984, the operation was extended to seasoned government bonds. The securities companies for their part have been offering deposit-like investment trust funds, and are planning to offer credit facilities with government bonds they hold for customers as collateral. They are also beginning to deal in bank CDs and BAs. Thus both banks and securities companies are vigorously seeking to expand their scope of operations.

Basically banks and securities companies are in competition, but there are also indications of cooperation between the two groups of financial institutions. Several smaller banks have recently offered cash management services combining demand deposits with medium-term government bond funds issued by securities companies. As of April 1985, 13 Shinkin and Sogo banks offered these sweep accounts, but the volume is still marginal. This type of innovative service has been made possible through a dramatic decline in the cost of financial transactions, and it indicates an important direction for financial innovation in the coming years.

As Japan has become deeply integrated in the world economy, developments in the international financial markets are one of the strongest forces that have prompted Type 1 innovations at home. One early consequence was liberalization of interest rates on foreign currency deposits in 1974. Borrowing by residents in foreign currencies was completely liberalized in 1980. Holding of foreign securities by residents as well as investment in domestic securities by non-residents have been freed of any restrictions. In addition, the development of the Euro-yen markets with their freedom from regulatory constraints strongly affects the basic framework of the domestic financial system. Monetary authorities normally have mixed feelings about their own national currencies becoming internationalized, and the Japanese authorities are no exception. But following the so-called U.S.-Japan Yen-Dollar Agreement in May last year, restrictions on Euro-yen transactions have been progressively relaxed; banks are now free to extend Euro-yen loans to non-residents. Only medium- and long-term Euro-yen loans to residents are still restrained, but relaxation of this rule is already under discussion. On the liability side, banks are now allowed to issue short-term Euro-yen CDs, with some conditions still attached. The implications of these developments for the remaining regulatory constraints at home are quite obvious. However, while it cannot be denied that the U.S.-Japan agreement gave the Japanese financial system a significant thrust toward a freer, less-regulated financial system, it should be noted that innovative moves in that direction have already been under way for some time.

IV. Implications of Financial Innovation for the Management of Banks

In this section, we first review the changes which financial innovation has brought about in the environment where banks operate. Then we survey prevailing views on the implications of innovation for the safety and soundness of bank management and the banking system. Ideally, we should review the developments in a number of major countries; however, the existing literature is heavily biased toward data from a single country, the U.S.; hence our study relies mainly on the U.S. experience. We believe that this approach can be justified to a certain extent since the rapid progress of innovation in the U.S. should have made the impact of financial innovation there much more pronounced than in any other country.

1. Changes in Financial Structure

As described in the previous sections, open markets have been undergoing rapid expansion and considerable deepening in recent years. The share of funds channeled through such markets has been increasing at the expense of the share of traditional banking channels. In terms of the assets of the non-financial sector, the share of cash and deposits (on an annual flow basis) has declined and that of market instruments has risen in most countries (Table 3.6). In terms of the composition of bank income, the relative share of profits from traditional banking operations has been declining and that of investment returns and service fees rising (Table 3.7).

In order to keep deposits from flowing out of the banking system, banks started to sell deposits carrying market-determined interest rates. In addition, banks have been making more use of short-term market funds for their operations (Table 3.8). The increased reliance on market-related funds has exposed banks to risks associated with interest rate fluctuations.

Table 3.6   Flow Composition of Financial Assets Held by Domestic Nonfinancial Sector

(% of annual flow)

		1967	1970	1975	1980	1982
Currency and deposits	U.S.	65.4	69.1	47.5	38.5	37.5
	Japan	70.0	67.8	71.9	56.3	62.2
	France	—	66.1	76.1	51.8	—
	Canada	—	36.4	37.7	37.1	13.4
	U.K.	—	47.6	42.2	49.4	49.8
	Germany	59.9	58.0	56.1	44.7	48.7
Market instruments	U.S.	6.4	5.4	29.1	38.7	37.7
	Japan	7.0	11.6	11.5	11.4	15.0
	France	—	27.0	18.3	40.6	—
	Canada	—	9.7	26.4	19.7	39.4
	U.K.	—	23.2	30.5	20.4	19.4
	Germany	24.0	32.9	25.9	41.0	37.7
Others	U.S.	28.0	25.6	23.4	22.8	24.8
	Japan	23.0	20.7	16.7	32.3	22.8
	France	—	6.9	5.7	7.6	—
	Canada	—	53.8	35.9	43.3	47.2
	U.K.	—	29.2	27.3	30.2	30.8
	Germany	16.0	9.2	18.0	14.3	13.6

Source: OECD Financial Statistics.

It could be argued that deregulation of deposit interest rates would reduce fluctuations of money market rates and associated risks, assuming that other things such as the behavior of banks and depositors

Table 3.7   Trends in Components of Various Income of U.S. Banks

(Annual average; % of total)

	1970–74	75–79	80–83
Interest received on loans minus interest paid on deposits	56	55	48
Other income	44	45	52
Income from market investments minus interest paid on borrowings	28	28	28
Income from trust departments	5	5	6
Income from charges	10	11	18

Note: Labor costs, occupancy expense, loan-loss provision, and other operating expenses are not included.
Source: FDIC, Annual Reports.

Table 3.8   Share of Interest-sensitive Components of Commercial Bank Liabilities   (%)

		1960	1980
United States		3	45
Japan		4	12
Germany		15	87
United Kingdom	(London clearing banks in 1960; all banks in 1980)	9	74
France		19	36

Note: Interest-sensitive liabilities include:
U.S.   FF, RP, CP, CD, MMC, SSC
Japan   Call money, bills sold, Gensaki sold, borrowings from financial institutions, CD, non-resident yen deposits, foreign currency deposits.
Germany   Borrowings from financial institutions and bank debentures issued in 1960. All liabilities other than demand deposits in 1980.
U.K.   All liabilities other than deposits in 1960. All liabilities other than demand deposits in 1980.
France   All liabilities other than deposits and borrowings from financial institutions (mainly borrowings from the Bank of France).
Source: Statistical reports published by central banks of respective countries.

remain unchanged. However, if interest rate behavior changes as a result of deposit rate liberalization, this may not hold true. The supply and demand curves for bank deposits may become less elastic with respect to market interest rates (Davis 1982). In this case, changes in market interest rates resulting from shifts in the demand and supply curves would be larger in magnitude.

In addition to interest rate risks, financial innovation has increased another type of risk-liquidity risk. As indicated in Figure 3.1, the M1 velocity has shown an upward trend in most countries. This is partly a reflection of the fact that savings deposits have become more liquid as financial innovation has progressed, permitting the public to economize on non-interest-bearing cash and low-interest demand deposits. Increased liquidity of savings deposits means increased risk exposure for banks.

Risks may also arise under the EFT payments system. Under EFT, transfer of funds between customers' accounts precedes settlement between the agent banks involved, so that the agent bank of the payee has net claims on the agent bank of the payer during the period between

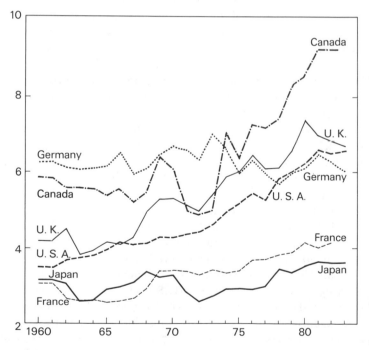

Figure 3.1
Trends in M1 Velocity in Selected Countries

payment and settlement. If a bank with a net debit position becomes insolvent, the liquidity of other banks having a net credit position in the interbank settlement system could be seriously affected.

2. Implications for Safety and Soundness of Banks and the Banking System

What is the effect of the changes mentioned above on the safety and soundness of bank management and the banking system? In an attempt to find an answer to this question, we shall proceed by examining in turn their impact on the level and variability of bank earnings.

In many countries, the introduction of interest rate regulations was prompted by episodes of financial panic in the early twentieth century and by the collapse of the U.S. banking system during the Great Depression in the 1930s. Excessive competition among banks pushed the cost of funds acquisition to an extraordinarily high level. The generally accepted view is that banks invested in high-yielding assets without adequate attention to the risks involved, in order to compensate for these high funds acquisition costs (Cargill and Garcia 1982). In the United States, as the depression began, banks incurred losses on a scale which made the collapse of the banking system inevitable and made regulation of deposit rates desirable. Financial innovations that aim at circumventing interest rate regulations—and also measures which relax such restrictions—thus mean higher costs.

The squeeze on bank profits resulting from the introduction of deposits carrying market-related interest rates, however, may be partially offset by economizing on implicit interest payments, i.e., free gifts and exemption from various service charges. The results of past studies with respect to demand deposits in the United States vary (Figure 3.2), but according to Judd and Scadding (1982), implicit corporate deposit yields since the second half of the 1970s have come close to the level of market interest rates. Implicit interest rates also apply to household deposits. In addition, enhanced price competition tends to help eliminate so-called "X-inefficiency" within banking organizations (e.g. inefficient branch offices and idle employees), contributing to lower costs and higher profits. Banks compete not only with one another but also with nonbank financial institutions conducting banking activities. For example, U.S. securities companies offering MMMFs could establish POS and CBCT network with their customers and link them with the Fed Wire to provide EFT payment services bypassing bank accounts. Since networks linking securities companies with customers can also be used for conventional securities operations, the real sunk cost to securities companies (the cost of entry that cannot

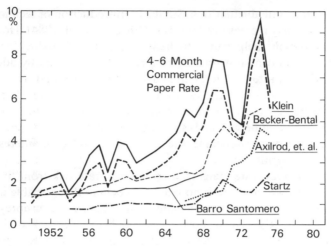

Figure 3.2
Estimates of Implicit Interest Rates on Demand Deposits in the United States
Source: Judd and Scadding (1982).

be recovered upon exit) of establishing an EFT system may be small. The significant decline in sunk cost as a result of technological innovation has raised the shadow cost of legal restrictions on scope-of-operations. As long as sunk costs are close to zero, the banking industry can be considered a contestable market—one in which potential entry leads to competitive results—where organizational efficiency is essential for the survival of market participants.

As banks diversify into a wider range of activities, they may enjoy "economies of scope," reduction of marginal costs accompanied by increasing scale of operations ("multiproduct scale economies"), and reduction in costs resulting from joint production of different services. The existence of "multiproduct scale economies" has been confirmed in empirical studies by Benston, Berger, Hanweck, and Humphrey (1983) and Mullineaux (1978). On the other hand, the cost-reducing effect of joint production seems much less clear. For example, Murray and White (1983), studying the case of Canadian credit unions, have argued that economies of scope existed with respect to mortgages and other loans, while the above-mentioned study by Benston et al. on U.S. member banks does not indicate significant results.

The impact of financial innovation on profit variability is also multi-faceted. As mentioned earlier, if bank assets are less liquid than liabilities, an increase in the share of market-yield liabilities may raise the risk of interest rate fluctuations. Similarly, introduction of technologies such as EFT may increase system risks (McEntee et al. 1984). However, some innovations help banks to hedge against such risks. Thus, for example, banks can shift interest rate risks to customers by adopting variable interest rates, or they can hedge in the futures markets.

Flannery (1981, 1983) analyzed the relationship between changes in interest rates and the ratio of current operating net revenues to total assets of U.S. commercial banks for the period 1960–1978, and found that maturity matching made the risk associated with interest rate fluctuations insignificant.

Variable interest rate loans transfer interest rate risk from banks to borrowers. However, there is no reason to believe that variable interest rate loans are necessarily associated with higher bankruptcy risks (Jacobs 1983). Risk-averse borrowers can hedge the risk of interest rate fluctuations in the futures markets. Since banks can also hedge in this way, it might seem best to allow the market to determine which agent has a comparative advantage in hedging risks.

The increase in bank liquidity risks may be offset by the decline in transaction costs (search cost, investigation cost, etc.) involved in borrowing and selling assets, made possible by the expansion of markets and development of institutions that facilitate such transactions (intermediation through brokers, establishment of credit lines, etc.). The decline in transaction costs provides banks with a buffer against illiquidity.

Product line diversification has also been suggested as a means of reducing risk that banks face in the new environment. In the United States, a number of empirical studies examined the effects of product line diversification of bank holding companies (BHC). In the 1960s, one-bank holding companies (OBHC) with nonbank subsidiaries engaging in securities, insurance, real estate, etc., emerged. However, legislation in 1970 stipulated that subsidiaries of bank holding companies had to confine their activities to fields closely related to banking. Boyd, Hanweck, and Pithyachariyakul (1980), in their study of bank holding companies for the period 1971–1974, found that the risk-reducing effect of product line diversification was insignificant. Based on the covariance matrix of profits of BHCs' bank and non-bank subsidiaries, they calculated the share of non-bank assets in the BHC's total assets (on a consolidated basis) which would minimize the probability of bankruptcy of the BHC in question, and found that it was very small (at most 0.65% of total assets, when the nonbank subsidiary happened to be a consumer credit company).

Eisenbeis, Harris, and Lakonishok (1984) also examined whether the establishment of a one-bank holding company led to an upward revaluation of the bank's equity value. The authors concluded that in the 1960s the announcement of an OBHC was closely linked to an unusual rise in the bank's stock price, while no such relationship has been identifiable since 1970. To the extent that bank shareholders and creditors have similar interests, this test should provide an indication of expected bank risks as well as profits. In short, the magnitude of the risk-reduction effect of product line diversification depends very much on the nature of the newly introduced activities. Income from such nonbanking activities as are permitted under the 1970 U.S. legislation (mortgage loans, leasing, and financial data processing) is so closely tied to income from traditional banking operations that the additional risk-reduction effect is very limited.

Cost-benefit analysis is not always easy, particularly in the field of finance. There seems to be a consensus among economists that financial innovation is conducive to enhancing efficiency as it invariably reduces the costs of constraints, leading to improved allocation of financial resources. In general, financial innovation is not without its own costs, and therefore it can have both positive and negative effects on bank profit and risk. In the United States, where significant financial innovation has taken place, commercial bank profits were generally larger and their variance smaller in the 1970s than in the 1950s and 1960s (Table 3.9). Smirlock (1984) studied the impact of the introduction of large CDs and MMCs on the solvency risk of commercial banks and found no evidence that such developments endangered the soundness of individual banks or the banking system as a whole.

On the other hand, the performance of U.S. thrift institutions, which concentrated on long-term fixed-interest-rate loans, deteriorated sharply in recent years. This seems to be a typical case where regulations and tax incentives which once contributed to maintaining the soundness of financial institutions now tend to work in the opposite direction. Existing regulations restricting the ability of financial institutions to adapt to the new environment could become a factor that impairs the soundness of the institutions and of the financial system.

Further empirical studies are needed, but past studies seem to indicate that the costs of innovation are not so serious as to undermine benefits. Casualties are of course inevitable as inefficient or inadequately managed institutions fail to adjust themselves to new conditions, but this does not justify going backwards, by tightening regulations. As a tentative conclusion we are inclined to argue that if sufficient measures are taken to deal with systemic risk, then total social welfare will definitely increase.

Table 3.9 Profitability of Insured Commercial Banks in the United States

| Year | Net Income as % of | | |
	Total Assets	Total Capital	Equity Capital
1952	0.55	8.07	
1953	0.55	7.93	
1954	0.68	9.50	
1955	0.57	7.90	
1956	0.58	7.82	
1957	0.64	8.30	
1958	0.75	9.60	
1959	0.63	7.94	n.a.
1960	0.81	10.02	
1961	0.79	9.37	
1962	0.73	8.83	
1963	0.72	8.86	
1964	0.70	8.65	
1965	0.70	8.73	
1966	0.69	8.70	
1967	0.74	9.56	10.14
1968	0.72	9.70	10.31
1969	0.84	11.48	11.98
1970	0.89	11.89	12.37
1971	0.87	11.85	12.39
1972	0.83	11.60	12.25
1973	0.85	12.14	12.86
1974	0.81	11.89	12.53
1975	0.78	11.19	11.75
1976	0.70	10.66	11.41
1977	0.71	10.93	11.72
1978	0.77	11.96	12.80
1979	0.81	13.01	13.89
1980	0.80	12.85	13.66
1981	0.76	n.a.	13.20
1982	0.71	n.a.	12.20
1983	0.67	n.a.	11.20
1952–69 (Average)	0.69 (Standard deviation: 0.087)		
1970–83 (Average)	0.78 (Standard deviation: 0.065)		

Source: Kaufman et al. 1983.

If this argument is correct, then what is being asked of the authorities seems clear: to eliminate as completely as possible those regulatory constraints that have created the circumventive by-products which we call Type I innovations. Circumvention itself is a waste of resources. However, care has to be taken to avoid monetary and financial instability in the transitionary phase; here, the pace of deregulation is of vital significance.

Even if all regulatory constraints are removed or relaxed, system risks will remain, for they cannot be avoided by the efforts of individual financial institutions. System risks are already a potential problem in the interbank market, and are expected (as we indicated earlier) to increase with the introduction of EFT payments services.

In order to cope with system risks, particular attention has to be paid to fostering the already existing precautionary mechanism and safety network. In particular there is an acute need for improving the quality of official supervision and consultation, and for restructuring the existing deposit insurance scheme. It may also be necessary to strengthen certain balance-sheet requirements or to introduce restrictions on off-balance-sheet activities. This kind of preventive mechanism is in itself a regulatory framework, and therefore places constraints on bank management. We, however, believe that these constraints are least restrictive of competition, and a are price that must be paid if financial stability is to be maintained.

The precautionary measures outlined above may not be entirely sufficient to prevent instability. Past experience shows how crucial it is for the central bank to act quickly and decisively in an emergency. Given the progress in financial innovation, the role of the central bank as monitor of bank management and interbank market transactions and as provider of last resort will become more and more important.

Acknowledgment

The authors are indebted to Mr. Kermit L. Schoenholtz, a Visiting Scholar at the Institute for Monetary and Economic Studies of the Bank of Japan during 1984–85, for his valuable comments and advice.

Appendix: Abbreviations used in this paper

ASC	All Saver's Certificate
ATM	Automated Teller Machine
BA	Banker's Acceptance
BHC	Bank Holding Company
CBCT	Customer-Bank Communications Terminal

CD	Negotiable Certificate of Time Deposit
CHAPS	Clearing House Automated Payment System
CMA	Cash Management Account
CP	Commercial Paper
EFT	Electronic Fund Transfer
FF	Federal Fund
MMC	Money Market Certificate
MMDA	Money Market Deposit Account
MMMF	Money Market Mutual Fund
NOW	Negotiable Order of Withdrawal
OBHC	One Bank Holding Company
POS	Point of Sale
RP	Repurchase Agreement
SICAV	Société d'Investissement à Capital Variable
SSC	Small Saver's Certificate
SWIFT	Society for Worldwide Interbank Financial Telecommunication

References

Akhtar, M.A. 1984. Financial Innovation and Monetary Policy: A Framework for Analysis. In *Financial Innovation and Monetary Policy*, BIS, Mar. 1984.

Baudewyns, Jacques and Pierre Petit. 1984. Financial Innovation and Monetary Policy in Belgium. In *Financial Innovation and Monetary Policy*, BIS, Mar. 1984.

Beguelin, Jean-Pierre. 1984. Financial Innovation and Monetary Policy: The Swiss Non-Case. In *Financial Innovation and Monetary Policy*, BIS, Mar. 1984.

Benston, George J., Allen N, Berger, and David B, Humphrey. 1983. Economies of Scale and Scope in Banking. In *Proceedings of a Conference on Bank Structure and Competition*. Federal Reserve Bank of Chicago, May 1983, pp. 432–455.

Boreham, Gordon F. 1984. *Financial Innovation in Canada*. Societé Universitaire Européènne de Récherches Financières,

Boyd, John H., Hanweck, Gerald A., and Pithyachariyakul, Pipat. 1980. Bank Holding Company Diversification. In *Proceedings of a Conference on Bank Structure and Competition*. Federal Reserve Bank of Chicago, May 1980, pp. 105–121.

Bruneel, D. and J-M. Facq. 1984. Financial Innovation and Monetary Policy in France. In *Financial Innovation and Monetary Policy*, BIS, Mar. 1984.

Cargill, Thomas F. and Gillian G. Garcia. 1982. *Financial Deregulation and Monetary Control*. Stanford: Hoover Institution Press.

Cargill, Thomas F. 1985a. Financial Reform in the 1980's. Stanford: Hoover Institution Press.

Cargill, Thomas F. 1985b. A U.S. Perspective on Japanese Financial Liberalization. In *Monetary and Economic Studies*, Vol. 3, No. 2, pp. 115–161.

Davis, Richard G. 1982. Monetary Targeting in a 'Zero Balance' World. *Proceedings of Asilomar Conference on Interest Rate Deregulation and Monetary Policy* sponsored by the Federal Reserve Bank of San Francisco, Nov. 1982.

Dudler, Hermann-Josef and H. Herrmann 1984. Financial Innovation and Monetary Policy: The Case of Germany. In *Financial Innovation and Monetary Policy*, BIS, Mar. 1984.

den Dunnen, Emile and Gertjan Hogeweg. 1984, Financial Innovation and Monetary Policy in the Netherlands. In *Financial Innovation and Monetary Policy*, BIS, Mar. 1984.

Eisenbeis, Robert A., Robert S. Harris, and Josef Lakonishok. 1984. Benefits of Bank Diversification: The Evidence from Shareholder Returns. In *The Journal of Finance*, Vol. 39, No. 3, July 1984, pp. 881–892.

Flannery, Mark J. 1981. Market Interest Rates and Commercial Bank Profitability: An Empirical Investigation. In *The Journal of Finance*, Vol. 34, No.6, Dec. 1981, pp. 1085–1101.

———. 1983. Interest Rates and Bank Profitability: Additional Evidence. In *Journal of Money, Credit and Banking*, Vol. 15, No. 3, Aug. 1983, pp. 355–362.

Frazer, Patrick and Vittas, Dimitri. 1982. *The Retail Banking Revolution – An International Perspective*. London: Michael Lafferty Publications Ltd.

Freedman, Charles. 1984. Changes in the Canadian Financial Structure over the Last Decade. In *Financial Innovation and Monetary Policy*, BIS, Mar. 1984.

Golembe, Carter H. and Davis S. Holland. 1983. *Federal Regulation of Banking 1983–84*. Golembe Associates, Inc.

Hansson, Lars and Mats Josefsson, 1984. Financial Innovation and Monetary Policy in Sweden. In *Financial Innovation and Monetary Policy*, BIS, Mar. 1984.

Jacobs, Rodney L. 1983. Fixed-Rate Lending and Interest Rate Futures Hedging. In *Journal of Bank Research*, Autumn 1983, pp. 193–202.

Judd, John P. and John L. Scadding. 1982. Financial Change and Monetary Targeting in the United States. In *Proceedings of Asilomar Conference on Interest Rate Deregulation and Monetary Policy* sponsored by the Federal Reserve Bank of San Francisco, Nov. 1982.

Kane, Edward J. 1977. Good Intentions and Unintended Evil, The Case against Selective Credit Allocation. In *Journal of Money, Credit and Banking*, Vol. 9, No. 1, pp. 55–69.

———. 1981. Accelerating Inflation, Technological Innovation, and the Decreasing Effectiveness of Banking Regulation. In *The Journal of Finance*, Vol. 34, No. 2, pp. 355–367.

Kaufman, George G., Larry R. Mote. and Harvey Rosenblum. 1983. Implications of Deregulation for Product Lines and Geographical Markets of Financial Institutions. In *Journal of Bank Research*, Spring 1983, pp. 8–24.

————. 1984. Consequences of Deregulation for Commercial Banking. In *The Journal of Finance*, Vol. 39 No. 3, pp. 789–803.

McEntee, Elliott C., Jeffrey C. Marquardt Gilbert T. Schwartz, Edward C. Ettin, David B. Humphrey, and Joseph R. Alexander. 1984. Risk Reduction on Large Dollar Transfer Systems. Federal Reserve press release, Mar. 29, 1984.

Mitsui Bank EB Kenkyūkai. 1983. *Electronic Banking Jidai* (in Japanese). Tokyo: Nihon Keizai Shinbun.

Mullineaux, Donald J. 1978. Economies of Scale and Organizational Efficiency in Banking: A Profit-Function Approach. In *The Journal of Finance*, Vol. 33, No. 1, pp. 259–279.

Murray, John D. and White, Robert W. 1983. Economies of Scale and Economies of Scope in Multiproduct Financial Institutions: A Study of British Columbia Credit Unions. In *The Jounal of Finance*, Vol. 38, No. 3, pp. 887–902.

Silber, William L. 1975. Towards a Theory of Financial Innovation. In Silber, William L., ed., *Financial Innovation*. Lexington Books. 1975.

————. 1983. The Process of Financial Innovation. *American Economic Review*, Vol. 73, No. 2, pp. 89–95.

Simpson, Thomas D. and Patrick M. Parkinson. 1984. Some Implications of Financial Innovation in the United States. In *Financial Innovation and Monetary Policy*, BIS, Mar. 1984.

Smirlock, Michael. 1984. An Analysis of Bank Risk and Deposit Rate Ceilings, Evidence from the Capital Markets. In *Journal of Monetary Economics*, Vol. 13, No. 2, pp. 195–210.

Suzuki, Yoshio. 1984a. *Kinyū Kakushin no Uneri* (in Japanese). Tokyo: Nihon Keizai Shinbun.

————. 1984b. Financial Innovation and Monetary Policy in Japan. In *Financial Innovation and Monetary Policy*, BIS, Mar. 1984.

Uejo, Toshiaki. 1983. *CMS Senryaku* (in Japanese), Kinyū-Zaiseijijo-Kenkyūkai.

Wenninger, John. 1984. Financial Innovation in the United States. In *Financial Innovation and Monetary Policy*, BIS, Mar. 1984.

4

Financial Liberalization and Innovation in Seven East Asian Economies

John G. Greenwood

This paper provides a survey of developments in financial deregulation and innovation in seven East Asian countries: Taiwan, the Republic of Korea, Hong Kong, and four of the five ASEAN nations—Malaysia, Singapore, Thailand, and Indonesia. The seven countries contain a wide diversity of economic and financial systems, ranging from a high degree of centralization and government control (South Korea, Singapore) to economies where market mechanisms are the prevalent means of allocating resources (Hong Kong, Thailand). To handle such diversity within a short space, some means of classification is necessary, and some simplification is inevitable. This paper adopts a two-fold classification to describe the *sources* or *influences* making for financial deregulation and innovation in the seven East Asian countries, and a further two-fold classification to describe the *types of liberalization* or innovation which have occurred.

The experience of these seven East Asian countries over the past decade suggests that there have been two broad sets of influences operating to induce financial deregulation and innovation. The first influence, which I shall call the *foreign influence*, usually comes from the presence of foreign bank branches in the country concerned, and is often associated with the financing of trade transactions rather than with the movement of capital. The wide fluctuations in interest rate differentials between foreign—usually U.S. dollar—interest rates and local interest rates since 1979 radically altered the position of foreign banks. In most cases their traditional business was the financing of exporters or importers using "cheap" U.S. dollar or other foreign-sourced credit. It was cheap first because U.S. interest rates were lower than local interest rates, and second because the foreign bank could borrow in the Euro currency markets at more favorable rates than any Asian bank. With the rise in nominal U.S. dollar interest rates, especially since 1979, many Asian countries have enjoyed lower interest rates than are available in U.S. dollar markets, and it therefore no longer makes sense for an Asian importer to borrow U.S.$ funds. Foreign banks have therefore had to struggle to find new areas of business and, frequently with the backing of their home governments, have exerted pressure on Asian governments to obtain access to interbank markets for funds in local currencies. In Taiwan and Indonesia pressures of this kind have led to the emergence, often for the first time, of wholesale money market instruments (bankers' acceptances, commercial paper, and certificates of deposit), and these have on the whole been priced according to supply and demand. The next step in the process is that arbitrage occurs between the money market and the institutional deposit market (e.g. in Taiwan), and this in turn creates pressure for deregulation of the purely domestic market for funds. In one case, Thailand, roughly the same chain of events has occurred, though it has not involved foreign banks specifically.

The second set of influences originates from the *domestic side*, deriving from governmental efforts to develop a money market or to mobilize resources such as savings, sometimes in an attempt to reduce the need for foreign borrowing (e.g. in Indonesia), and sometimes in response to distortions or problems which have arisen on account of excessive rigidity in the past (e.g. in Hong Kong). The deregulatory steps in this area, such as the removal of deposit interest ceilings or the elimination of credit allocation, can also be viewed as an attempt to overcome "financial repression" where it was considered to hamper economic development. With some exceptions in specific areas of the financial sector, the achievements of the seven East Asian countries are quite recent and modest, though there are definite signs of a generalized shift towards market-based solutions to the credit and capital allocation problem. One reason the results are so limited is that there remain serious distortions which the authorities fully realize will take time to untangle (e.g. in Korea), and extensive residual controls, especially on the scope of business of financial intermediaries, controls on capital transactions, and foreign exchange controls, all of which tend to maintain the segmentation or compartmentalization of domestic financial markets and to insulate the local market from overseas markets. This in turn hinders arbitrage between the various types of financial asset or instrument. The limited achievements in this domestic area mean that it is still very costly for households and firms in two of the seven Asian economies surveyed here—Korea and Taiwan—to hedge themselves against the risk of depreciation in their financial asset portfolios, except perhaps by increasing their domestic debt.

To describe the types of financial deregulation and innovation, it is again useful to adopt a two-fold classification, dividing the changes into (1) those affecting the *pricing* of deposit interest rates and other financial assets and instruments and (2) those which affect *the other conditions of competitiveness* such as barriers to entry, controls on the scope of financial intermediaries' business, ownership restrictions, etc. For each country it is only possible to highlight a few of the main changes which have occurred, and in each case an attempt is made to classify the steps towards deregulation according to whether or not they are associated with overseas developments and/or the presence of foreign banks.

My survey permits some tentative conclusions as to the sources of financial deregulation. The experiments in financial liberalization in the seven East Asian countries surveyed here do not appear to derive from the advent of floating exchange rates in the early 1970s since every one of these seven countries still operates a fixed or managed exchange rate (with the exception of Hong Kong between 1974 and 1983). However, increased interest rate volatility abroad (not at home) and hence large changes in interest rate differentials between local and foreign markets clearly have been a factor in promoting financial liberalization via the foreign route referred to earlier. The fact that most of the changes documented below come after 1979 suggests that they have more to do with the volatility of interest rate differentials than with the advent of floating rates. Nor is it possible to say in the case of these seven Asian countries that large government budget deficits have been a significant factor in promoting financial liberalization since most of these countries (with the exception perhaps of Indonesia and Malaysia) have generally maintained healthy budgetary positions. On the other hand, the desire to limit the growth of foreign indebtedness has been a factor behind interest rate liberalization in some cases (e.g. the Philippines, although that country is not included in this survey) but not in others (S. Korea). The influence of technical changes (the introduction of computers, electronic fund transfers, data communications, etc.) in lowering transaction costs and encouraging keener arbitrage among different financial markets and instruments has clearly been a factor in some cases, but it is not clear that it has been decisive. The fact that these East Asian countries as a group have displayed the highest real economic growth rates in the world despite the existence of interest rate controls and numerous impediments to the development of free capital markets suggests that free markets in credit and capital are not a *sine qua non* of rapid economic development. Nevertheless, as economic development has brought financial deepening and a build-up of financial assets, the distortions in the credit markets due to excessive regulation have become more apparent (e.g. in Korea, Taiwan, Thailand, Malaysia, and Hong Kong), and various devices have been introduced to overcome the regulatory obstacles (e.g. unorganized "kerb" markets, swaps into foreign currency, etc.). For the present, however, the removal of the obstacles to free markets in credit and capital from the domestic side is only partial and, in several cases, reluctant.

Fundamentally this reluctance to move towards fully deregulated markets reflects some predisposition in favor of a particular pattern of resource allocation. Instead of using fiscal means to achieve a desired resource distribution the government is using the financial system to achieve the desired result. In using the financial or credit system to achieve a pattern of resource allocation which is different from the solution that would be achieved by the free market, there is always a risk that the government concerned will undermine the integrity of the monetary unit as a medium of exchange or store of value. Those governments which most clearly separate the allocative function of prices (including the price of credit) from their monetary function—i.e., preserving the value of the medium of exchange—also tend to be those which achieve the greatest degree of deregulation.

None of the countries surveyed has a completely free market in all financial instruments, or across all financial markets. On the domestic side governments are generally moving ahead slowly in order to minimize the disturbances due to the transition from a regulated to a deregulated environment. The most striking changes in the recent wave of innovations have therefore generally occurred in response to foreign influences which are by definition beyond the power of the Asian governments to control. It seems, therefore, that the coincidence of the volatility in interest rate differentials and the technological improvements which have made it possible to exploit those differentials have been among the key factors precipitating the trend towards financial liberalization in these seven Asian economies.

Financial Deregulation in the Republic of South Korea

Taking first the ability of banks to freely price bank credit and deposits, the approach of the Korean authorities appears to have been to avoid permitting too much competition too soon. Given the extent of existing controls, there is understandable apprehension at the prospect of any drastic changes in financial conditions on the part of both financial intermediaries and their highly leveraged clients. Thus, although in April 1984 the authorities announced a timetable for several cautious moves toward liberalization for foreign banks, none of the announced measures implied any increase in the freedom of foreign banks (or others) to set the level of interest rates on deposits or loanable funds more freely. At present foreign banks can raise local funds through foreign currency swaps by arrangement with the central bank, but only up to 3% of total Won assets. Aside from this, foreign banks have been so restricted in their activities as to have a negligible influence on the interest rate structure in Korea. Even the size of compensating balances with which foreign banks previously attempted to obviate the lending rate ceilings is now restricted to 10% of the loan amount so that effective loan rates can only be 10/9 of the permitted rates. In November 1984, when bank interest rates were raised, they were set for the first time at a uniform level rather than at discriminatory levels for different classes of borrower, and the authorities permitted banks to set loan rates within a narrow margin (10–11.5%). Recently (in April 1985) the range of discretion has been widened to 3.5% (10–13.5%). On the other side of bank balance sheets, the government has continued to set all deposit interest rates in the commercial banking sector.

Another element in the strategy of the Korean authorities seems to be to allow a quasi-banking sector to emerge between the commercial banking sector—in which deposit and lending rates are virtually government-mandated—and the unofficial kerb loan market where interest rates are market-determined. The intermediate group of quasi-banks, called STFCs (Short Term Finance Companies), are permitted to set rates between the unofficial kerb market rates and the banks' rates, and, not surprisingly given the problems of credit quality in the kerb loan market, have been rapidly gaining market share at the expense of the banks. In 1983, for example, the interest rates on deposits in this non-bank sector were set at 13.5% while the comparable savings rates offered by banks were set at 10%. Consequently deposits in the non-bank sector rose by 28% in 1984 compared with just 9.8% for deposits at the commercial banks, and the market share of recognized non-bank financial institutions rose to 45.6% (see Table 4.A).

Turning to other measures affecting competition in the banking sector, there have been a series of measures taken since 1981, the most important of which are on the domestic side, notably the decision to privatize the five large state-owned banks. These have all now been sold to private interests, the last being the Choheung Bank which was sold in March 1983. Although it is to be hoped that in time the Korean banks will start to behave like true private sector banks, they are still

Table 4.A.   Market Share of Korean Financial Institutions
(In terms of outstanding deposits)   (%)

	1975	1980	1983	1984
Commercial Banks	55.0	43.2	35.4	33.0
Specialized Government Banks	25.4	26.0	23.7	21.4
Non-bank Financial Institutions	19.6	30.8	40.9	45.6
Total	100.0	100.0	100.0	100.0

very much agents of governmental policy. Their staff were trained in a banking system which was entirely government-controlled and owned, and even following privatization they have been obliged to march to the tune of government policy. For example, following the collapse of the Kukje conglomerate group at the end of 1984, the five privatized banks were required by the government to step in and absorb the component companies in the group. Also, the presidents of the four largest commercial banks were reshuffled following the latest National Assembly elections, in February 1985, according to government wishes. Thus aside from the six state-owned Special Banks, the commercial banks, though privatized, are still quasi-government organizations. It is readily admitted that bankers who have learned their trade in an environment of pervasive state direction will take time to learn the skills appropriate to a free-market environment, but it does seem that this transition is going to proceed at the pace directed by government and will therefore take considerably longer than the free-market lobby had anticipated.

More substantive but still limited measures have been implemented with respect to expanding the scope of banks' activities. In 1982 new regulations were introduced to permit commercial banks to enter the trust business, factoring, leasing, and dealing in government securities. An important allocative measure referred to earlier was the move in November 1984 to make bank lending rates uniform, thus removing the preferential rates for specified borrowers. However, the significance of this is considerably undermined by the continuation of extensive preferential rediscounting facilities offered by the Bank of Korea to banks which lend to exporters and other strategically important industries. Also, since it is still only well-established firms which can obtain these preferred credits from the central bank and since the commercial banks and the Special Banks have little incentive to lend to less well-established borrowers (except to meet the requirement that some 20% of their loans must go to so-called medium or small companies), the *raison d'être* for the large unorganized kerb loan market remains strong both for lenders and borrowers. In a recent retrogressive step, in November 1984 the authorities outlawed the unofficial "wanmae" (repurchase) market which had grown in three years to a size of Won 1.5 trillion (US$1.8 billion) in outstanding volume. As long as the authorities remain overly restrictive about the pricing, the quality, and the direction of commercial bank lending, it must be regarded as extremely unlikely that Korea will have any long-term success in unifying its various credit markets.

In summary, despite numerous well-publicized moves towards more liberal conditions in the credit and capital markets in Korea, the reality is that government controls remain a pervasive feature of the system, forcing unqualified, new borrowers and lenders to operate outside the officially recognized markets. Korea's credit markets, more than most others in Asian economies, continue to be carefully segregated from the outside world by specific credit controls, rigid compartmentalization, and strict foreign exchange and capital controls. Under these conditions arbitrage and competition in the provision of financial services will remain severely hampered.

Financial Deregulation in Taiwan

By far the most important developments in the deregulation of Taiwan's financial markets concern the moves towards greater freedom in the pricing of credit through the issue of commercial paper (CP), bankers' acceptances (BAs), and swaps. Most of these developments have come about through the coincidence of two sets of needs on the part of foreign banks and domestic banks. When US$ interest rates exceeded local NT$ interest rates for the first time in 1981, foreign banks sought access to the local credit market to fund their traditional trade financing loans. At the same time depressed conditions in the domestic Taiwanese economy in 1982–83 and a series of bankruptcies left local banks flush with funds but reluctant to lend. The squeeze on foreign banks' margins combined with their willingness to take risks led to an extension of maturities in the interbank market as local banks funded foreign banks, and a big increase in BAs and swaps. In part the growth of BAs was also a direct response to the ceiling imposed on CP issues by the Ministry of Finance in 1981 whereby banks' holdings were restricted to five times their paid-in capital. While CP issues have stagnated since 1982, NT$156 billion in BAs were issued in 1982 (equivalent to US$3.9 billion). In June 1983 BAs exceeded CPs for the first time and have now become an important source of working capital for numerous Taiwanese companies.

The case of Taiwan is clearly one where competitive pricing is setting the pace, and other regulatory changes arc definitely lagging behind. One consequence is that when monetary conditions are tight, the credit markets which are market-determined expand rapidly at the expense of the regulated deposit and lending sectors, as occurred in 1981. A government study of the kerb market in Taipei (which operates on the basis of post-dated cheques) found that in the second half of 1983 as much as 40% of private sector credit requirements were met through this illegal channel. The pressure on the regulated sector is therefore coming from two directions—the legal and officially sanctioned competitive, wholesale money market as well as the illegal kerb loan market. As volume in each market grows and credit evaluation skills improve, no doubt these pressures will intensify.

The reluctance to expand competitive forces in areas other than pricing in Taiwan appears to be politically (or militarily) motivated. There is strong desire on the part of the Taiwanese authorities to maintain a firm hold on the ownership of strategic industries (which includes banking), to prevent capital flight from Taiwan, and to maintain very tight controls on international communications for military purposes. The result is that controls on the ownership of financial intermediaries, controls on entry and on the scope of business are likely to continue to be tightly enforced. Theoretically Taiwan should be able to maintain a fixed exchange rate and move to a regime of free capital movement which welcomes foreign ownership along the lines practiced in Hong Kong. In practice political and military considerations are likely to mean that the controls remain in place indefinitely. Accordingly the extent of further progress in Taiwan's progress towards a deregulated financial system other than in the area of pricing may turn out to be limited.

Addendum on OBUs

Starting in 1984 the Taiwanese authorities decided to allow local and foreign banks to establish offshore banking units (OBUs). These are business units of banks which accept deposits and make loans in foreign currencies at free market interest rates. They maintain accounts separate from the domestic unit. In May 1985 only seven out of the thirty foreign banks and four local banks were participating in the OBU market. Total assets of OBUs at 31st May 1985 amounted to US$5.1 billion, of which only US$135 million were loans to nonbank customers, while interbank credit lines accounted for US$4.9 billion, or over 90% of OBU portfolios. While this provides "safe" business, margins are minuscule. The importance of OBUs in Taiwan appears to be more as a training ground for personnel than as a means of liberalizing domestic money markets. However, if domestic borrowers and lenders are granted unrestricted access to OBU credit this must accelerate the pace of liberalization in the local NT$ markets.

Financial Deregulation in Hong Kong

Since the formal abolition of residual exchange control in December 1972, Hong Kong's capital markets have been among the least restricted in Asia, particularly in respect to external transactions. Excepting controls on the entry of banks and other deposit-taking companies, and the compartmentalization of deposits under the present three-tier structure of the Hong Kong Association of Banks (HKAB) discussed below, the range of non-price controls on financial intermediation has been reduced to a minimum. These statements apply both during the periods when Hong Kong has maintained a fixed exchange rate regime (in the years up to November 1974 and then again since October 1983) and during the decade 1974–1983 during which the HK$ exchange rate was freely floating. The experience of Hong Kong therefore suggests that the choice of exchange rate regime (fixed, managed, or floating) is not in itself important for the progress of financial deregulation: substantial deregulation is evidently attainable under both floating and fixed rate systems.

More fundamental than the choice of exchange rate regime is the choice between a rule-based system, such as Hong Kong's floating and fixed exchange rate regimes, and discretionary types of monetary system in which the monetary authorities act as permanent arbiters, allocating the supply of new high-powered money and new credit among the private sector, the government sector, and the overseas sector. Hong Kong has operated an essentially rule-based system in which the authorities were generally prepared to allow market forces to determine the allocation of credit and capital. During the decade when the currency was floating (1974–1983), this "positive non-interventionist" policy was extended (mistakenly, in the author's view) to incorporate a rationale for allowing the value of the currency to be freely determined in the foreign exchange market. As the pace of economic activity accelerated in the late 1970s and banks continued to create credit unrestrained by any control on the monetary base or by any balance of payments constraints, there was inevitably increasing debate in Hong Kong about the appropriate level of interest rates and the need for some method of monetary control. Gradually the government departed from its traditional role of leaving the problem of resource allocation to the free market by taking a series of interventionist measures intended to control monetary growth, but which in practice only distorted the pattern of credit growth. Following the run on the Hong Kong dollar in September 1983 and its subsequent stabilization in October 1983, the problem of preserving the currency as store of value was finally solved by the adoption of a traditional gold standard-type convertible currency mechanism which uses the U.S. dollar instead of gold. Even in the face of widespread anxieties about the future of Hong Kong after 1997, the new system has withstood both external drains (October 1983, July 1984), and internal drains (December 1983/January 1984), without serious ill effects on the domestic economy. Provided the system is maintained in its present form it should be feasible for the Hong Kong authorities to return to their traditional non-interventionist role. In keeping separate these two fundamental ideas—the role of free markets in allocating resources and the role of currency as a medium and store of value—the Hong Kong authorities can preserve a very large measure of financial freedom for firms and individuals in Hong Kong.

Concerning the pricing of bank deposits and bank lending, the first point to make is that the distinction between foreign influences and domestic influences on the Hong Kong banking system is not particularly appropriate since the Hong Kong government maintains a non-discriminatory position vis-à-vis domestic and foreign institutions (once they have gained entry). Nevertheless, as in Taiwan, the primary agent for change has been competition in the wholesale credit markets. Second, a dominant feature of the Hong Kong scene has been the existence of an interest rate agreement among the licensed banks. Introduced originally in July 1964 to bring to an end to the so-called "interest rate war" among the banks, the agreement was retained and strengthened in January 1981 when the banking system was reorganized into a three-tier structure consisting of licensed banks, licensed deposit-taking companies, and registered deposit-taking companies (DTCs). Under the new structure all licensed banks are required to adhere to the interest rate agreement of a statutory body known as the Hong Kong Association of Banks, a kind of bankers' parliament. Briefly, all deposits at banks up to a value of HK$500,000 (approx. US$64,000) and with a maturity of up to 18 months are subject to the agreement. For deposits over HK$500,000 of any maturity there is now free competition. Licensed deposit-taking companies are also entitled to compete for deposits in excess of HK$500,000 and for any maturity, but they may not offer demand deposit accounts or checking facilities. The third group, registered deposit-taking companies, can accept deposits in excess of HK$50,000 (approx. US$6,400) providing they have an original maturity of 3 months or more. Deposits at both types of DTC are exempt from the interest rate agreement.

On the lending side there is no mandatory price fixing, but two of the largest banks, Hong Kong and Shanghai Bank and Standard Chartered Bank, exercise effective price leadership and have been able to maintain a substantial 3%–5% spread between the typical savings rate and their Best Lending Rates, depending on the general level of interest rates. In the competitive sectors (i.e., among the DTCs) lending is done at some spread over the interbank rate, the spread depending on the borrowers' creditworthiness.

Even with the rapid growth of nominal income in Hong Kong it will be many years before the officially sanctioned interest rate agreement begins to be eroded because the HK$500,000 (approx. US$64,000) minimum size of deposit which can benefit from freely competitive interest rates is approximately ten times the level of per capita income in Hong Kong. The appeal of sweep accounts is therefore likely to be limited for some while. However, alternative methods of overcoming the interest rate agreement are available, such as pooled trust accounts and the increasingly popular foreign currency swaps which enable depositors to obtain the market rates of return available on US$ or Euro-dollars deposits less the transactions cost. In February 1985 swap deposits accounted for some HK$23.4 billion (approx. US$3 billion), about 15% of all HK$-denominated deposits at licensed banks in Hong Kong. A further point is that so long as the demand for credit is weak, the interest rate agreement may not be subject to much erosion, but at a later stage in the cycle when the demand for credit is much stronger and the differential between regulated rates and free rates widens it is likely that market forces will draw funds away from the licensed banks.

The interest rate agreement therefore continues to discriminate primarily against the small retail depositor; it encourages the misallocation of bank capital (it has probably been responsible for the growth of unusually large branch networks of retail banks in Hong Kong), and it hinders the development of a longer-term capital market in debt instruments by supplying the banks with cheap, captive deposits. It is nevertheless true that since the linking of the Hong Kong dollar to the U.S. dollar in October 1983, changes in deposit interest rates under the interest rate agreement in Hong Kong have become more frequent, and more sensitive to those set by market forces. Also, through the linking of the two currencies and the resultant convergence of HK$ interest rates with US$ interest rates, Hong Kong depositors have gained some of the benefits of high real interest rates available to U.S. depositors. It should be emphasized that it is the absence of foreign exchange controls and the presence of the offshore currency markets in Hong Kong that have provided the necessary conditions for Hong Kong residents to enjoy the benefits of being able to arbitrage among a wide choice of financial assets.

As a consequence of studies currently in progress, some revision of the methods of prudential supervision in Hong Kong is likely, and there may even be changes to the three-tier banking structure, but is seems unlikely that the artificial compartmentalization of deposits under interest rate agreement will be abolished for some time, partly because it is still officially regarded as a cornerstone of the safety of small local banks. In conclusion, we may note that aside from the discriminatory interest rate agreement, deregulation in Hong Kong has already progressed much further than in most other countries in Asia, but that additional deregulatory steps will be significantly dependent upon the degree to which a free market approach is adopted in the current re-examination of prudential supervision in Hong Kong.

Financial Deregulation in Malaysia

Among the ASEAN countries, Malaysia was the second to embark on a program of deliberate financial deregulation. Except for the stimulus provided by the presence of foreign merchant banks, the sources of change were almost entirely domestic, in contrast to the Korean and Taiwanese cases described earlier. Starting in August 1973, finance company deposit interest rates were freed, and the discount rate on Treasury bills was determined by open tender. The deposit and lending rates of merchant banks were already determined by free competition. In the October 1978 Budget the Minister of Finance announced a set of four monetary measures designed to change the character of banking and finance in Malaysia. These involved making bank interest rates more market-oriented; reforming the liquidity requirements to eliminate distortions in the money market; bringing the merchant banks within the framework of the 1973 Banking Act; and introducing BAs and NCDs. Particular care had already been taken since the early 1970s to create the conditions necessary for effective competition, including strengthening of bank management and the consolidation of smaller banking units. The Association of Banks in Malaysia was encouraged to draft rules for its members stressing the standardization of maturities, the uniformity of deposit and loan pricing, and the prominent display and public announcement of the borrowing and lending rates of each bank, all of which would promote homogeneity in the credit markets.

The process of deregulation and the continuation of regulation in Malaysia are very clearly linked to the attainment of national goals. For example, BAs and NCDs were introduced partly to develop the money (i.e., credit) markets, but also to mobilize domestic savings and to provide alternative investment media for short-term funds. As a consequence, and despite the price competition so carefully fostered, allocative requirements are regularly imposed. Thus in the area of non-price factors determining competititve conditions there are extensive annual guidelines for funding priority sectors which severely restrict the composition of banks' loan portfolios. In 1984, for instance, the credit guidelines required that 20% of all loans be allocated to Bumiputras (indigenous Malays), 5% to small-scale enterprises, and 6% to agricultural food production. No less than 50% of the loans to small-scale enterprises were required to be extended to Bumiputras. The commercial banks were required to make new firm commitments to individuals to finance at least 20,000 newly constructed houses, 6,000 of which were to be for Bumiputra individuals. Within these priority sectors, loans to small-scale enterprises and Bumiputras were pegged at 9%, and individual housing loans at 10%. There are also preferential terms for housing loans for Bumiputras as compared with other sections of the population. Similar requirements amounting to 45% of total loans (20% to Bumiputras, 25% to small-scale enterprises) were imposed on finance companies and foreign banks.

In view of the difficulty of satisfying some of these strictures placed upon them, banks have come into open conflict with the authorities over several matters in recent years. This has led Bank Negara Malaysia (the central bank) to amend the Banking Act giving it new powers to direct banks to achieve more "balanced" loan portfolios. Also, dissatisfied with the banks' apparent lack of flexibility—i.e., their unwillingness to lower bank lending rates in 1982–83, Bank Negara sought and obtained a commitment from the Association of Banks in Malaysia that as from November 1983 the interest rates on bank loans would be tied to a Base Lending Rate (BLR). Revisions to this BLR may occur "periodically," but housing loan interest rates may not be adjusted more than once every six months.

The overall picture in Malaysia is therefore an unusual mixture. On the one hand the authorities have fostered freely competitive pricing; on the other they have retained extensive and onerous priority lending requirements, some of them involving preferential lending rates. A full analysis is obviously not possible here, but the require-ment to subsidize loans to certain sectors with funds from other sectors clearly reduces allocative efficiency in the economic sense, even though it may enhance the achievement of national goals. In addition Mal-aysia operates a large forced savings scheme, under which 20% of an employee's aggregate monthly wage is contributed to the Employees Provident Fund. In 1984 88% of the assets of the E.P.F. were invested in government securities, and accounted for 73% of the net domestic financing requirements of the federal government. Gross contributions amounted to 3.4% of the GNP. Again, national goals take precedence over individual preferences or technical economic efficiency. Malaysia's distinctive policy mix of market mechanisms combined with specific allocation constraints is well illustrated by a paragraph on exchange control in the Bank Negara Malaysia's 1984 Annual Report:

> Consistent with the policy of allowing market forces of supply and demand to determine the exchange rate of the Ringgit, the exchange control policy of Malaysia remains liberal and non-discriminatory. This liberal system of exchange control allows a free inflow of funds and outflow of payments on current account. As a matter of policy, even for capital outflows, payments are readily permitted so long as these are not financed by borrowings in Malaysia. While corporations and individuals might wish to do whatever they desired with their own money (not borrowed funds), they should not do so with the savings (borrowings) of other nationals, the first priority of which must be to finance, through the banking system, the increase in productive capacity in the country. Such a policy has worked to the country's advant-age, especially in encouraging the inflow of foreign investments.

Financial Deregulation in Singapore

Prior to July 1975 interest rates in Singapore were fixed by a cartel of the Association of Banks in Singapore in consultation with the Monetary Authority of Singapore; Since 15 July 1975 banks have been able to set their own rates depending on supply and demand. Under government supervision and encouragement a diverse and sophisti-cated money market has grown up, featuring a variety of instruments (CDs, bills of exchange, promissory notes, Treasury bills, etc.) and a variety of financial intermediaries which is remarkable for a city of some 2.5 million inhabitants. The only serious distortion from free market pricing has stemmed from the liquid asset ratio requirements imposed on banks, which has resulted in persistently low yields on Treasury bills, the compulsory CPF savings scheme which provides captive funds at artificially low rates to the Statutory Boards, and some distortions occasioned by banks' need to meet reserve requirements. (These were structured in such a way that it was more profitable for banks to reduce their liabilities than to bid for assets, leading to an unusual interest rate pattern at monthly make-up dates.)

Alongside the domestic Singapore dollar market the authorities have fostered the Asian dollar market, an offshore currency market where rates are also freely determined and which has become a major center for the funding of foreign currency credits in the Southeast Asian region, rivalling Hong Kong. However, whereas the Hong Kong authorities have not attempted to limit nonresidents' use of the local currency, the Singapore authorities have strictly segmented the two markets, limiting certain types of banking license to the offshore market only (ACUs) and making it almost impossible for nonresidents to borrow Singapore dollars. As Singapore abolished Exchange Control in June 1978 the retention of this strict division between local currency transactions and offshore currency transactions may seem rather unnecessary, but the Singapore authorities appear anxious to prevent an offshore Singapore dollar market growing up outside their control and supervision, and one effective way to prevent such a development is to proscribe the ability of Singapore banks to lend to nonresidents.

Unlike Malaysia, Singapore does not impose credit quotas on the commercial banking system. Thus although the banking system is very strictly supervised, the pricing and allocation of credit is largely free. However, like Malaysia, there is also a large forced savings scheme (the Central Provident Fund) under which all workers other than those self-employed are required to contribute a fixed proportion of their monthly wages up to a certain salary level, half being "paid" by the employer and half by the employee. Both the combined percentage contribution and the limiting salary levels have been raised progressively since the start of the scheme in 1955 and currently stand at 50% of salaries up to S$5,000 (approx. US$2,250). Like the Malaysian EPF, the CPF invests mainly in government securities, but in the last 2–3 years there has been some liberalization. Members of the scheme are now permitted to make withdrawals for house purchases as well as for retirement income. In recent years savings channelled into the CPF have formed 5–6% of gross domestic product.

Competition in the banking industry has been intensified recently by the aggressive entry of another government institution, the Post

Office Savings Bank, into traditional banking areas. The POSB now offers checking accounts and automatic fund transfers, as well as new products such as point-of-sale ATMs (where debits to a customer's account are instantly credited to the account of the supermarket or other vendor). However, although the entry on the POSB into the banking arena has put additional pressure of private sector bank margins, this cannot be termed a move towards deregulation. The POSB is a government institution exploiting a natural monopoly—its extensive branch network of post offices. Thus while the competitive environment for Singapore banks and finance companies is extremely tough, this is more because the government prompts a large proportion of the savings flow (through the CPF) and undermines the position of the banks (through the POSB) than because of any significant recent moves to deregulate financial markets. To conclude, Singapore deregulated the pricing in most of its financial markets as long ago as 1975, and ever since then it has been tightening up the supervisory system, the amendments to the Banking Act of 1984 being just one example. The visible, heavy hand of the regulatory authorities therefore coexists with free, but limited, competition.

Financial Deregulation and Innovation in Thailand

Thailand is another Asian economy where foreign influence has been of key significance in initiating the process of financial deregulation. The large change in interest rate differentials between domestic and foreign interest rates has again been the source of these first cautious steps towards a more liberal financial environment. The Thai Baht had been tied rigidly to the U.S. dollar with only two changes in the parity since 1970. There was one devaluation in July-August 1981, and another in November 1984 when the Baht was devalued 14.8% against the U.S. currency. At that time the Bank of Thailand announced that the Baht would henceforth be linked to a basket of currencies, though the weight of each currency in the basket was not specified. In practice the Baht has traded in an extremely narrow range, suggesting that the change in exchange rate regime has been less significant than the public announcements suggested. As a result of the virtually fixed exchange rate regime and the absence of controls on capital movements, the combination of domestic monetary arrangements in existence in Thailand—which included credit controls and interest rate ceilings—was unsustainable in the face of large and variable international capital flows.

Under the fixed exchange rate regime the trend of monetary growth in Thailand was principally determined by the trend in the balance of payments. In turn the wide fluctuations in the balance of payments in the last five years—from large surplus in 1980 to large deficit in 1981, and back to surplus in 1982—have been primarily determined by large swings in the private net borrowing component of the capital account of the balance of payments. Shifts in private net foreign borrowing have resulted from large shifts in interest rate differentials as U.S. interest rates fluctuated widely and Thai rates remained essentially rigid. Thus in 1981 when U.S. rates were at record levels, a sharp decline in foreign borrowing and debt repayments took the Thai balance of payments into deficit, and in 1982 after U.S. interest rates had fallen below Thai rates, a build-up of foreign borrowing caused the balance of payments to switch to surplus again. In 1981 monetary growth (M2) tumbled from 25% to 15%, and in 1982 it surged again to 24%. In 1983–84 the cycle was repeated with the trade deficit more than doubling as imports rose and foreign borrowings declined in 1983, until the situation was reversed in 1984. However, although the direction of monetary changes was repeated, the magnitude of the changes was not as great as in the previous cycle. In short, the course of monetary growth in Thailand has been a direct consequence of the rigidity of the exchange rate and the rigidity of Thai interest rates.

The instability resulting from these rigidities has caused the Thai authorities to introduce some measure of flexibility both in the setting of interest rates and in the setting of the exchange rate in order to weaken the linkages between the behavior of the monetary aggregates and the level of U.S.-Thai interest rate differentials. These measures are set out in Table 4.6.

Unfortunately, however, not all of the Thai authorities' measures have been in the direction of greater liberalization and deregulation. Indeed, concerned at the tendency of domestic credit to fluctuate so much in response to these external developments, the authorities have also resorted to direct credit controls, imposing a ceiling of 18% on the extension of bank credit in 1983/84, although this was suspended in August 1984. Along with the imposition of overall credit ceilings, commercial banks were requested "to restrain unproductive credit extension, especially lending for consumption, stock accumulation and ... construction," and borrowings by commercial banks in the repurchase market against government securities were limited. One side-effect of the credit controls has almost certainly been to encourage the growth of Thailand's unofficial credit markets, which have included some ill-starred "chit-fund" (i.e., kiting or Ponzi) schemes— a situation that has parallels in both Korea and Taiwan.

To sum up, Thailand is a clear case where the foreign influence is forcing changes in the domestic interest rate structure and in the conduct of domestic monetary policy. While some changes have been in the direction of more regulation rather than less, they have led to further distortions which in time will surely produce responses from either the government or the private sector which will lead in turn to more competition and more flexibility in the banking sector. Once again, as with Singapore and Hong Kong, the absence of foreign exchange controls has been a significant necessary condition linking developments in financial markets abroad to financial conditions in Thailand.

Financial Deregulation and Innovation in Indonesia

The process of financial deregulation in Indonesia started on the domestic side, but, following extension to the wholesale local money markets and through them to the overseas money markets, the foreign influence has now become a substantial factor promoting liberalization.

From the end of the Indonesian hyperinflation of the mid-1960s until 1983, the Indonesian financial system was notable for its many rigidities. Forty years of state dominance of the banking industry had led to a grave lack of responsiveness to market needs. As a result black markets for foreign currency and for credit were commonplace. Foreign banks were very tightly controlled, and were prohibited from lending outside the capital, Jakarta. However, following the 27.6% devaluation of the Rupiah against the U.S. dollar in March 1983, a series of steps was taken to mobilize domestic savings, to reduce subsidies, and to move towards market pricing of commodities and credit. Initially the interest rates on deposits at state banks for maturities of up to 6 months were freed, leading to competition on the funding side while fixed rates were maintained on the lending side. Efforts were also made to improve the management of the state banks.

In June 1983 the interest rates on deposits at state banks were freed for all maturities. Effectively one-year deposit rates were raised from 8–9% to between 16% and 18%. At the same time Bank Indonesia, the central bank, abolished credit ceilings on all commercial banks (state, private national, and foreign). The end of deposit interest rate controls caused a flood of deposits (they rose by 85% in 1984) into the state banks, which were ill-equipped to find borrowers and consequently started searching for ways to use their funds through the money market. In February 1984 the central banks issued new instruments known as SIBs (Sertifikat Bank Indonesia) to absorb some of this excess liquidity. About the same time it opened two discount windows with facilities for 15 and 30 days. In September 1984 there was a miniature crisis in the foreign exchange market consequent upon large sales of local currency. The shortage of Rupiah funds in the spot market drove overnight rates up to over 85%, forcing some banks to make use of the new discount window facilities and prompting Bank Indonesia to arrange additional special credits of 6 months and 12 months maturity.

In January 1985, ahead of the repayments due on the 6–month facilities, the central bank announced the formation of a new market in short-term instruments, known as SBPUs, to start in February. SBPUs are promissory notes or trade bills of 30–90 days maturity, endorsed by a bank which is the guarantor of payment no matter how often the bill or note is traded. A 95% government-owned discount house, Ficorinvest, specializes in making the market in these instruments, but direct interbank trading has rapidly become the more significant part of the market. To avoid any bank becoming too dependent on this source of funds, Bank Indonesia restricts borrowing through Ficorinvest to 10% of a bank's deposit base, and direct interbank borrowing is limited to 7.5% of a bank's deposit base.

There have been two important results of these developments. First, as a by-product of the new instruments the central bank now has new methods at its disposal for monetary control, buying SBPUs and SBIs when it wishes to ease monetary conditions, or selling them when it wishes to tighten monetary conditions. Second, not only have interest rates in the recognized interbank market fallen substantially below institutional deposit and lending rates, but intermediation costs have been greatly reduced by these new facilities.

As with Hong Kong, Thailand, and Singapore, one reason the rigidities in the Indonesian credit markets have been broken down so quickly is that Indonesia no longer imposes foreign exchange control. Thus, for example in September 1984 when there were widespread fears of another Rupiah devaluation, the banking system experienced a serious external drain. However, because the central bank stood its ground and was prepared to see overnight rates rise to 85% p.a., the capital flows soon reversed themselves and the crisis passed. An important conclusion from the Indonesian experience is therefore that reliance on market forces must be consistent. If the Indonesian authorities had compromised and resorted to direct controls to solve the September scare, that would only have led to further distortions which in turn would have required other measures to solve.

Finally, and also concerning consistency: one Indonesian bank

(BPA) has failed following the start of deregulation, and it is widely believed that others may follow. The authorities in Indonesia appear to recognize that use of the market mechanism implies that there will be profits and losses, or winners and losers in the process of financial liberalization.

Conclusion

A recurrent theme in each of the seven Asian countries surveyed is that financial deregulation and innovation has come about and is coming about through two different but gradually merging routes: the foreign route and the domestic route. In each case two types of measures were noted: those which dealt with increasing the competition among financial intermediaries in the pricing of financial instruments, and measures which enhanced other conditions of competitiveness. Reluctance on the part of governments to foster these other conditions of competitiveness hinders deregulation as much as price-fixing because it helps to maintain segmented or compartmentalized markets and thereby obstructs arbitrage among financial instruments.

A second theme emerging from this survey is that any government which uses the financial system to achieve allocative goals jeopardizes efficiency in other sectors of the economy. The essential role of government in the monetary sphere can be narrowed down to one single objective: the preservation of the integrity of the unit of account as a store of value and as a medium of exchange. Where they confuse their allocative goals with their monetary role, Asian governments render their people a disservice.

Third, it is evident from this survey that foreign exchange controls (e.g. in S. Korea and Taiwan) represent a major impediment to the process of deregulation. Capital movements are an integral part of the process of achieving an optimal portfolio of financial and other assets; the inability to arbitrage or shift assets between financial centers by moving capital prevents the achievement of an international equilibrium of yields on financial assets, and misallocates resources internationally. Moreover, where national goals are in conflict with the optimum international distribution of capital there will be distortions and inefficiency. The abolition of foreign exchange controls breaks down the segmentation or compartmentalization of capital markets on an international basis and is therefore a necessary condition for full-scale financial deregulation.

Table 4.1   SOUTH KOREA: Financial Liberalization and Innovations by Type and Source

Type \ Source	Foreign	Domestic
Pricing of Bank Credit, Deposits, and Other Instruments	Swaps permitted, but only to a market share of 3% of banks' Won assets.	Call market and CP market partially liberalized, but no proper money market exists.
	Foreign banks permitted to require compensating balances, but these may not exceed 10% of loan amount.	Lending rates still fixed by govt., but from Nov. 84 rates may be set within a narrow range (10%–11.5%).
		STFCs gaining market share at expense of commercial banks owing to more favorable rates.
Other Factors Affecting Competition in the Provision of Financial Services — 1. Credit Allocation/ Preferential Lending/ Other Asset & Liability Constraints		Preferential credit allocation by banks stopped Nov. 1984, but preferential rediscounting still available from central bank.
2. Barriers to Entry	KorAm (1982) and Shinhan (1983) banks started in conjunction with U.S. and Korean/ Japanese interests.	Restriction on formation of STFCs and MSFCs eased July 1982. (8 and 42 respectively authorized in 1982–83.)
3. Scope of Business		Factoring, leasing, trust services, dealing in government securities, more branches permitted.
4. Ownership		Privatization of 5 state-owned banks since 1981. But 6 state-owned Special Banks still remain.
5. Market Share	Foreign banks are believed to be restricted to 10% of all bank assets.	
6. Other		Exchange controls remain in force. Capital flows highly restricted.

Table 4.2   TAIWAN: Financial Liberalization and Innovations by Type and Source

Type \ Source	Foreign	Domestic
Pricing of Bank Credit, Deposits and Other Instruments	July 1981: BAs pioneered by Citibank. 1982–83: Access of foreign banks to local funding via BAs, interbank market, and swaps dramatically improved. 1983: Foreign banks permitted to offer time deposits up to 6 months. Interbank maturities extended from up to 1 week to 6 months in response to local banks having surplus funds, and foreign banks being short of funds.	Legal maximum lending rates set by Bankers' Assoc. of Taipei (floors + ceilings). March 1985: "Prime rate" system permitted 5 big banks to vary lending rate within narrow range. Money market: Freely determined CPs and BAs swelled to US$5.6 bn and US$1.1 bn equivalent in 1981 when market rates exceeded ceilings.
Other Factors Affecting Competition in the Provision of Financial Services 1. Credit Allocation/ Preferential Lending/ Other Asset & Liability Constraints 2. Barriers to Entry 3. Scope of Business 4. Ownership 5. Market Share 6. Other	Foreign banks permitted to hold CPs up to 5 times net worth. No ceilings on quantities of BAs that may be guaranteed; hence huge expansion. 1981–85: 21 foreign banks admitted.	Central bank offers extensive preferential "accommodation" for export financing, etc. Still largely govt./Kuomintang ownership. NT$ not convertible for residents. Exchange controls remain in force, capital flows restricted.

Table 4.3 HONG KONG: Financial Liberalization and Innovations by Type and Source

Type \ Source	Foreign	Domestic
Pricing of Bank Credit, Deposits, and Other Instruments	1970s: DTCs permitted to offer free market interest rates on HK$ deposits over HK$50,000. March 1982: Deposits in excess of HK$500,000 (US$64,000) exempted from HKAB interest rate agreement. March 1981: Foreign currency interest withholding tax abolished. HK$ interest withholding tax reduced to 10%. 1982–83: Foreign currency swaps growing rapidly. Oct. 1983: HK$ interest withholding tax abolished. Oct. 1983: HK$ linked to US$ by gold standard mechanism (banknotes convertible to US$ at fixed price of HK$ 7.80 per US$), making money market interest rates in Hong Kong converge to US$ rates in Euromarket. 1983: CP issues permitted.	
Other Factors Affecting Competition in the Provision of Financial Services		
1. Credit Allocation/ Preferential Lending/ Other Asset Constraints	25% Liquid Asset Ratios, but easy to fulfill; these do not significantly constrain bank behavior.	Home Ownership Scheme loans guaranteed by government. 25% Liquid Asset Ratios.
2. Barriers to Entry	March 1978: Moratorium on issue of foreign bank licenses lifted. DTCs only subject to registration requirements.	
3. Scope of Business	No significant restrictions for banks. Only banks may offer checking accounts.	No significant restrictions for banks. Only banks may offer checking accounts.
4. Ownership	No restrictions.	No restrictions.
5. Market Share	Compartmentalization of deposit types under 3-tier banking structure.	Compartmentalization of deposit types under 3-tier banking structure.
6. Other		

Table 4.4   MALAYSIA: Financial Liberalization and Innovations by Type and Source

Type \ Source	Foreign	Domestic
Pricing of Bank Credit, Deposits, and Other Instruments		August 1973: T/bills determined by market tender. August 1973: Finance company deposit interest rates freed. Oct. 1978: Bank lending rates freed, except to priority sectors. Deposit rates also freed. 1979: BAs, NCDs introduced. Lending rate ceilings for priority borrowers still retained. Nov. 1983: Base Lending Rate introduced. 1985: IMF completed study on interest rate liberalization.
Other Factors Affecting Competition in the Provision of Financial Services — 1. Credit Allocation/ Preferential Lending/ Other Asset & Liability Constraints	1985: Gap between merchant bank and commercial bank reserve requirements narrowed.	Annual guidelines for funding priority sectors still enforced. 1982: 52% of loans to priority sectors. 1984: 31% of loans to priority sectors. Liquid Asset Ratios: 20%. Feb. 1983: Banking Statute amended giving power to BNM to insist on "balanced" loan portfolios.
2. Barriers to Entry		Merchant banks, finance companies offer wholesale services competitive with banks but are excluded from interbank market.
3. Scope of Business	Merchant banks soon to be permitted to enter foreign exchange market, and enter stock broking.	1983: Leasing permitted.
4. Ownership	Malayanization of foreign bank interests still sought.	
5. Other		Oct. 1981: Interest on deposits at nonbanks up to M$10,000 tax exempt, up to M$1,000 at banks. All interest on fixed deposits over 1 year tax exempt.

Table 4.5 SINGAPORE: Financial Liberalization and Innovations by Type and Source

Type \ Source	Foreign	Domestic
Pricing of Bank Credit, Deposits, and Other Instruments		1972: Treasury bill issue system changed from tap to tender.
		July 1975: Bank deposit and lending rates freed from fixing by Association of Banks in Singapore and M.A.S.
1. Credit Allocation/ Preferential Lending/ Other Asset & Liability Constraints	1982: 2 Foreign banks penalized for (legal) avoidance of reserve requirements.	1974–75. Selective credit controls: directives on loan growth and sectoral allocation abolished 1975.
2. Barriers to Entry	Subject to satisfaction of specified criteria and M.A.S. approval.	Merchant banks, discount houses, money brokers, and finance companies all operate in defined spheres.
3. Scope of Business	1968–75: Asian Dollar market established. ACUs remain separate from domestic banking units.	Scope defined by full, restricted, and offshore banking licenses.
4. Ownership		Public sector financial institutions (POSB and CPF) play large role in financial system.
5. Market Share		1983–85: Post Office Savings Bank (110 + branches) retail banking sphere. POSB is exempt from Banking Act.
6. Other	1976: Asian Bond Market developed. 1984 Banking Act requires daily reporting of foreign exchange positions.	June 1978: Exchange control abolished. Since 1955: Large forced savings scheme (CPF).

(Rows 1–6 grouped under the side label: Other Factors Affecting Competition in the Provision of Financial Services)

Table 4.6 THAILAND: Financial Liberalization and Innovations by Type and Source

Type \ Source	Foreign	Domestic
Pricing of Bank Credit, Deposits, and Other Instruments	1980–84: Wide fluctuations in Thai-U.S. interest differentials cause large private sector capital movements, resulting in pressure to liberalize domestic deposit and lending rates.	Legal interest rate ceilings still apply. Jan. 1983: Bank lending ceiling lowered for first time (to 17.5% from 19%). Deposit ceiling left unchanged. March 1983: 1-year deposits offered at 11.5–12% and 13% on provident funds: i.e., some flexibility introduced. March 1983: Prime rate introduced for term loans (cf. overdrafts) at more favorable rates. 1984: Preferential lending rates apply to priority sectors.
Other Factors Affecting Competition in the Provision of Financial Services 1. Credit Allocation/ Preferential/ Lending/ Other Asset & Liability Constraints	Liquidity ratio. Mandatory bond holding requirements for banks, also used as collateral for BOT borrowings.	Bank of Thailand supplies concessionary credit (e.g. for foreign exports). 1983/84: Bank credit growth restricted to 18%. 1984: Thai banks' use of repurchase market limited to 14% of total deposits. Banks obtain preferential treatment (e.g. new branches permitted) if loans are extended to poor rural areas.
2. Barriers to Entry	Embargo on new foreign entrants under review (1984).	
3. Scope of Business	Securities and finance companies able to issue promissory notes, etc., hence in competition with banks.	
4. Ownership		1979: Commercial Banking Act required family-owned banks to divest 50% of shares to the public. Deadline March 1982 extended to March 1984.
5. Market Share		Sigdificant public sector financial institutions: IFCT, BAAC, Govt. Savings Bank, Govt. Housing Bank.
6. Other		Active finance companies, kerb market and chit-fund systems. Foreign exchange control largely in abeyance.

Table 4.7 INDONESIA: Financial Liberalization and Innovations by Type and Source

Source Type	Foreign	Domestic
Pricing of Bank Credit, Deposits, and Other Instruments		March 1983: Interest ceilings on deposits at State banks with maturity up to 6 months abolished.
		June 1983: Interest ceilings on all deposits at State banks ended.
		February 1984: SBIs issued by Bank Indonesia.
	Jan. 1985: Two new instruments (promissory notes/trade bills, known as SBPUs) authorized to trade at free market yields, enabling foreign banks to access money markets. N.B. limits on issue volume (7.5% of deposits).	January 1985: SBPUs introduced, effectively extending free market interbank interest rates to other borrowers.
1. Credit Allocation/ Preferential Lending/ Other Asset/ Liability Constraints		June 1983: Credit ceilings on all commercial banks (State, private, national and foreign) abolished.
2. Barriers to Entry		
3. Scope of Business		
4. Ownership		State owned banks still predominate.
5. Market Share		
6. Other	June 1983: Abolition of withholding tax on foreign currency deposits.	Feb. 1984: Bank Indonesia opens two discount window facilities.

Other Factors Affecting Competition in the Provision of Financial Services

Comments

Thomas F. Cargill

The past decade has witnessed a growing incompatibility between established monetary and financial arrangements and an economic environment characterized by inflation, high and uncertain interest rates, changes in established flow-of-fund patterns, increasing government deficits, oil-price shocks, shifts from fixed to more flexible exchange rate systems, increasing international integration, and advances in computer and telecommunications technology. The conflict resulted from the clash between monetary and financial frameworks that were inflexible because of restrictions on financial behavior and an economic environment that demanded greater flexibility in the allocation of funds. The conflict also posed problems for monetary control. The new economic environment forced a reevaluation of the role of monetary policy in maintaining price stability. In response to these forces, a number of countries embarked on a process of "financial reform" designed to remove or relax key constraints on competitive behavior in the financial system, to allow market forces a greater role in allocating funds, and to alter the structure and conduct of monetary policy.

The paper by Greenwood and the paper by Yumoto, Shima, Koike, and Taguchi (hereafter referred to as Yumoto et al.) provide an interesting review of some of these changes for both developed and developing economies. The Greenwood paper is especially useful in this regard since it provides detailed information on a number of countries not easily accessible to the foreign researcher. The task of surveying the reform experiences of diverse economies is formidable to say the least; however, several issues can be raised with regard to each paper. These comments will be confined to three areas. First, why should we be interested in a multicountry survey of financial reform efforts? Beyond a mere listing of reforms, is the survey based on a set of common hypotheses about financial reform, and does the survey reject one or more of these hypotheses? Second, how can one judge the two papers with respect to this issue as well as judge some of the specific points raised in each paper? Third, what are the major implications that can be drawn from multicountry comparisons in general?

Perspectives On a Multicountry Survey of Financial Reform

The social, cultural, institutional, and economic differences between the countries discussed at this conference are obvious to everyone, and yet multicountry surveys suggest the existence of an underlying hypothesis that each country is responding to similar catalysts, each country is starting from a similar set of initial conditions, each country is proceeding along a similar path, and each country is converging toward a common goal. Despite the differences among countries, the common effort to remove or relax some of the constraints on financial transactions suggests that the similarity hypothesis might be a useful starting point. A second set of hypotheses that would appear appropriate as a framework for multicountry comparisons concerns the relative pace of financial reform between domestic and international finance, especially in the light of theoretical literature that argues that international finance should be deregulated at a slower pace than domestic finance assuming highly regulated initial conditions. What do we learn about this hypothesis from the present surveys? A third set of hypotheses concerns the relationship between financial reform and monetary control. To what extent is the misbehavior of the monetary authority responsible for generating reform, and what is the relationship between structural change in the financial system and the conduct of monetary policy? A fourth set of hypotheses concerns the relationship between financial market behavior and tax structure. Should changes in the tax structure be incorporated into financial reform efforts in light of the importance of capital account movements?

Greenwood and Yumoto et al. have provided a useful service by their detailed enumeration of financial reform efforts. Greenwood provides much insight into the experiences of specific developing countries, and his detailed knowledge is evident as one reads the concise accounts for each country. At several places, the author steps back to abstract some general principles from the survey; for example, Greenwood cautions against expecting meaningful shifts toward less constrained financial systems when more market-sensitive financial flows conflict with government industrial and social policies. Other generalizations are more controversial; for example, it is not at all clear that international finance should be liberalized at the same pace or faster than domestic finance, as implied by Greenwood. Related to the international issue, one should be cautious about generalizing from the experience of Hong Kong that the pace of reform is not influenced by the type of exchange rate system. Nor is it clear that government deficits have played little importance in the reform process. Work by Michael Hutchinson (1985) at the Federal Reserve Bank of San Francisco suggests that government deficits in the Pacific Basin have had a rather significant impact both as a cause of financial reform and as an influence on the specific reforms adopted. It is also not clear that Hong Kong and Singapore should be regarded in the same light as other Pacific Basin countries since their respective financial reforms arose more from a desire to become international financial centers and less from the economic conditions that generated reforms in the other countries.

Two other issues can be raised with respect to the Greenwood paper. First, the paper does not adequately incorporate monetary policy issues. To what extent have the reforms involved the monetary authority and to what extent have failures of past monetary policy been a catalyst in the reform process? In the case of Indonesia, for example, financial reform has been importantly concerned with the restructuring of monetary policy in response to the significant structural changes in the financial system. Second, a more extended discussion of Hong Kong in the light of China's economic liberalization program would have been useful. Greenwood is in a position to offer useful insights about the future development of Hong Kong's financial system in the light of this event.

The Yumoto et al. paper is more ambitious than the Greenwood paper in that it attempts to categorize financial innovations in an economically meaningful manner, survey the reforms in several industrialized economies, provide specific insights into the experiences of the United States and Japan, and investigate the impact of reform on bank profits with respect to the United States. At the same time, the more ambitious the task, the more likely that problems will be encountered.

The specific classification scheme used to separate innovations into those that avoid existing regulation (Type 1) and those that reduce the cost or risk of existing transaction media (Type 2) may not be as useful as the authors suggest. The basic problem is that it cannot clearly categorize a wide variety of innovations; for example, NOW accounts in the United States represent both a new means of transaction not subject to existing regulation (zero interest rate ceiling on demand deposits held by households); at the same time, NOW accounts reduce the liquidity or disintermediation risk of the financial institution. Other examples could be offered. One can understand the basic idea that the authors are trying to convey; however, a more careful rationale of the particular taxonomy for financial innovations should be developed.

The authors provide a concise overview of financial reform in Japan as well as highlight some of the major events in the United States. There are several aspects of the discussion that may generate misconceptions about the comparative reform process in the two countries. First, the role of monetary policy has not been adequately incorporated into the discussion. Perhaps both papers assumed that monetary policy issues would be discussed elsewhere in the conference; however, these are survey papers and as such should incorporate the relevant issues for each country. Second, Yumoto et al. suggest that liquidity risk has increased as a result of deregulation in the United States. Perhaps the authors have something else in mind, but as it stands, the statement is incorrect. Liquidity risk or disintermediation has been greatly reduced, though interest rate risk has increased because regulators in the United States have adopted an unbalanced approach to the liberalization of the uses and sources of funds for depository institutions. This has become an especially serious problem for thrifts and largely accounts for the continuation of a thrift-problem. Third, the authors suggest that EFTs in the United States has increased bank risk. It is debatable about the alleged risk-increasing effects of EFTs; however, the development of EFTs has been rather slow in the United States compared to Japan, and its importance for the United States is overstated in the paper.

In summary, both papers offer important insights into the reform process and provide useful enumerations of the significant changes. Aside from specific issues raised above with respect to each paper, the main issue that can be raised with both papers is the failure to adequately deal with the relationship between monetary policy and financial innovation. Misbehaved monetary policy has sometimes been the catalyst of reform, and, in general, reform itself raises significant issues for the conduct of monetary policy.

General Issues

These comments can be concluded by turning to three general issues regarding financial reform in terms of multicountry comparisons. First, the term "deregulation" is constantly employed as a description of the recent events. A more accurate terminology would be desirable. In many cases, the recent changes have involved increased regulation and supervision, especially in the United States. More accurately, the reform process is directed toward removing or relaxing a *few* binding constaints on interest rates and the portfolio operations of market participants. Deregulation is the least likely activity one can expect from a regulatory agency! Second, the impetus to financial reform is almost always attributed to a conflict between existing regulation and economic conditions; however, many of the reform actions have been preceded by intellectual changes about the role of government in society. The interplay between ideas and events is complex, but the concept of liberalization as something good will only persist as long as economic conditions remain reasonably stable during the reform process and the reform process does not significantly interfere with established property rights. Counterreform is likely in those cases where prudential concerns about the safety of banks become paramount or a more market-oriented financial system allocates funds in conflict with government industrial and social policies. Third and last, the two papers raise the issue as to how far one can emphasize the common elements of the experiences of a variety of countries. Despite the broad similarities, the differences dominate; in the future, one may want to consider a less ambitious approach and focus on only a few countries for which strong arguments of comparative treatment can be advanced. Even in these cases, the comparative approach must be cautiously pursued. To illustrate, consider the United States and Japan. A close analysis (Cargill 1985) of the catalysts of reform, the process of reform, and the likely ending point of the reform process suggests that the differences are far more important than the similarities even for these two reasonably comparable economies.

References

Cargill, Thomas F. 1985. In *Financial Policy and Reform in Pacific Basin Countries*, Hang-Sheng Cheng (ed.), forthcoming from D.C. Heath and Co.

Hutchinson, Michael. In *Financial Policy and Reform in Pacific Basin Countries*, Hang-Sheng Cheng (ed.), forthcoming from D.C. Heath and Co.

Comments

Warren D. McClam

The Bank of Japan paper provides us with a very informative comparative survey of financial innovations as well as important insights into the process of innovation and some of the problems it poses.

The background and causes of financial innovation can, of course, be viewed from several perspectives. In the BOJ paper, I believe it fair to say, one finds essentially two complementary, but different, approaches. The first of these is presented in Section II. Here the authors divide financial innovations into two categories: Type 1 innovations directly reduce the shadow cost of regulatory constraints, and Type 2 reduce physical transaction costs or improve allocation of risk. This two-type taxonomy sees financial innovation as occurring on the initiative of *private* financial institutions motivated by profit and cost considerations. It is recognized that the effectiveness of the innovation may depend upon official approval, which is seen to be forthcoming often because of private pressures for change.

In part 3 of Section III, the authors offer a second approach. Here the emphasis shifts to the "process of financial innovation" but the analysis is confined to Japan. In a more general framework of financial flows, the pressures for innovation are implicitly seen to depend partly on changes in the size and composition of sectoral portfolios and their influences on direct lending and the financial intermediation process.

In some ways I find the second approach more congenial. As I see it, pressures for innovation can come from non-financial as well as financial sources, from the public as well as the private sector, from foreign as well as domestic influences, from financial markets as well as financial intermediaries. Innovation can be induced as well as spontaneous, defensive as well as aggressive, market-share as well as profit-oriented. Innovations may find official sanction or they may be discouraged. Competitive forces may be greater or less, depending on market structure and the degree of regulation. Distinctions such as these would seem essential to any further comparative study of the causal process in a historical setting.

By way of constructive comment, I would add that it might have been useful if these sections had given more attention to the background causes of financial innovation. I refer here to the so-called exogenous factors summarized under the heading "social and economic conditions and technological developments" but not discussed in any detail. I say this for two reasons. One is that a better understanding of causes could be helpful in deciding what particular policies, if any, might be needed to help cope with innovation. The second is that, in a wider context, some of the listed causes are closely interrelated. High and volatile interest rates—one might also add exchange rates—may, in particular, be the outcome of other forces, one of them being public-sector deficits, which are listed as a separate exogenous factor.

Indeed, focusing on the 1970s and 1980s, I would be inclined to lay considerable stress in many countries on the causal role of public-sector deficits and related regulatory attitudes. This has been a period when structural—or at least large—public-sector deficits emerged and brought new pressures for financial change in a number of countries. Thus it might be useful to look quickly at the specific ways in which public-sector behavior and attitudes have been closely intertwined with the innovation process.

In the first place, one must consider the public sector as an innovator in its own right. Various authorities (for example, the United Kingdom, Italy, France, Spain, Sweden, and Japan) have developed a number of new debt instruments, often with quite novel features.

Secondly, public-sector financial innovation has generally been designed, whether for monetary control reasons or simply to facilitate government borrowing, to promote the role of open markets. The paper describes this development in Japan, and its more general relevance is evident from my Figure 1. The figure suggests that, parallel with increases in the share of government borrowing, the role of markets has grown in most countries, though in Belgium and Japan financial intermediaries still seem to take up a large proportion of government paper.

Thirdly, public-sector deficits may have indirectly stimulated innovation through their influence, concurrent or expectational, on inflation and interest rates. Although country situations have differed widely in this respect, the link, as I see it, runs in terms of the effect of deficits on the current and prospective behavior of total credit. In my Figure 2 you may get a visual impression for six countries of the contribution of public-sector credit to total new credit and of the behavior

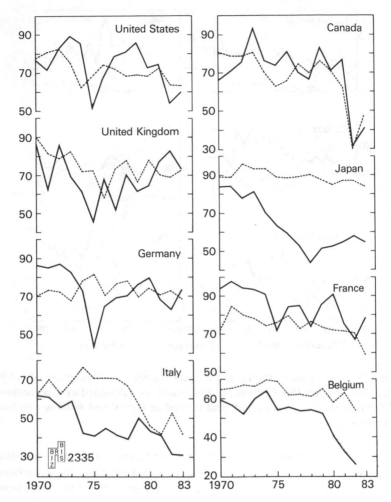

Figure 1
Changing Patterns of Borrowing and Financial Intermediation
Source: OECD, *Financial Accounts of OECD Countries.*
——— Private-sector borrowing as a proportion of credit-market funds raised
by domestic non-financial sectors.
------ Financial institutions' share of total credit-market funds supplied.

of total credit in relation to nominal gross national expenditure.

Fourthly, public-sector deficits have had an important private-sector counterpart in terms of asset accumulation which, with or without some Ricardo-equivalence effect, has tended to encourage innovation.

Fifthly, public sectors in a number of countries continue, partly via

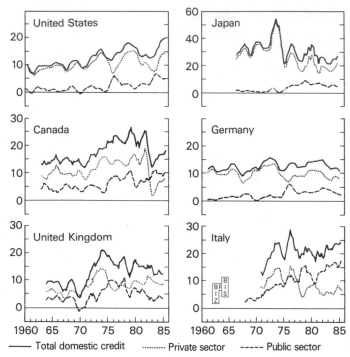

Figure 2
Total Domestic Credit: Public and Private Sectors as a Percentage of GNP. Quarterly changes (for German, semi-annual) are calculated as a percentage of GNP in the previous period, and plotted as uncentered moving averages over four quarters.

public credit institutions, to maintain protected, privileged financial circuits, in terms of both fund collection and lending. By definition, this limits the scope for market-related flows and may at the same time encourage financial innovation in the private sector.

Taking all these points into consideration, the induced effects of public-sector deficits on private-sector innovation have been extensive. They have contributed to pressures on intermediaries to offer more market-related interest rates, to a proliferation of bond-based investment funds and deposit accounts, to the emergence of new intermediaries, and to the blurring of boundaries between old ones. In some cases governmental borrowing abroad may have shifted the locus of innovation influences from the domestic to the external sector.

Two additional points concern the regulatory authorities. Firstly, the government's willingness to accede to pressures from private-sector sources for innovation and change has almost surely had something to do with the relative size of its own borrowing requirements. On the other hand, some authorities have also had a fairly clear conception of how far and fast they want to go along the paths of innovation. In Germany, the Netherlands, and Switzerland, for example, my impression is that the authorities have not been very receptive to certain new financial instruments that might, say, unduly blur the distinctions between money and other financial assets.

Secondly, mention can be made of the official efforts, consistent with the Kane thesis discussed in the paper, whereby countries compete with one another internationally in promoting their own financial centers. One recent example was the abolition of the withholding tax on interest income from non-resident holdings of securities by the United States, Germany, France, and Japan. Another was the decision by Germany to give foreign banks based in Germany the right to lead-manage DM Euro-bond issues and also to look more favorably on swaps and issues with variable rates or zero coupons. Still another is the forthcoming "big bang" that is designed to make U.K. capital markets more competitive internationally.

In terms of broader implications, it seems to me arguable, at least, that the interplay between public-sector deficit and financial innovation has, in important cases, led to an acceleration of total credit expansion. I would therefore side with those who feel that innovation is pushing us towards giving greater attention to the broad credit and asset aggregates. While the relationship is obviously a very loose one, it would broadly appear from Figure 2 that countries which have had a high rate of financial innovation (the United States, the United Kingdom, Canada, and Italy) have had wider—and less satisfactory as a trend—movements of total credit expansion than countries where innovation has not proceeded so fast (Germany and Japan).

Turning briefly to Section IV, the authors first present some comparative data on changing financial structures, nicely complementary to Section III, before going on to discuss the implications of innovations for the stability of the banking system. The analysis is, as the authors point out, mainly based on evidence from the United States. But the situation might look different in other countries, especially if considered in the light of the possible *benefits* of deregulation and financial reform. In a number of countries the expected gains in terms of efficiency and competition may outweigh by a wide margin any perceived costs in terms of system stability.

Moreover, at the systemic level, the paper notes that recourse to interest rate regulations was prompted by episodes of financial panic earlier in this century and by the collapse of the U.S. banking system in the Great Depression. But economic structures and policy attitudes have since changed in quite fundamental ways, and macroeconomic policies have become such that the risk of a systemic liquidity problem is no longer of the same order. The main dangers today, I think, are dangers of the kinds mentioned in Pierce's paper: unregulated, or poorly regulated, scope-of-operations activities and, in a more competitive environment, specific cases involving questionable practices and excessive risk-taking.

As far as new financial instruments are concerned, the implications of different innovations differ, and they depend on other changes that are occurring. Innovations that seem to increase risk often induce others that can be used to reduce it. Incidentally, the paper addresses the question whether deposit rate deregulation increases the variability of interest rates but finds the answer inconclusive. At all events deregulation has generally helped to counteract wide swings in the pattern of intermediation, enabling the banks better to maintain their share of the credit market when interest rates change.

Although an increase in competition seems bound on balance to squeeze profit margins, this need not threaten the soundness of banks. As stated in the paper, the effects on profits and profit variability also depend very much on the nature of the newly introduced activities. Moreover, despite added pressure on bank profitability, cautious portfolio management can help to minimize solvency risks. Nevertheless, competition seems in many instances to breed excessive risk-taking, and the quality of both asset and liability portfolios has turned up as a problem in certain recent cases. One might add that the recent tendency towards a tightening of bank supervision in many countries implies a new regulatory constraint of a different order. It may itself prompt new types of innovation: witness the various new kinds of off-balance-sheet activity which are designed partly to circumvent balance-sheet and capital requirements. With this development, which is closely linked with a new wave of innovation in international markets generally, the problems for the supervisory side of monetary policy are only beginning to be better appreciated.

For these reasons, and because the debate on financial innovation has been shifting to broader questions concerning the reform of financial systems, it seemed to me appropriate to stress the role of background causes of innovation. If, as I have argued, public-sector needs, high and volatile interest rates, financial innovation, and total credit expansion are partly interrelated, it would seem to follow that more consistent macro-policies could render the innovation process less frenetic and more amenable to rational manipulation and control.

The experience of various countries where innovation has been slow and deliberate would seem to confirm this. But it also follows that any attempt to influence the innovation process by macro-policies implies, as it also would in the case of such composites as total credit expansion, real interest rates and nominal GNP, the need for consistent policy-mix approaches, and not simply central-bank policies as such.

Comments

Norbert Bub

Innovations in the financial system are not simply a feature of our own days. The financial markets have always been subject to changes, but it was from about the mid-1970s onward that financial innovations began to attract greater attention. This probably owed something to the fact that new instruments and methods started to appear more frequently at that time. These developments had to be seen against the background of inflation rates that reached quite unprecedented levels and of higher and sharply fluctuating market interest rates, while in many countries the adaptability of the traditional financial intermediaries was impeded by administrative measures. This topic caused particular upheaval, however, in the Anglo-Saxon countries, where in the course of this process considerable doubt arose as to the reliability of the target variables used until then for monetary policy.

Problems of this kind did not occur in the Federal Republic of Germany. Since the beginning of monetary targeting in the mid-1970s the Bundesbank has been able to use the central bank money stock virtually without qualifications as its key target variable, and it has generally achieved the goals set.

There are a number of reasons for this. In contrast to the situation in many of the more seriously affected countries, the flexibility of interest rates in Germany was not impaired by regulations at any time during the 1970s. The Bundesbank had already abolished the ceilings for bank interest rates during the 1960s, towards the end of the reconstruction phase. That move was in line with its liberal basic stance of not intervening in the operation of the markets as long as fundamental principles of monetary policy, meaning in particular the maintenance of price stability, are not at risk.

Another favorable factor was that the Bundesbank had been assigned, as its primary function, the task of safeguarding the currency.

This was an essential precondition for keeping inflation rates in Germany distinctly lower than those in most other countries. As a result, fluctuations in interest rates—a cause of some innovations—tended to be small by international standards. Furthermore, under these conditions savers could with good reason depend on the financial assets they had invested at long term yielding a positive real rate of interest, so that they did not have to hold financial assets in short-term forms for fear of galloping inflation rates, and hence rising interest rates, in the future.

However, higher and more sharply fluctuating interest rates left their marks on the pattern of financial investment in the Federal Republic of Germany, too. Traditional savings deposits, the interest rates on which were adjusted only sluggishly by banks, lost ground to new forms of investment which were geared more to market rates of interest. This process was, however, also affected by trends in government savings promotion. Up to 1974 the government strongly encouraged long-term savings contracts. The phased reduction of this promotion in the ensuing period directed savers' attention more strongly to the yields offered by the market.

It is true that all this has contributed to the rising share among German banks of liabilities bearing interest at market-related rates, to which Yumoto et al. have pointed. The crucial factor is, however, that this has not led to a migration of savings from the universal bank system to other institutional investors.

The fact that the Bundesbank has been able to keep to its original target variable no doubt also owes something to the circumstance that, in the central bank money stock, it had chosen from the outset a broadly defined statistical aggregate that corresponded rather well to the concept of money under the conditions obtaining in Germany. This monetary aggregate is affected far less than M1 by fluctuations in short-term interest rates and the consequent shifts between sight deposits and short-term time deposits that bear interest at market-related rates.

Needless to say, German monetary policy has not been entirely spared certain disruptions. Yumoto et al. have pointed to the development of the Euro-DM markets and the sharp growth at times—albeit from a very low level—in short-term bank bonds. The effects of these innovations have been watched carefully by the Bundesbank. It can be said today, though, that the disturbances they caused were not lasting or severe.

The strong growth of short-term bank bonds remained limited to a period of steep rises in interest rates. Moreover, the expansion of the

Euro-DM markets did not seriously endanger the orientating function of the central bank money stock. The deposits of German nonbanks on these markets have so far been of secondary importance. For the rest, quite a number of circumstances have contributed to the evolution of these money and credit markets, and in my view the attempt to circumvent the minimum reserve regulations was hardly the most significant of them. Another important factor, to my mind, was that, given the rising inflation rates and the more restrictive monetary policy stance at that time, the profit margins of the banks and their own-capital ratios contracted, and these then migrated in an attempt to circumvent the regulations of the supervisory authorities.

Yumoto et al. have discussed the implications for the profitability and stability of the German banking system of the increased proportion of deposits bearing interest at market-related rates. In this respect Germany may serve as an example of the conditions obtaining on unregulated financial markets.

In the past, one consequence of interest rate rises in Germany has often been that the liabilities side of banks' balance sheets has been affected first by them. Initially, the banks have been unable or unwilling to pass on the increase in their costs in full on the assets side. However, the ensuing deterioration in their profit situation then made adjustment measures more and more imperative: the propensity to extend credit diminished, requirements for creditworthiness became more stringent, and finally the lending rates were raised as well. In the event of falls in interest rates, the opposite applied. For monetary policy, this mode of operation implied a certain lagging of effects; on the other hand, the system managed with smaller fluctuations in interest rates than would otherwise have been the case.

In external economic questions, too, Germany's behavior is characterized by liberal principles. Thus, at the beginning of the 1970s it advocated floating exchange rates, which helped it materially in pursuing its stability target. Under these conditions, the remaining controls on capital movements could be run down as well. Today German residents are completely free to acquire assets in foreign currencies or to take up corresponding credits. Conversely, non-residents can borrow in D-Marks and build up all kinds of D-Mark creditor positions.

To be sure, hopes of a smooth functioning of floating exchange rates, e.g. in the sense of the theory of purchasing power parity, failed to come true. This was felt by the German economy particularly keenly in the 1970s, when the D-Mark, as a freely convertible currency, was suddenly faced with undue international demand. For a comparatively small and open economy, the role of a substitute reserve currency could not but pose problems. Consequently it appeared to be inadvisable to abolish at once all the restrictions still surviving from the period of fixed exchange rates.

Given the changed exchange rate situation obtaining in the 1980s, some "surviving features" of that period have now been finally done away with. The general public has sometimes termed this, not quite aptly, the "rest-liberalization of the German capital market." The most significant measure was, I think, the abolition of withholding tax on the interest income of non-residents from domestic bonds.

The abolition of what was known as the "Gentlemen's Agreement" must also be mentioned in this context. Under this agreement between the Bundesbank and the German banks, which dated back to 1968, foreign D-Mark bonds were to be issued only with a German bank as the lead manager. The Bundesbank formerly tried in this way to exercise a slightly dampening influence on the strong growth of the international role of the D-Mark and to restrain the overvaluation of the German currency. Since May 1 there has been nothing to prevent the lead management being effected by foreign banks domiciled in Germany. This applies, at least, if similar facilities are granted to German-owned banks in the home country of the bank in question.

The Bundesbank took the opportunity presented by this change to authorize the introduction of a number of innovations that are already well established on capital markets outside Germany. These include floating rate bonds, bonds issued in connection with currency swaps, and so-called zero bonds. Switching into short-term loans and loans with variable interest rates has been common practice in Germany for a long time. Hence these new instruments hardly present any new problems for monetary policy.

Comments

Y. C. Jao*

John Greenwood's paper provides a concise but comprehensive analysis of financial liberalization and innovation in seven East Asian economies—the famed "four little dragons" plus Malaysia, Thailand, and Indonesia. The author's analytical device is to distinguish between two broad sets of influences, foreign and domestic, making for financial deregulation and innovation, which in turn are divided into two major types: those affecting the pricing of deposit rates and financial instruments and those affecting other conditions of competitiveness. The material in the text is then most lucidly and usefully summarized in an appendix of tables, using the aforementioned taxonomic scheme.

At the purely factual or institutional level, I find it very difficult to disagree with Mr. Greenwood. What I propose to do in my comments are, firstly, to fill in a few gaps and, secondly, to try to extend the author's analysis of the causes or origins of financial innovation.

Let me first start with a few supplementary remarks about Hong Kong and Taiwan. In his paper, Mr. Greenwood briefly mentions the currency stabilization scheme instituted in Hong Kong on October 15, 1983, which he characterizes as a "traditional gold standard-type of convertible currency mechanism." In essence, the new arrangement amounts to a return to the system that prevailed in Hong Kong before July 1972, but the mechanism of "arbitrage and competition" that ensures the convergence of the market rate to the official rate of US$1 = HK$7.8 is a remarkable innovation. The scheme has not only saved Hong Kong from near collapse; its success and innovative aspect have, in my view, invested it with more than parochial significance. The author's modesty has prevented him from mentioning his role in the

*Professor Jao was unable to attend the conference but submitted his Comments for inclusion in this volume.

reform, but he is widely known to be its intellectual architect through his incisive and persuasive articles on the subject (see, *inter alia,* Greenwood 1982, 1983). The section on Taiwan however seems to me to be too brief. I am also puzzled that the establishment of the Taipei Offshore Banking Centre in 1984 is not mentioned in the paper. While Taipei lags very much behind Hong Kong and Singapore, the fact that offshore banking units are formally permitted to operate there can be regarded as an important experiment in financial deregulation and in- novation. It is also noteworthy that Taiwan has opted for the Singapore rather than the Hong Kong model, in that onshore and offshore opera- tions are clearly and strictly segregated (Sun 1984).

Coming to the general themes of the paper, I agree with the author that monetary policy and the financial system should not be used for achieving allocative goals, otherwise economic efficiency is bound to suffer, and that foreign exchange controls are a major impediment to financial deregulation. Mr. Greenwood, however, tends to discuss financial innovations in conjunction with deregulation, and I wonder whether this approach is not unduly restrictive. It is of course true that financial innovations often come about in an environment of financial liberalization; but it is also true that financial innovations can just as often be caused by attempts to evade or circumvent onerous govern- mental regulations and restrictions (e.g. the Xeno-currency markets). Other important causes are technological advances and agents' desires to protect themselves against risk or uncertainty (e.g. financial futures).

Perhaps because the author is primarily concerned with deregulation, which is implicitly regarded as highly desirable, he is silent on the im- plications of financial innovations for the implementation and effec- tiveness of monetary policy. However, in those economies where sub- stantial deregulation has been achieved, financial innovations do pose serious problems for the monetary authorities. In Hong Kong, for instance, during the interregnum of 1972–83 between gold-standard- type regimes, sophisticated techniques of "liability management" and new financial products like "swap deposits" had gravely undermined the authorities' ability to control monetary aggregates.

The preoccupation with deregulation also shows up, I think, in the explanation of the causes of financial innovations. Although theories are not explicitly discussed, the passing references to "financial repres- sion" and "financial deepening" seem to imply tacit approval of the McKinnon-Shaw model (McKinnon) 1973; Shaw 1973). This model, in exhorting less developed countries to liberalize their financial systems, is a prescriptive one as far as financial innovations are con- cerned. But as mentioned earlier, the origins of financial innovations are complex, and given the growing integration of world financial markets, a wider view of financial innovations and their implications is warranted.

This is not the place for a detailed review of theoretical models of financial innovations. All I wish to do is give a sketch of alternative theories to supplement Mr. Greenwood's treatment.

I suppose that no one can seriously discuss innovations without being inspired by Schumpeter, the progenitor of the view that economic development is essentially a process of discontinuous and disruptive innovations, a process of "creative destruction." Innovations can occur in both the real and financial sectors, and it is the interaction between both sectors that provides the driving force for dynamic development. However, neither in his famous early work on development (1911, 1935) nor in his posthumous work on monetary theory (1970) did Schumpeter explicitly explain the causes of innovations: they seem to have been treated as an exogenous variable that generated business cycle fluctuations. Paradoxically, an endogenous theory of inventions and innovations was adumbrated in his later work on comparative systems (1942), in which he espoused the view that market structure may make a decisive difference in the sense that large, monopolistic firms are much more likely and able to introduce inventions and innovations which will be subsequently imitated and diffused. As is well known, this hypothesis has generated a huge and controversial empirical literature. As an illustration, a recent study (Hannan and McDowell 1984) shows that market concentration did have a positive impact on the diffusion of new technology in the U.S. banking industry during the 1970s. However, Schumpeter's model cannot statisfactorily explain financial innovations arising from an environment of deregulation and fierce competition.

If financial innovations were entirely motivated by agents' desire to hedge against risk or uncertainty, the Arrow-Debreu model (Arrow and Debreu 1954; Arrow 1964; Debreu 1959) would seem to have anticipated everything in the financial services industry during the past two decades. Arrow and Debreu proved rigorously that an equilibrium exists for a complete system of competitive markets in which commodties are defined not only by their physical characteristics but also by the "states of the world" at which they are to be exchanged. However, as Arrow himself emphasized, the competitive allocation of risk-bearing is guaranteed to be viable if agents are risk-averse (their utility functions must be quasi-concave). But financial innovations are known to have originated from causes other than risk-reduction or insurance. Even for those securities that are supposedly Arrow-Debreu in conception, there is a tendency for the new options and contracts to be mainly exploited by short-term speculators and arbitrageurs, according to Tobin (1984). Thus, even though the model is extremely elegant, it can at best explain a small subset of financial innovations.

Neither Schumpeter nor Arrow-Debreu, in developing their theories, however, had financial innovations specifically in mind. As is well known, Schumpeter was more concerned with "real" innovations, while Arrow and Debreu's primary interest was the mathematical proof of the Invisible Hand. Explicit theorizing about financial innovations has been a relatively recent development. Greenbaum and Haywood (1971), using the Gurley-Shaw framework, stress the secular rise in non-human wealth as the primary demand stimulus to financial innovation, especially as fixed costs in portfolio management enables scale economies to be reaped in portfolio diversification. In contrast, Silber (1975) emphasizes the supply factors by postulating the hypothesis that "innovation of financial instruments and practices occurs in an effort to remove or lessen the financial constraints imposed on firms." Government regulations and restrictions constitute only one form of constraint: there are other self-imposed or market-imposed constraints as well. This hypothesis receives support from a study by Ben-Horim and Silber (1977), who find that major U.S. financial innovations did occur in response to significant increases in the costs of financial constraints on banks. While these theories can account for a number of important causes of financial innovation, they cannot fully explain innovations which are primarily designed to reduce risk or uncertainty in an environment of greater interest rate and exchange rate volatility. In their study of international financial markets, Dufey and Giddy (1981) therefore place greater emphasis on "defensive" innovations in response to changes in relative prices or relative risks that give rise to a gap in the range of available financial instruments.

Another school of thought, which one might loosely call the historical-institutional approach, is represented by Davies and North (1971), Davies (1975), and West (1982). This school regards financial innovations as a part of institutional change that interacts with the economic system. Financial innovations may come about because of income-enhancing or income-redistributing motives; in other words, financial innovations are dominated by two pervasive motivations: the reduction of transaction costs and the preservation of the stability of the financial system. Without going into the details of this approach, two salient features may be noted. One is that the adherents to this approach are strongly critical of the "ahistorical" attitude of contemporary economists, who tend to regard financial innovations principally in terms of the private sector's response to governmental regulations or an adverse economic environment, forgetting that financial innovations have been as ancient as human economic history itself. Secondly, instead of viewing governmental regulation as the antithesis of financial innovation, the institutionalists regard regulatory change itself as an innovation designed to eliminate or reduce instability or other deficiencies of the financial system. For instance, West argues that major milestones in U.S. financial history, such as monopoly of note issue by the federal government, the creation of the Federal Reserve System and the Federal Deposit Insurance Corporation, were pro-stability innovations in response to the abuse of note issues by private banks and recurrent financial panics. The primary reason why these innovations have been undertaken by the public sector is the "public good" or "externalities" aspects of financial stability.

These points deserve serious consideration, but there are other questions that require further clarification. For instance, what is the relationship between social framework and financial innovations? At one extreme, in command economies where financial repression is complete, no financial innovation is possible. This explains why the menu of financial services available to consumers is so meager, and also why no international financial center has ever existed in command economies. At the other extreme, in a pure *laissez faire* economy, there is no need to innovate in order to evade or circumvent official controls. It seems therefore that the social framework most conducive to financial innovations is a market economy where the financial services industry is subject nevertheless to considerable regulation.

Furthermore, granted that financial innovations have been a long and continuous historical process (one need only recall the use of money in lieu of barter, the evolution of paper currency, and the emergence of bank deposits as the principal means of payment), the intensity and acceleration of financial innovations in the past thirty years still requires an explanation. One of the most frequently given reasons, interest rate and exchange rate volatility, is not a real answer, since such volatility had also existed in previous historical periods, notably the interwar period in this century. One suspects therefore that the acceleration of financial innovations may have something to do with structural changes in the world economy—the growing integration of world financial markets, the spectacular advances in electronic and telecommunication industries, and the gradual but persistent trend in mature economies towards a new stage of economic development variously called "post-industrial society," "information society," "New Industrial Revolution," etc. Clearly, the origins and causes of financial innovations are more complex than commonly realized, and economists have so far failed to come up with a model general enough to account for all such complexities.

These theoretical excursions however represent only a discussant's afterthought. Mr. Greenwood's valuable paper enables us to understand better the process of financial deregulation and innovation in the major East Asian economies which now constitute, by general agreement, an important growth center in the world economy.

References

Arrow, K.J. 1964. The Role of Securities in the Optimal Allocation of Risk-bearing, *Review of Economic Studies*, Vol. 31, pp. 91–296.

Arrow, K.J. and G. Debreu. 1954. Existence of An Equilibrium for a Competitive Economy, *Econometrica*, July, No. 3, pp. 265–90.

Ben-Horim, M. and W.L. Silber. 1977. Financial Innovation: A Linear Programming Approach, *Journal of Banking and Finance*, Vol. 1, pp. 277–296.

Davies, L.E. 1975. The Evolution of the American Capital Market, 1860–1940: A Case Study in Institutional Change. In Silber (1975).

Davies, L.E. and D.North. 1971. *Institutional Change and American Economic Growth*. New York: Cambridge University Press.

Debreu, G. 1959. *Theory of Value*. New Haven: Yale University Press.

Dufey, G. and I.H. Giddy. 1981. Innovation in the International Financial Markets, *Journal of International Business Studies*, Fall, pp. 33–51.

Greenbaum, S.I. and C.F. Haywood. 1971. Secular Change in the Finnacial Services Industry, *Journal of Money, Credit and Banking*, May. pp. 571–589.

Greenwood, J.G. 1982. Hong Kong's Financial Crisis: History, Analysis, Prescription, *Asian Monetary Monitor*, November-December, pp. 2–69.

Greenwood, J.G. 1983. How to Rescue the HK$: Three Practical Proposals, *Asian Monetary Monitor*, September-October, pp. 11–40.

Hannon, T.H. and J.M. McDowell. 1984. Market Concentration and the Diffusion of New Technology in the Banking Industry, *Review of Economics & Statistics*, November, pp. 686–691.

McKinnon, R. 1973. *Money and Capital in Economic Development*. Washington: Brookings Institution.

Schumpeter, J.A. 1911, 1935. *Theorie der wirtschaftlichen Entwicklung*. Berlin: Duncker und Humblot; English edition entitled *Theory of Economic Development*, translated by R. Opie. Cambridge, Mass: Harvard University Press.

Schumpeter, J.A. 1970. *Das Wesen des Geldes, aus dem Nachlass herausgegeben und mit einer Einführung versehen von Fritz Karl Mann*. Göttingen: Vandenhoeck und Ruprecht.

Shaw, E.S. 1973. *Financial Deepening in Economic Development*. New York: Oxford University Press.

Silber, W.L. 1975. *Financial Innovation*. Lexington: Lexington Books.

Tobin, J. 1984. On the Efficiency of the Financial System. *Lloyds Bank Review*, July, pp. 1–15.

Sun I-shuan. 1984. Prospects of the Taipei Offshore Banking Center, *Bulletin for International Fiscal Documentation*, No. 6, pp. 259–60.

West, R.G. 1982. A Theory of Financial Innovation in the United States, Research Working Paper 82–07, Federal Reserve Bank of Kansas City.

The Process of Financial Deregulation, Monetary Reform, and the Financial System of the Future

5

International Financial Intermediation: Underlying Trends and Implications for Government Policies

Ralph C. Bryant

This paper analyzes the international dimensions of financial inter-mediation. It focuses in particular on international aspects of the reg-ulation and supervision of financial institutions.*

Section I presents summary observations about the progressive internationalization of financial intermediation during the last few decades. Section I also discusses alternative explanations for this inter-nationalization and offers a summary judgment about how far it has progressed as of the mid-1980s. Section II summarizes some basic rationales for the regulation and supervision of financial intermediaries and the extensions of those rationales made necessary by cross-border and cross-currency financial transactions. Section III identifies inter-national collective-goods problems in the regulation, taxation, and supervision of financial intermediaries and discusses nascent inter-governmental cooperative efforts to deal with them. The paper con-cludes with some brief speculations about alternative possible evolu-tions of the world financial system.[1]

* The research on which this paper is based was financed by an experimental grant for the study of international economic policy issues, made to the Brookings Institution by the U.S. National Science Foundation. The views expressed are en-tirely my own and should not be attributed to the National Science Foundation or to the officers, trustees, or other staff members of the Brookings Institution. I am grateful to Linda L. Mix for excellent research assistance.

[1] The paper draws upon a longer manuscript, *International Financial Intermedia-tion: Analysis and Public Policy*, prepared as part of the author's research program at the Brookings Institution. A published version of that manuscript should be available shortly after the publication of this paper. Readers interested in an ampli-fication of the argument here, in particular of the material summarized in Section I, should consult that manuscript.

I. The Progressive Internationalization of Financial Intermediation

In modern complex economies most decisions to save are made independently of decisions to invest in tangible physical assets. Ultimate savers (primarily households) set aside some fraction of current income rather than spending it on current consumption so as to increase their or their children's future possibilities for consumption. Ultimate investors (primarily businesses) purchase and employ tangible capital goods to facilitate their production of goods and services; they borrow—issue financial instruments as liabilities—to be able to employ more physical capital than would otherwise be possible.

Financial intermediation is the complex process through which the differing needs of ultimate savers and ultimate investors are reconciled. Financial intermediaries are institutions that facilitate this reconciliation. The assets of a financial intermediary are the obligations of the ultimate investors (and, in an increasingly complex financial system, of other intermediaries as well). The liabilities of a financial intermediary are the assets of the ultimate savers (and of other intermediaries). Unlike the ultimate investors whose main assets are physical capital goods, the financial intermediaries have both their assets and their liabilities predominantly in the form of financial instruments.[2]

An economy without financial instruments would severely constrict the behavior of spending units. No unit would be able to indulge its needs and preferences for an intertemporal pattern of consumption that differed from the time profile of its income. Resources would be allocated inefficiently and the economy-wide levels of saving and investment, and hence the growth rate of output, would be substantially less than under arrangements where ultimate investors can borrow through the issuance of "primary securities" (financial obligations issued directly by ultimate investors).

Although to a lesser degree, an economy in which the only financial instruments were primary securities would also be constricted in its possibilities for growth and efficient resource allocation. By issuing claims against themselves, financial intermediaries offer ultimate savers a wider menu of risk-return combinations than would be available if the savers had to lend directly to the ultimate investors. Many intermediaries engage in "maturity transformation" so that their liabilities have shorter maturities than their assets. And the liabilities of inter-

---

[2] For a more detailed description of the activities of financial intermediaries, see for example Tobin and Brainard (1963) or Gurley and Shaw (1960, chap. 6).

mediaries tend to have smaller default risk and greater predictability of value than their assets. Ultimate savers can therefore hold financial assets of greater liquidity than the primary securities issued by the ultimate investors.

Financial intermediaries can accomplish this transformation between primary securities and the financial assets held by the ultimate savers because of, for example, reduction of risk per dollar of lending through the pooling of independent risks and specialized expertise in risk evaluation. Financial intermediaries can also reduce the costs associated with the transformation through their greater efficiency in negotiating, accounting, and collecting. The activities of financial intermediaries thus enable ultimate investors to finance their purchases of tangible assets at lower rates and easier terms than if they were forced to borrow directly from the ultimate savers. Similarly, financial intermediation provides ultimate savers much greater flexibility than they otherwise could have to adopt intertemporal paths of consumption different from the intertemporal paths of their income.

The existing literature on financial intermediation has focused on domestic aspects—that is, intermediation where the lenders, the borrowers, and the intermediating parties are all residents of a single nation and the asset-liability relationships are assumed to be denominated exclusively in the national currency unit. The international aspects have frequently been neglected. Increasingly, however, this relative lack of attention to the international dimensions has become an anomaly.

Increasing Interdependence: Broad Trends

From our vantage point in the mid-1980s, we can perceive that increasing economic interdependence is one of the key economic facts characterizing the world economy in the second half of the twentieth century. The most familiar manifestations of the greater openness of national economies are those involving international trade in goods and services. Exports from and imports into most nations have been growing more rapidly than national output. Correspondingly, the aggregate flow of trade across national borders for the world as a whole has been increasing faster than total world production.

The international debtor-creditor relationships of national economies are less well documented and understood than international trade in goods and services. But increases in *financial* interdependence have been even more rapid than those for trade.

International lending and borrowing by *banks* has been the cutting edge of this growing financial interdependence. Other types of financial intermediaries such as insurance companies, pension funds, and security dealers have also contributed importantly to the trend. So far, however, commercial banks and merchant banks have played a role overshadowing nonbank financial institutions.

I have presented and analyzed evidence about these important trends elsewhere. For the purposes of this paper, therefore, I omit all discussion of the empirical evidence and turn instead to a discussion of possible explanations for these trends.

Why Has Progressive Internationalization Occurred?

To provide a benchmark for analysis, consider first a hypothetical self-contained economy whose financial markets are fully integrated. In such an economy, all financial intermediation is "domestic" (by assumption the economy is completely closed to the rest of the world). The financial system may be likened to a reservoir. When the current-period consumption of households and other economic agents falls short of their income, the resulting savings flow into the reservoir. Businesses whose current-period spending exceeds their income draw funds out of the reservoir as they borrow to finance their excess spending. The existence of the reservoir permits saving and investment decisions to be taken independently. The risk pooling, risk evaluation, and maturity transformation activities of financial intermediaries play a central role in maintaining the reservoir. In effect, the intermediaries attract and funnel the savings into the reservoir and make it easier for ultimate investors to withdraw funds out of it. Without the intermediaries, the economy's financial transactions would be fragmented into numerous local puddles partially or wholly disconnected from each other.

In a super-efficient financial system having no market imperfections and very low communications and transactions costs, the fluid in the reservoir would behave like water. Following a change in underlying circumstances somewhere in the economy, the fluid would adjust almost instantaneously to re-establish a single uniform level. In other words, savers would move funds so adeptly from low-return to higher-return locations and borrowers would shift so promptly from high-cost to lower-cost sources of financing that market interest rates and yields on investments (adjusted for risk premia) would speedily become equalized throughout the reservoir.

Given asymmetries in the distribution of information and in access to financial markets, and given significant communications and transactions costs, however, the fluid in the reservoir should be imagined as viscous—more like thick molasses than water. Given sufficient time for adjustment to changes in underlying circumstances, a uniform level of the viscous fluid will prevail. Nonetheless, if in one region the "taking out" activity during any particular short run substantially exceeds or falls short of the "putting in" activity, the level in that region can be temporarily lower or higher than elsewhere in the reservoir.

Suppose investment opportunities become more favorable in a particular region of the economy. In an *ex ante* sense, the region will have an excess demand for savings: desired withdrawals from the reservoir by its residents will be temporarily larger than planned inflows. The region will pull savings from other parts of the reservoir as investors in the projects with higher-than-average expected returns successfully bid funds away from investors whose projects in other regions are less promising. Investment in the favored region will not be limited by the current flow of regional savings; during the transitional adjustment period there need be little relation between the investment and saving of the region's residents. If one could calculate balance-of-payments accounts for the favored region, one would observe a net savings inflow (a current-account deficit). Eventually, rates of return on investment will converge (adjusted for risk premia) throughout all regions of the economy. But while perceived rates of return are unusually high in the favored region, the reservoir will not have a uniform level and funds will flow away from the rest of the reservoir to the favored region.

National Financial Markets After World War II. The depression of the 1930s and World War II caused severe disruptions in world economic activity. In the early postwar period, cross-border transactions in goods and services were thus hampered by many frictions and obstacles. Financial transactions between nations were impeded even more; in numerous cases they were prohibited altogether by exchange and capital controls. Individual national economies were partially isolated from each other.

The financial system of each nation was in effect a different reservoir. Within each national reservoir, savings flows were viscous and in some instances impeded by market imperfections. But internal conditions were sufficiently flexible to encourage an eventual convergence of returns on investment projects throughout most parts of each nation's economy. In any case, the mobility of funds within each reservoir was much greater than the mobility of funds from one reservoir to another.[3]

[3] The analogy of a single reservoir in which rates of return (adjusted for risk) were relatively uniform throughout each nation does violence to the facts, even for the immediate postwar period. For the discussion here, however, I simplify by omitting any further mention of the market imperfections and lack of complete integration within each nation. My analogy of reservoirs and viscous savings flows is similar to the "hydraulic" imagery in Harberger (1980).

The reasons for the separation of national reservoirs can be classified into two broad groups. *Nonpolicy factors*—geography, technology, information and education, and even cultural and social traditions—interposed large "economic distances" between the national reservoirs. Second, *governmental policies* inhibited the cross-border transfer of funds; in effect, nations' governments erected and maintained a "separation fence" around their reservoirs.

Communications and transportation costs were the most important nonpolicy factors interposing economic distance between nations. Financial transactions across borders require the transmission of messages. The physical transport of pieces of paper, and often people themselves, is also required. Money and time are expended in this transmission and transport. The greater the economic distance, the larger the fraction of the total costs of a transaction due merely to communications and transportation.

The various nonpolicy factors inhibited movements of funds across borders, but not by design. In contrast, the governmental policies embodied in separation fences were explicitly intended to disconnect the reservoirs. Some countries maintained separation fences that were high and nearly insurmountable. Others had fences that were lower and partially permeable. Very few nations, however, had no separation fences at all.

Postwar attitudes about international capital flows were supportive of government policies to maintain separation fences. The most widely accepted economic analyses of the 1920s and 1930s identified "disequilibrating" capital flows as a prime cause of the unfavorable economic performance of those years. Writing in 1941 about prospective postwar arrangements, Keynes insisted that "nothing is more certain than that the movement of capital funds must be regulated" (1980, vol. 25, pp. 30–31). Virtually all countries came out of the war with extensive exchange and capital controls.

Attitudes about international trade in goods and services were markedly different. All countries shared the aspiration to liberalize trade transactions after the war. To be sure, rhetoric went well beyond actual practices. Many trade barriers did not come down promptly. The existence of barriers to trade transactions reinforced the separation of national financial reservoirs due to policy barriers against capital flows.

The analogy of relatively isolated national reservoirs is helpful when analyzing financial activity in the world economy of the early postwar period. But it has increasingly diminished validity as analysis moves forward in time toward the present. Indeed, one can classify explanations for the rapid growth in cross-border financial intermediation in terms of the different ways in which the separateness of the national reservoirs has progressively eroded.

Alternative explanations fall under three broad headings according to whether cross-border financial activity (1) followed real-sector transactions, (2) led real-sector transactions, or (3) responded to regulatory, tax, and supervisory incentives.

Financial Activity "Following" Real-Sector Transactions. The faster expansion of cross-border trade than of incomes and outputs occurred because governments reduced barriers to trade. Even more important, it occurred because the effective economic distances between nations were shrinking for nonpolicy reasons such as a sharp fall in the relative price of transport.

The faster growth of trade than of output would by itself have given rise to a growth in cross-border financial activity more rapid than the growth of domestic financial activity. To pay for cross-border shipments of goods and services, for example, a nation's residents needed to hold, borrow, or otherwise acquire cash balances denominated in foreign currencies (or foreign residents needed to acquire home-currency balances). Thus the transactions-balance requirements of trade alone would have induced a significant increase in international assets and liabilities. In many instances, traders sought credit to finance trade transactions. Non-financial traders could have extended credit directly to each other, and to some degree did so. At least as much as in domestic transactions, however, they resorted to financial intermediaries. Hence financial transactions such as bankers' acceptances and short-term bank loans against trade collateral expanded with the growth in international trade.

When cross-border financial activity is merely the financing counterpart of trade transactions, the goods trade may be said to "drive" the financial activity that is supporting it. An imbalance in the current account of a country's balance of payments associated with such transactions may be described as the causal result of the export and import transactions; the capital flows can be considered a passive accompaniment. Any resulting net transfers of savings between countries are the byproduct of the real-sector transactions and the incentives that drive those transactions.

The simplest international economic relationships involved arms-length transactions between a home resident and a foreign resident, each of whose business was primarily domestic in orientation. But as the postwar period progressed, some nonfinancial firms developed a much deeper involvement in foreign business. Rather than merely engaging in limited export or import transactions, some firms oriented their business primarily to foreign residents. And to facilitate this more ambitious involvement they established production facilities or sales and trading offices abroad.

Because some of their nonfinancial customers were establishing offices abroad, banks and other financial intermediaries themselves had incentives to set up physical facilities abroad—branches or separately incorporated subsidiary banks—to supplement the support they could give to customers from the home economy. Some part of the transactions with their customers were then booked on the balance sheets of the foreign offices.

As with the simple financing of international trade identified above, here too financial transactions were driven by real-sector economic decisions. The financial institutions setting up foreign offices "followed" their existing customers to retain, or to participate in the growth of, the customers' financial business.

Financial Activity "Leading" Real-Sector Transactions.   Although the nonpolicy factors shrinking the economic distances between nations encouraged international trade in the postwar period, those forces had, arguably, an even more dramatic impact on international financial transactions.

New developments in communications technology were especially important. Innovations in electronic equipment—computers, switching devices, telecommunications satellites—permitted the transmission of information, the confirmation of transactions, and the making of payments for transactions in a progressively less costly manner. Sophisticated methods of using the new equipment—such as computer software for electronics funds transfer and accounting—revolutionized the delivery of financial services. Entirely new possibilities for financial transactions became available.

Partly in response to such technological innovations, information and education about financial opportunities in foreign countries became much more readily and cheaply available. Those changes in turn helped to alter consumers' and producers' tastes. Foreign goods, foreign financial investments—virtually anything foreign—became much less a rarity than had been true early in the postwar period.

The implications for financial activity were far-reaching. Economic agents became more sensitive to, and had improved capacities to take advantage of, incentives for arbitrage among the national financial reservoirs. Financial instruments denominated in different currencies and issued by borrowers in different nations became less imperfect substitutes in the portfolios of increasingly sophisticated investors. Accordingly, cross-border ladling of funds began to increase. Moreover, many types of this ladling were not directly related to cross-border trade in goods and services or other real-sector transactions. Saving units could decide to take advantage of higher expected yields on financial assets in foreign reservoirs by purchasing foreign assets or making loans to foreigners rather than investing the funds somewhere in the home reservoir. Investing units could borrow from foreign reservoirs if they could thereby obtain more favorable loan terms than was possible at home. Increasingly, decisions about the country location of the investment and borrowing of funds were divorced from decisions about the country location of real-sector activity.

The economic distances between reservoirs were effectively shrinking for everyone. But financial intermediaries, and most of all large commercial banks, were the best-equipped to exploit the enhanced arbitrage opportunities. They had more and higher-quality information about foreign financial markets. They were better placed to introduce new communications technology. The relative costs of cross-border financial transactions thus fell most rapidly for banks and other financial intermediaries.

Ladlings of funds between reservoirs that were directly induced by newly profitable arbitrage calculations or newly perceived opportunities for arbitrage may be described as leading rather than following real-sector transactions. The gross financial flows and the resulting net transfers of savings were (*ex ante*) independently initiated. The ensuing imbalance in current-account and real-sector transactions was a passive byproduct of the capital flows.

In addition to arbitraging among national reservoirs by initiating financial transactions from their home bases, some financial intermediaries—again on their own initiative—moved abroad to establish actual physical offices within foreign reservoirs. Such offices enabled them to conduct arbitraging and intermediation activities directly from foreign locations. For example, banks with head offices in a home ("parent") country could, by the establishment of foreign branches, facilitate their collection of funds from and their lending of funds to the residents of foreign ("host") countries. Many of those foreign residents might have no real-sector transactions with economic agents in the parent country. Such internationally oriented banks would want not merely to service home customers with international transactions or home customers who themselves had foreign facilities. The banks would want new, foreign customers and would want to become active borrowers and lenders in host-country financial markets.

Regulatory, Tax, and Supervisory Explanations. From the perspective of private-sector agents, the existence of a government-erected separation fence around their home reservoir imposed extra costs on cross-border financial transactions. For reservoirs around which the fence was high and effectively maintained, the cost of transferring funds in or out was prohibitive.

For given economic distances between reservoirs attributable to nonpolicy factors, government actions to lower separation fences caused a decline in the differential costs required to get across the fence. Incentives were thereby enhanced for the ladling of funds between reservoirs. The partial dismantling of policy-erected barriers to international capital flows is thus another conceptually distinct category of explanation for the rapid growth of international financial intermediation in the last four decades.

Still other incentives due to governmental policies were important. They resulted from the interaction of nonpolicy technological innovations with regulatory, tax, and supervisory restraints on the financial systems *within* some of the economies. Such incentives would have been operative even if the separation fences themselves had not been altered.

These latter stimuli were important in nations having a domestic regulatory, tax, and supervisory environment that was more constraining than the environments in some foreign countries. High reserve requirements against deposit liabilities, binding interest-rate ceilings on deposits, high ratios of required capital to assets, and unusually strict examination procedures are examples of such constraints. Financial intermediaries in nations with these constraints had incentives to locate affiliated offices outside their home country and to book transactions through those offices to take advantage of the less constrained operating environments abroad.

By locating offices abroad, a financial institution gained access to possibilities for financial intermediation in the wider world economy without the encumbrances of the home environment. To be sure, financial intermediaries with offices in foreign host locations still had to cope with the domestic operating environments in the host nations. Those environments often prevented them from carrying out business with host-country customers in an unhampered way. And the intermediaries still had to cope with getting across the separation fences of third nations to conduct business with residents of those nations.

The incentives for getting outside the home regulatory environment were related to, but not the same as, the incentives for getting over the home nation's separation fence. The distinction is between continuously shuttling over the home separation fence (engaging in profitable cross-border transactions in and out of the home reservoir on an ongoing basis) versus jumping over the separation fence once and then staying outside it.

Important variants of getting-outside-the-fence behavior occurred as regulatory authorities permitted banks to establish special "offshore" facilities—typically, segregated accounting units—for conducting transactions with foreign customers or transactions in foreign currencies. In effect, banks were permitted to carry out "offshore" transactions as though the facility were "just outside" the home separation fence—even though the facility was physically located in the home nation. Regulations, supervision, and taxation were altered to discriminate in favor of the offshore transactions. For example, in contrast with the treatment of "domestic" deposits, banks were not required to hold fractional reserve balances at the central bank against deposits. In exchange for the ability to operate offshore facilities, the banks agreed to limit transactions between the facilities and domestic residents (including their own "onshore" offices), thereby protecting the integrity of the separation fence.

Prominent examples of this phenomenon have included the creation of Asian Currency Units in Singapore and International Banking Facilities in the United States. But a similar phenomenon has occurred implicitly whenever national regulations or taxation were changed to discriminate in favor of transactions with foreigners or transactions denominated in foreign currencies.

The Relative Importance of Different Explanations. To recapitulate, three categories of explanations for the progressive erosion of the separateness of national financial systems can be distinguished:

(1) Financial activity following real-sector transactions:

    (1a) Cross-border financial transactions, many of them conducted from home-country offices of financial intermediaries, that were closely associated with and driven by cross-border trade in goods and services.

    (1b) Establishment by financial intermediaries of affiliated offices abroad to improve services for existing nonfinancial customers who themselves had established operations abroad.

(2) Financial activity leading real-sector transactions:

    (2a) Cross-border financial transactions, conducted from home offices of financial intermediaries, that proceeded in advance and independently of cross-border trade in goods and services;

    (2b) Establishment by financial intermediaries of affiliated offices abroad in advance and independently of the current requirements of existing nonfinancial customers in the home country.

(3) Regulatory, tax, and supervisory explanations:

(3a) Lowering of national separation fences;

(3b) Establishment by financial intermediaries of affiliated offices abroad to escape from more stringent regulation, taxation, and supervision in the home environment.

It is convenient to refer to categories (1) and (2) as the basic nonpolicy hypotheses about international financial intermediation and to category (3) as the government-policy hypotheses.

The (a) variant of each explanation can partially account for the more extensive movement of funds from one national reservoir to another. But the (b) variants were probably at least as important. The (b) variants presupposed a still deeper involvement in foreign activities through the establishment of actual bricks-and-mortar presences outside the home-nation reservoir. Such ownership and locational penetrations of foreign economies represented more than a mere ladling of funds among the reservoirs. In effect, financial intermediaries installed pipes, siphons, and pumping stations to facilitate their interreservoir transfers of funds.

Which category of explanation best describes the actual facts in the last four decades? I believe that each of the three was important. If forced to rank them, I would tentatively put the second category of explanation in first place. But no one of the three can be ignored.

In particular, neither the nonpolicy hypotheses nor the government-policy hypotheses can alone carry the whole burden of explanation. The technological nonpolicy factors were so powerful, I believe, that they would have induced a progressive internationalization of financial activity even in the absence of changes in government separation fences and even without the inducement of regulatory, tax, and supervisory environments that differed substantially across nations. But I also conjecture that government-policy changes were important enough to have promoted a significant integration of national financial markets even if there had been no shrinkage in the economic distances between reservoirs due to nonpolicy innovations. Indeed, it is likely that the *interaction* between nonpolicy innovations and changes in government policies was itself an important part of the history. Each set of evolutionary changes reinforced the effects of the other.[4]

---

[4] When each of two interacting variables changes by a large factor, the combined change requires analysis to take into account not only the partial effects of each change considered separately but also the interaction of the two changes. (More formally, the third term in the identity $d(AB) = A(dB) + B(dA) + (dA)(dB)$ is

No doubt exists about the qualitative fact that many governments lowered their separation fences over the last four decades. After the reconstruction period of the late 1940s and 1950s, for example, many European countries restored "convertibility" for current-account transactions in 1958. Those policy actions inevitably undermined the early postwar distinction between current-account payments that were welcome from capital-account transactions that were not, which in turn loosened governmental restraints on capital flows generally. Some new controls on international capital movements were imposed in the 1960s (for example, in the United States). Viewed in retrospect, however, the predominant trend was to reduce or eliminate such restrictions.[5]

Prevailing attitudes about international capital flows also changed gradually. In contrast with the early postwar period, by the 1970s more emphasis was placed on the possible benefits associated with cross-border financial transactions. In the initial years after the onset of floating among the major currencies, the potential costs seemed less worrisome. Many governments also came to doubt the administrative feasibility of controlling capital flows (whatever the potential benefits and costs).

By the mid-1980s the salience of government restrictions on capital flows—especially among the industrial countries—was altogether different from what it had been four decades earlier. The United States was strongly against any form of capital controls; it was even leaning on other major nations to reduce their remaining controls on domestic as well as international transactions. The United Kingdom removed its remaining exchange controls in 1979. Germany was an advocate of relatively unfettered capital movements. Some industrial countries, it is true—for example, France, Italy, and Japan—were less than ardent enthusiasts for complete freedom for international capital movements. But even those countries were experiencing increasing difficulty in implementing their own remaining controls; much less could they persuade countries like the United States, the United Kingdom, and Germany to reverse the general trend away from such controls.

Many developing countries retained some form of separation fence for cross-border financial transactions. Yet some had eased earlier restrictions. In Latin America, for example, although Brazil and Co-

---

far from negligible when dA and dB are themselves large in relation to A and B.)

[5] Japan is the most important example of a major industrial nation that relaxed its capital controls at a pace markedly slower than the average for all industrial countries.

lombia kept their exchange and capital controls more or less intact, Argentina and Chile experimented with the relaxation or abandonment of such restrictions.

These generalizations do not take us very far. Economists have not done a good job of marshalling the evidence about government separation fences and generating analytical estimates of their effects. If we could accurately assess the relative importance of changes in government policies in the past four decades, we would be on much stronger ground in forming judgments about future trends and in framing recommendations for appropriate public policies.

What weights should be assigned to the nonpolicy explanations in categories (1) and (2) above? Did finance follow or independently lead real-sector transactions in the internationalization of financial intermediation?

The distinction between following and leading is conceptually helpful. With sufficient information about the decisions of particular financial institutions in specific contexts, one could give it empirical content. When evaluating financial history in the large, however, it is difficult to disentangle the two.

Whether international finance has been following or leading real-sector activity is an issue related to the proposition that financial intermediation tends to grow faster than output in the earlier stages of economic development (see Goldsmith 1969; Gurley and Shaw 1957). That proposition does not rest on behavior that is peculiarly domestic in nature. And financial activity with an international dimension has been growing much faster than either output or trade. As already observed, if cross-border real-sector transactions had been growing faster than purely domestic real-sector transactions, international financial activity would have grown faster than domestic financial activity merely because of the increasing openness of the real sectors of national economies. But since international financial activity has been growing markedly faster than international trade, one is tempted to infer that the Goldsmith-Gurley-Shaw proposition can be validly extended to the world economy as a whole.

The facts on relative growth rates are consistent with the presumption that international finance has tended more to lead than to follow real-sector activity. Observers of foreign-exchange and interbank-funds markets can cite numerous instances of financial transactions that are independently initiated in response to cross-border and cross-currency arbitrage opportunities. Conversations with bankers about the location decisions for foreign branches and subsidiaries often portray their organizations behaving in an anticipatory way, seeking new customers and profit opportunities in advance of the current-services requirements of existing customers.

The combination of this evidence persuades me that financial intermediaries themselves have often been the cutting edge of internationalization and that finance has been much more than a passive veil draped over and molded by real-sector activity. In the absence of a better understanding of the effects of changes in government policies, however, this conclusion remains uncertain, albeit plausible.

How Interconnected Are Financial Markets in the Mid-1980s?

Have national reservoirs today become so well connected that we must now picture nations as participants in a single world reservoir, having a more or less uniform level throughout its extent, thereby leaving little scope for autonomous financial conditions within individual national economies?

Existing knowledge does not yet permit a satisfactory answer to this question. On the basis of my analysis so far, however, I venture a preliminary, eclectic judgment along the following lines.

The financial structure of the world economy underwent a sea change in the last four decades. Nonpolicy technological innovations dramatically reduced the effective economic distances between national markets. Separation fences around them were partially or wholly dismantled. Indisputably, therefore, the conceptual analogy of nearly autonomous national reservoirs is no longer appropriate. To a much greater extent than in the early postwar years, the levels in national reservoirs tend to be pulled together toward a common level. A disturbing event originating in one nation's economy or financial system causes substantially larger ripples—or even waves—in other nations' reservoirs.

Even so, financial activity in many parts of the world is still significantly segmented. The conceit of a unified world capital market, implying a nearly uniform level throughout a single world reservoir, is also an inappropriate conceptual analogy for analyzing most aspects of international financial intermediation.

The actual situation, I believe, can only be characterized as an intermediate position not approximating either of the polar cases. On the spectrum running from completely separated national markets at one extreme to a fully unified world market at the other, the major nations and currencies are probably some two-thirds or three-fourths of the way—but not further—toward the single world reservoir.

This untidy state of affairs is a conceptual vexation for analysts and policymakers. Each group must mentally simplify a complex reality when trying to understand events and reach conclusions. The easiest simplifications to apply are the assumptions of the "nearly closed" paradigm, which presumes almost autonomous national markets, or the assumptions of the "small and open" or "supranational" paradigms, which presume the polar case of a unified world reservoir. Yet the assumptions of each of those approaches clashes too greatly with the actual, intermediate facts. If theorists and empirical researchers hope to illuminate actual experience, they must struggle more directly with the analytical difficulties of intermediate interdependence. Similarly, if policymakers hope to avoid seriously overestimating or seriously underestimating the autonomy of national economic policy, they too must abandon the polar assumptions as a basis for analysis.[6]

II. The Regulation and Supervision of Financial Intermediaries

In virtually all nations, financial intermediaries are subjected to tighter regulation and supervision than other types of business organization. Commercial banks often attract even closer secrutiny than other financial institutions. Yet the reasons for this special attention are seldom identified clearly. Before discussing the international dimensions of regulation and supervision, therefore, I first review the rationales that have been used to justify government intervention in a domestic context.

Basic Motives for Supervision and Regulation

The possible motive for supervision and regulation of financial intermediaries include: (a) prudential oversight of the stability of the financial system as a whole (a "macro-prudential" rationale), (b) prudential oversight of the payments mechanism (a corollary rationale that is also macro-prudential); (c) prudential protection of depositors and investors (the "micro-prudential" rationale), (d) policy control of the financial system and the economy, (e) prevention of undue concentration of economic power and promotion of competition among financial intermediaries, (f) achievement of sectoral allocation objectives for credit flows, and (g) preservation of indigenous and small financial institutions.

Prudential Oversight of the Financial System. The macro-prudential

---

[6] For discussion of alternative paradigms for studying international economic events, including the "intermediate interdependence" paradigm, see Bryant (1980, chap. 10).

rationale is integrally associated with the role of a central bank as "lender of last resort." Policymakers and economists at least since the time of Walter Bagehot have argued that, because society is prone to panicky crowd behavior in times of distressed financial conditions, some central financial institution is necessary that can provide banks and other intermediaries with temporary liquidity assistance during crises (Bagehot 1873; Kindleberger 1978; Kindleberger and Laffargue 1982; Hirsch 1977).

This rationale for a lender of last resort need not presume that individual economic agents act "irrationally." Careful analysts of economic and social behavior have identified numerous instances in which noncooperative competition and unconstrained maximization by individual agents, while rational for each individual, can be irrational for all individuals together. In the context here, the contention is that a financial crisis unchecked by a lender of last resort is a situation in which each financial intermediary and each customer can behave rationally and yet still produce a collective outcome that is highly undesirable for society as a whole.

If accepted, this argument for action in crises by a lender of last resort creates a fundamental dilemma. If intermediaries can confidently count on the ready availability of assistance from a lender of last resort on a rainy day, on sunny days they will have insufficient incentives to behave prudently. Financial intermediation necessarily entails the assumption of risks. Ultimate investors may not be able to service their borrowing, or may even go bankrupt. Ultimate depositors may unexpectedly withdraw their funds, requiring sudden and costly adjustment of the intermediaries' asset portfolios. *Some* level of risk-taking by the intermediaries is of course socially desirable. But the intermediaries will be tempted to take excessive risks if they believe that emergency funding will always be readily available to bail them out of trouble. This temptation to excessive risk-taking is a salient illustration of the general problem referred to by economists as "moral hazard."

This moral hazard dilemma thus leads many analysts to the prudential-oversight rationale for supervision and regulation of financial intermediaries. These analysts argue that the government cannot acknowledge its residual responsibility for stability of the financial system unless it also engages in oversight of the intermediaries to ensure sound practices and to prevent excessive risk-taking.[7]

---

[7] Essentially similar considerations are at stake when governments provide deposit insurance. The classic case against a guarantee of the deposits of financial

Prudential Oversight of the Payments Mechanism.   A modern exchange economy is unimaginable without at least one financial asset that serves as a widely accepted means of payment and generalized store of value. As checkable demand deposits in financial intermediaries became the predominant means of payment in modern economies, procedures for facilitating transactions through and among the intermediaries correspondingly assumed an increasingly vital role in the financial system. In future years, electronic arrangements for making transactions are likely to account for a progressively larger fraction of all payments and receipts. As that happens, the role of financial intermediaries in operating the society's "payments mechanism" is likely to become still more important.

Some analysts, laying great stress on the importance of a smoothly operating payments mechanism, would therefore supplement the preceding macro-prudential rationale with a corollary. In their view, the government—as part of its role as lender of last resort and supervisor of the soundness of the financial system—should regulate, and thereby protect the integrity of, the society's payments mechanism. If pressed to state their position more formally, such analysts would describe the payments mechanism as a "collective good" (or "public good") that will not be supplied in an optimal way for society as a whole in the absence of governmental supervision.

For most of the nineteenth century, commercial banks have been the main, if not exclusive, type of financial intermediary supplying payments services. In recent history, the payments mechanism in many countries has changed significantly. Merchant banks, nonbank financial institutions, and even nonfinancial businesses have encroached on the traditional domain of commercial banks. These developments have demonstrated in practice a point that monetary economists have long appreciated in theory, namely that there is no logically inevitable correlation between commercial banking and the provision of the payments mechanism (see, for example, Tobin 1963).

Prudential Protection of Depositors and Investors.   In contrast to

---

intermediaries is that such a guarantee will mitigate the threat of withdrawal of deposits, thereby removing a check on imprudent risk-taking and irresponsibility by the management of the intermediaries. If made, however, a decision to provide deposit insurance leads logically to concomitant regulation of the intermediaries to avert the moral hazard problem that would otherwise exist. (The moral-hazard issue arises in its most acute form with "level-premium" insurance. Proposals for the reform of deposit insurance that recommend relating the premium paid by a financial intermediary to the riskiness of its asset portfolio are intended to mitigate the moral-hazard problem.)

macro-prudential justifications for regulation and supervision, which emphasize *systemic* stability, a different set of arguments can be given for "micro-prudential" protection of depositors and investors in financial intermediaries. This rationale emphasizes *individual* institutions—for example, the risks of failure of particular financial intermediaries and the regulations or supervisory oversight that might avert such failures.[8]

A substantial part of the legal regulation of ordinary nonfinancial corporations is designed to ensure disclosure of relevant information to investors and to inhibit insider misconduct. In many respects, therefore, a prudential-protection rationale for the regulation of financial intermediairies does not raise issues or problems peculiar to the financial industry. Some defenders of such a rationale, however, do believe it to be peculiarly applicable to banks and other financial intermediaries (Clark 1976).

Policy Control of the Financial System. This set of arguments appeals to the role of central banks in influencing financial and economic activity in "normal" times as well as in situations of financial crisis.

Even in the absence of financial crises, financial activity can exert powerful influences on the pace of real activity and on the general level of prices. It is also widely acknowledged that a nation's central bank— more generally, its monetary authorities—can strongly influence the volume of overall financial activity. The monetary authorities have this power because, in effect, the financial system is like an inverted pyramid balanced on a small tip, the balance sheet of the monetary authorities.

The relationships between the tip of the pyramid and all the upper layers of the structure (the balance sheets of the various private-sector financial intermediaries) are complex and elastic. The inverted pyramid is a flexible rather than rigid structure. Especially over a long period, it is capable of dramatic changes in size and shape that are independent of changes in the small tip controlled by the monetary authorities.

The flexibility of the pyramid does not mean, of course, that the monetary authorities are unable to influence the rate at which the national financial system expands. Other things being equal, an incremental expansion of the central bank's balance sheet will stimulate an expan-

---

[8] Examples of the regulations intended to achieve this micro-prudential protection include the various legal guidelines forcing intermediaries to disclose adequate information about their activities. Still other examples are the guidelines for capital-to-assets ratios imposed by government examiners and the restrictions pertaining to self-dealing, conflicts of interest, and other types of insider misconduct by the managements of intermediaries.

sion of the pyramid as a whole, and vice versa for an incremental contraction. Nonetheless, the authorities can "control" the financial pyramid only within some range of tolerance. When international economic interdependence is strong, the degree of imprecision in the control may be large.

These observations lead to a possible further rationale for the regulation and supervision of financial intermediaries. The general argument asserts that the monetary authorities should regulate the activities of the intermediaries to facilitate control of the financial system. More specifically, it is argued that the monetary authorities should be empowered to use supplementary devices—for example, reserve requirements against the deposit liabilities of the intermediaries—that would render their main control instrument, the expansion or contraction of their own balance sheet, more powerful or less uncertain than it would otherwise be.

An extension of this line of reasoning asserts that financial markets, especially when unregulated and unsupervised, are capable of generating asset prices that "fluctuate excessively" or that get "out of line with fundamental valuations." Equity prices vary by a multiple of the underlying variability in dividends and earnings. The prices of long-term bonds fluctuate more than can be justified by the variability in short-term interest rates. More generally, transient speculation in financial markets that is motivated only by short-run considerations can unhitch asset prices from the long-term profit risk calculations that are the fundamental determinants of whether investments are socially advantageous.[9]

If someone believes that government institutions have the requisite information and capacity for carrying out market transactions to offset excessive variability or misalignment in asset prices, he may then also believe that a strong public-policy case exists for such intervention. Similarly, a belief that governments can establish socially beneficial deterrents to short-sighted and inefficient speculative transactions can lead to a policy-control argument for particular types of regulations or supervisory procedures for financial intermediaries.

Concentration and Competition. A further family of arguments used to justify the regulation of financial institutions may be labeled the concentration-competitive rationale. Those accepting this rationale tend to believe that regulation is required to obviate an undue con-

---

[9] For a clear statement of these general arguments, see Tobin (1984). For research on the "excessive" fluctuations in asset prices, see Shiller (1979, 1981, 1984) and LeRoy and Porter (1981).

centration of economic power. Such a situation could develop, it is feared, unless governmental restraints prevent a few financial institutions from becoming very large and thereby acquiring an excessively dominant position in the financial system. A related line of reasoning asserts that regulation can promote or manage competition among financial intermediaries, thus improving the allocation of the economy's financial and real resources. Still another strand of thought, related but not identical, suggests that regulation can be helpful in assuring competitive equity among financial intermediaries. Bankers have competitive equity in mind when they say that the various categories of financial intermediaries should operate on a "level playing field" where like institutions are treated alike.

Unlike the prudential-oversight, the prudential-protection, and the policy-control rationales for regulation, this latter rationale is not peculiarly applicable to financial intermediaries. No doubt intermediaries pose some special regulatory problems because the nature of their business differs from that of nonfinancial organizations. But the same issues of concentration and competition arise in connection with virtually all types of economic activity in the private sectors of mixed capitalist economies.

Sectoral Allocation Objectives. The desire to achieve sectoral allocation objectives is yet another conceivable rationale for regulating financial institutions. For example, policymakers may seek to bolster activity in certain industries or regions of a country and discourage activity in other industries or regions. As one device for achieving this objective, they may design regulations intended to channel credit toward the favored destinations and away from those that are disfavored.

Indigenous and Small Institutions. A final set of arguments—the "indigenous-institution" and "small-institution" rationales—are less often encountered. But in some countries at some times they have been a significant factor in debates about regulation and supervision.

The indigenous-institution rationale asserts that it may be important for communities or regions to have financial intermediaries that are organized, owned, and controlled locally. Those making this assertion presume that intermediaries rooted locally will provide better financial services for the community or region than intermediaries not so rooted. This presumption depends on, among other things, the view that local residents have better information about the community or region and are more likely to be responsive to its needs and problems.

The small-institution rationale asserts that small intermediaries may perform valuable fuctions that would not be served, or not served so well, by a financial system composed entirely of large institutions. The underlying thought behind this assertion may be a presumption that small institutions help to foster innovation and entrepreneurship. Those holding this view may wish to preserve small institutions to affect the distribution of income and wealth (in favor of the owners and customers of the small institutions). Some may hold this view because they like to help the underdog.

The wish to maintain indigenous institutions can be logically differentiated from the wish to maintain small institutions. When one of the two is encountered, however, the other is often present as well. Note that the meanings of "indigenous" and "small" critically depend on the contexts in which they are used. A large, non-local institution from the perspective of a community may well be a small, indigenous institution from the perspective of a region or the nation as a whole.

Whether used singly or together, the indigenous-institution and small-institution arguments can become justifications for preferential regulatory treatment. Most often, the arguments appear when the activities of indigenous or small intermediaries seem threatened in some way. Proponents of the arguments then advocate regulatory actions designed to protect the intermediaries from the threatening pressures.

Costs of Regulation and Supervision

The preceding summary of rationales refers to regulation and supervision in general rather than specific types of regulatory devices and supervisory procedures.[10] Yet regulation of financial intermediaries can take a wide variety of forms—for example, mandatory reserve requirements, interest-rate ceilings, limitations on capital-asset ratios, requirements for disclosure of information, restrictions on entry and merger, differential tax or subsidy treatment on types of activities or types of intermediaries, geographical limitations on activities, and quantitative limitations of one sort or another on the amounts of particular categories of assets and liabilities. Supervision can be exercised in alternative ways—for example, through monitoring of accounting reports, on-site examinations, and consultations with high-level management. Self-evidently, some types of regulation, supervision, and taxation are more appropriate than others for any one of the rationales summarized above. Not much can be usefully said about financial regulation at a high level of generalization. Particular regula-

---

[10] My analysis pays only limited attention to the taxation of financial intermediaries, partly because I am not competent to deal with the tax aspects in any detail. The tax aspects, however, are probably as important as regulation and supervision.

tions, taxes, and supervisory procedures need to be evaluated in specific contexts.

Because of its focus on the potential benefits of regulation and supervision, the preceding review is limited in a second way. Each aspect of a government's relationships with financial intermediaries can be rationalized, initially if not also currently, as a response to externalities or market imperfections. One fundamental rationale for government institutions, after all, is to supply, or induce others to supply, collective goods that would not be provided at all, or would be provided inadequately, in the absence of the governmental catalyst. Alternatively, government can ameliorate collective "bads" (for example, through lender-of-last-resort assistance in distressed financial conditions). The identification of externalities, however, is invariably controversial. Where one observer perceives a presumptive need for collective action catalyzed by government, another may not. In the case of each motive for regulation and supervision summarized above, some group can be found that questions the motive's validity.

Even if agreement could be reached on the worthiness of a particular motive, it would be insufficient to focus only on the potential benefits of regulation and supervision. The fact that markets often fail in adequately supplying collective goods does not justify the presumption that government action can appropriately remedy the market failures. Regulation and supervision may not succeed in achieving its goals. The costs of government regulations can exceed the benefits. Unanticipated side effects can be adverse. Conceivably, regulation and supervision can induce sclerosis in financial institutions and markets, inadvertently inhibiting needed adjustments to changed circumstances. For example, a regulation may initially facilitate a specific goal (say, improved policy control of the financial system or the maintenance of indigenous institutions) yet may also, indirectly if not directly, undermine the adaptability of the financial system to new technology. More generally, even if a regulatory measure is an appropriate response when first implemented, a good solution to today's problem is an admission ticket to new problems created by the solution's interaction with changed circumstances. A balanced analysis of any regulation must therefore evaluate its costs and side effects, not merely its intended benefits, and must subject it to periodic re-evaluation.

For virtually all the specific regulations and supervisory procedures that can be devised, some groups or some individuals assess the intended benefits as less consequential than the costs and side effects. Some authors who have studied government regulation of financial intermediaries perceive a general pattern of overregulation that has inhibited economic development (see, for example, Shaw 1973; Mc-Kinnon 1973). This enthusiasm for deregulation of banks and other financial intermediaries, however, is not shared by many other observers (for example, Kareken 1981, 1984; Wojnilower 1980).

Public opinion about the regulation and supervision of financial interemediaries tends to be strongly influenced by recent experience. Lengthy periods unsullied by distressed conditions cause regulation issues to recede into the background. The failure or near failure of intermediaries—in particular, highly-publicized problems of large institutions such as those of the Franklin National Bank and the Herstatt Bank in 1974, the Continental Illinois Bank in 1984, and the state-insured savings and loan associations in Ohio in 1985—bring the issues back into prominence.[11]

Innovation in Response to Regulation

The operating procedures and services provided by financial intermediaries change over time. Significant innovations have occurred especially rapidly in recent decades.

The importance of changing technology as an inducement to new types of financial intermediation, not least across national borders, has already been highlighted above. Domestically and internationally, improvements in communications methods and in electronic data processing have made many former banking practices obsolete or inefficient. The more rapid and more variable rates of inflation experienced in recent years have also been a significant catalyst for change. Higher, more variable rates of inflation have caused a secular upward drift and a greater volatility in nominal interest rates, which in turn have forced financial intermediaries and the nonfinancial sectors of the economy to adapt their behavior.

Scarcely less important, however, have been private-sector innovations responding to the existing pattern of governmental regulation, supervision, and taxation. If regulations are successful in inhibiting changes in financial markets that would otherwise occur, financial intermediaries and their customers have incentives to circumvent the regulatory constraints. The more stringent the constraints, the stronger the incentives for circumvention.

When financial intermediaries develop a new type of contract or a new practice that undermines a regulatory constraint, the governmental

---

[11] The tendency of the public and financial intermediaries themselves to forget incidents of distressed conditions in the more distant past—dubbed "disaster myopia"—is analyzed in Herring and Guttentag (1984).

authorities responsible for the regulations may try to change the regulations to cover the new circumstances. If so, the private-sector intermediaries may in turn try to adapt their behavior in still other ways. The process of interaction in retrospect may seem like a disorderly scramble, with the intermediaries and the authorities each vainly trying to get one step ahead of the other (see, for example, Hester 1981).

International Aspects of Regulation and Supervision

The possible rationales for regulation and supervision of financial intermediaries, the costs of implementing such measures, and the tendency for private-sector innovations to erode existing regulations warrant analysis in a purely domestic context. And, for the most part, those domestic aspects have received the lion's share of attention. When the international aspects have been considered, they have been discussed independently in specialized and less publicized forums. This separate treatment of the domestic and international aspects, however, has become increasingly anachronistic.

The supervisory, regulatory, and tax environments governing the operations of financial intermediaries differ in important ways from one nation to another. These disparities generate competitive inequities among national financial systems. Financial intermediaries thus have strong incentives to locate their borrowing and lending activities in those countries with the lower taxes and the less stringent regulations and supervision. In a world where cross-border financial transactions are growing rapidly, the disparities in national regulatory and tax environments become still more difficult to maintain. As intermediaries compete, in home and third markets, they become increasingly aware of the way that the disparities produce competitive inequities. Those intermediaries at a competitive disadvantage see the consequences of the inequities reflected in their profits. Hence the incentives become still stronger for the disadvantaged intermediaries to shift their activities to the countries with the less stringent regulations and tax treatments.

All nations are affected in minor ways by the erosion of the disparities in national regulatory environments. A few large industrial countries are beginning to encounter serious problems because of their more stringent and more pervasive regulations. Some financial business that is primarily "domestic" in nature is being conducted through "international" transactions, thereby enabling intermediaries and their customers to avoid "domestic" regulatory restrictions. For practical purposes, the traditional distinction between domestic and international banking is becoming elusive. Scarcely a single regulatory issue that

formerly was viewed solely as a domestic matter can now be intel-
ligently discussed without reference to international flows of funds and
the regulatory environments in foreign countries.

The erosion of national regulatory environments associated with
the internationalization of financial intermediation is a salient example
of the general phenomenon of innovations in response to regulations.
In a closed domestic context, financial intermediaries trying to avoid
regulations must devise a new financial instrument or find some other
innovation that will escape the existing regulatory constraint. In an
open economy, another and potentially more powerful alternative
exists: a financial intermediary experiencing stringent regulation can
decide to move the regulated activities outside the jurisdiction of the
national regulators. Unless the home authorities can induce their counterparts in other countries to adopt a posture as stringent as that in
the home country, the financial intermediary may succeed in escaping
the home regulations. Alternatively, the national regulators may see
that they cannot prevent the relocation of the intermediary's activities,
and may therefore decide to relax the home regulations sufficiently
to keep the activities at home.

When the international aspects are acknowledged, the conventional
arguments for and against regulation of financial intermediaries acquire additional nuances and encounter new difficulties.

In a significantly open economy the prudential-oversight and prudential-protection rationales must take into account the many complexities associated with cross-border and foreign-currency transactions.
Individual intermediaries are exposed to new types of risks when they
have extensive asset-liability relationships with foreign residents. Similarly, denomination of assets and liabilities in foreign currencies as
well as in the home nation's currency introduces additional elements
of risk. To be sure, cross-border and foreign-currency transactions also
permit a greater diversification of risk. The *net* consequences of international intermediation for the safety and soundness of a nation's
financial institutions are thus complex. No simple generalization about
the consequences may be possible. At the least, however, it is clear that
the regulatory authorities of a single nation concerned with the micro-
prudential protection of that nation's depositors and investors have
a much more difficult job than would their counterparts in a hypothetical closed economy.

Similarly, macro-prudential oversight of the financial system in a
single national economy becomes increasingly problematic as the economy becomes more open. The moral hazard dilemma—the temptation of financial intermediaries with ready access to lender-of-last-

resort assistance to take risks that are excessive from a social point of view—may be heightened in an economic environment characterized by extensive cross-border and foreign-currency transactions. In any case, a single nation's decisions about the intensity of regulation and supervision and its formulation of criteria for the provision of lender-of-last-resort assistance become more complex.

For some circumstances, furthermore, a qualitatively new set of difficulties arises. When a banking office in nation A of a bank with head offices in nation B gets into financial trouble, *which* central bank should have responsibility for providing lender-of-last-resort support (assuming such assistance is merited)? Should the allocation of the central-bank responsibility differ according to the nature of the banking office in nation A—for example, whether the office is a branch or a subsidiary of the parent bank in nation B? How should consortium banks—joint ventures located in A but owned by banks or investors in B and several other nations—be treated? Is there a risk that national central banks will individually behave too timidly, thereby exposing the world financial system as a whole to inadequate provision of lender-of-last-resort assistance? If international agreement on lender-of-last-resort assistance is thought necessary to assure world financial stability, does the moral-hazard dilemma require a commensurate degree of international cooperation in the supervision and regulation of banks and other intermediaries?[12]

Analogous points could be made about macro-prudential protection of (speaking loosely) the world's payments mechanism. Existing clearing arrangements for foreign-exchange transactions and other cross-border payments are operated primarily by a small number of the world's largest banks. If unexpected disruptions in these arrangements should occur, the responsibility for managing the restoration of normal activity would necessarily have to be shared among the large private banks and central banks of several nations, not merely one nation.

The motive for regulation and supervision based on policy control of the financial system likewise acquires greater force and encounters new difficulties when international aspects are taken into account. The greater urgency and complexities stem from the basic fact that increasing openness of a nation's economy undermines the autonomy of national monetary policy and the controllability of the national economy (Bryant 1980, chaps. 11–13, 20–25).

As a central bank perceives its control of the nation's financial sys-

---

[12] For a recent study analyzing some of these issues, see Guttentag and Herring (1983).

tem weakening, and more broadly its control of the ultimate target variables for the nation's economy, it may conceivably decide that the benefits from economic interdependence are outweighed by the costs of the erosion of controllability of the economy. If so, it may attempt in one way or another to inhibit cross-border financial transactions. If the separation fence around the national financial system had earlier been lowered, it might now be raised. Such an effort to enhance the autonomy of national monetary policy is, analytically speaking, a particular case of the policy-control rationale for regulation. The various conceivable controls on international capital movements could include restraints on the nonfinancial sectors of the economy as well well as on financial intermediaries. However, because intermediaries play such a key role in financial markets—and not least in foreign exchange markets—the central bank is likely to assert that an especially strong case exists for regulating the intermediaries.

The indigenous-institution justification for regulation and supervision has a straightforward international extension, and invites a correspondingly straightforward rebuttal. In a world of numerous nations, "indigenous" is likely to be a synonym for "national." The maintenance of national institutions, including the prevention of significant inroads in domestic activity by foreigners, is an objective that may have significant political appeal to home citizens. "Local" control can be defended as desirable to keep financial institutions sensitive to national needs and problems. Some may even allege that indigenous financial intermediaries are essential for national security. The standard rebuttal to these arguments is based on the traditional objection to economic autarky, namely, that protective regulations encourage an inefficient allocation of resources and deny the nation as a whole the full benefits of commerce with the rest of the world.

The concentration rationale for regulation is usually advocated in a form implicitly presuming that concentration and competition should be measured and evaluated in a domestic context, that is within an individual nation. For a significantly open economy, that presumption needs to be severely questioned. Why should a national economy be the relevant geographical "market" for judging concentration rather than a regional economy or the world economy as a whole? Can national governments have separate and different anti-trust policies for their economies when firms and financial intermediaries engage in integrated activities across national borders?

III. International Collective-Goods Problems in the Regulation and Supervision of Financial Intermediaries

The issues discussed above are certainly germane for the industrial nations that have well developed financial systems. Everything that has been said, for example, applies in some degree to banking and other types of intermediation in such financial centers as New York, Tokyo, London, Zurich, Frankfurt, and Paris. But still other geographical loci for international intermediation have also become important. Indeed, issues about the internationalization of banking arise in an especially interesting way in the so-called offshore banking centers.

Offshore Banking Centers

The locations commonly referred to as offshore centers include Anguilla, the Bahamas, Barbados, Bermuda, the Cayman Islands, the Netherlands Antilles, and Panama in the Caribbean area; Bahrain, Lebanon, and the United Arab Emirates in the Middle East; Guam, Hong Kong, the Philippines, Singapore, and Vanuatu (New Hebrides) in Asia and Oceania; and Luxembourg, the Channel Islands (Jersey and Guernsey), and the Isle of Man in Europe.

Banking transactions conducted from, or booked in, these offshore centers have grown especially rapidly. Table 5.1 provides some selective data for the centers that now have the greatest volume of activity. Where available, two indicators are shown in the table. The first is a measure of the total size of the balance sheets of some or all of the banking offices located in the country, as published by the national monetary authority. The second is a measure of the claims of local banking offices on *foreigners* (nonresidents); the figures for this second indicator are taken from statistics published by the International Monetary Fund. For comparison, the final two lines in Table 5.1 give figures for two broad aggregates in international banking that *exclude* data from offshore centers.[13]

Consider first Singapore and Hong Kong. As proxied in Table 5.1, international banking activity in Singapore grew at a compounded rate of some 50–55 percent per year over the thirteen years 1970–83. The international dimensions of the balance sheets of banks in Hong

---

[13] Neither set of indicators in Table 5.1, especially those of the second type taken from the IMF's *International Financial Statistics*, is fully satisfactory as a yardstick for the growth of banking activities in the countries shown. The figures in the last four columns of the table, however, do give an overall correct impression of the relatively faster expansion in offshore centers.

Table 5.1   Indicators of Banking Growth in Selected "Offshore" Centers, 1970–1983

Country of location of banking offices	Billions of U.S. dollars at current exchange rates				Compound rate of growth, percent per year[a]			
	1970	1976	1980	1983	1970–76	1976–80	1980–83	1970–83
Singapore:								
Total assets of Asian Currency Units[b]	0.4	17.4	54.4	111.9	88.3	33.0	27.2	54.5
Banks' claims on foreigners (IFS)[c,d]	0.5	14.6	44.6	88.2	73.8	32.2	25.5	49.1
Hong Kong:								
Total assets of banks[e]	3.8	18.5	57.4	101.2	30.4	32.7	20.8	28.7
Total assets of deposit-taking companies[e]	n.a.	n.a.	27.3	42.0	n.a.	n.a.	15.4	n.a.
Total assets of all deposit-taking institutions[e]	n.a.	n.a.	84.7	143.2	n.a.	n.a.	19.1	n.a.
Claims of deposit-taking institutions on foreigners (IFS)[c,f]	1.2	12.4	38.0	67.6	46.8	32.3	21.2	36.3
Bahrain:								
Total assets of Offshore Banking Units[g]	—	6.2	37.5	62.7	n.a.	56.7	18.8	n.a.
Banks' claims on foreigners (IFS)[c]	0.1	6.1	31.4	54.6	115.7	50.9	20.2	68.9
Bahamas:								
Banks' claims on foreigners (IFS)[c]	7.2	78.7	122.4	131.8	48.9	11.7	2.5	25.0
Cayman Islands:								
Banks' claims on foreigners (IFS)[h]	n.a.	22.0	84.5	131.3	n.a.	40.0	15.8	n.a.
Panama:								
Banks' claims on foreigners (IFS)[c]	0.3	10.4	34.2	37.3	78.6	34.7	2.9	44.2
Netherlands Antilles:								
Banks' claims on foreigners (IFS)[c,i]	0.1	1.6	7.4	11.7[j]	53.2	47.8	25.7[j]	46.4[j]
Luxembourg:								
Total assets of banks[j]	4.8	47.5	124.3	118.5	46.8	27.2	–1.6	28.1
Banks' claims on foreigners (IFS)[c]	3.7	37.9	104.8	103.5	47.3	29.0	–0.4	29.2
MEMORANDA FOR COMPARISON:								
Aggregate claims on foreigners of banks in all industrial countries excluding Luxembourg (IFS)[c]	114.2	487.9	1252.6	1674.9	27.4	26.6	10.2	22.9
BIS series for net international bank credit extended by banks in BIS reporting area[k]	76	340	810	1085	28.4	24.2	10.2	22.7

Table 5.1 (footnotes)

n.a.: not available.

a. Rates of growth are calculated from unrounded data.

b. Balance-sheet data for Asian Currency Units (ACUs) (total assets, including claims on Singapore financial institutions and nonbank Singapore residents) as published in *Monthly Statistical Bulletin* of the Monetary Authority of Singapore.

c. These series appear in *International Financial Statistics* (IFS) published by the International Monetary Fund. In principle, they refer to "deposit banks'" claims on foreign residents; the foreign assets of monetary authorities are excluded. Figures for 1970 and 1976 are from the 1984 IFS Yearbook. Figures for 1980 and 1983 are from the January 1985 issue of IFS (p. 49).

d. Includes the foreign assets of Asian Currency Units (ACUs) and domestic banking units. This IFS series incorrectly treats the entire amount of the claims of ACUs on non-banks as claims on foreigners; in fact, a modest fraction of the ACUs' claims on nonbanks involves lending to *Singapore* residents.

e. Balance-sheet data for banks and deposit-taking companies as published in the *Hong Kong Monthly Digest of Statistics* (Census and Statistics Department, Hong Kong). Historical data for 1970 and 1976 for the banks have been adjusted by the author to the same conceptual definition as the 1980 and 1983 data (making use of unpublished data kindly supplied by the Hong Kong Commissioner of Banking). Data for the deposit-taking companies are available only for 1978 and subsequent years.

f. This IFS series for years after 1978 includes figures for the identified foreign assets of the deposit-taking companies as well as the identified foreign assets of the banks.

g. Balance-sheet data for Offshore Banking Units (total assets, including claims on domestic residents) as published in the *Quarterly Statistical Bulletin* of the Bahrain Monetary Agency.

h. Based on the revised series published for the first time in the January 1985 issue of IFS, which in turn is derived from the *Statistical Abstract* of the Cayman Islands Central Statistical Office.

i. Data for 1983 were not available at the time the table was compiled (due to an official revision of statistical series for the Netherlands Antilles). The figure in the 1983 column is thus the observation for December 1982, and the last two figures in the row refer to rates of growth for the 1980–82 and 1970–82 periods, respectively.

j. Balance-sheet data for all "etablisseements bancaires et d'epargne" in Luxembourg as published in the *Bulletin Trimestriel* of the Institut Monetaire Luxembourgeois.

k. Data as published by the Bank for International Settlements in their *Annual Reports* and quarterly statistical releases on International Banking Developments. The figure for 1970 is partially estimated by the author.

Kong grew at an annual rate of more than 30 percent during that period. Even during 1980–83, a troubled time for the world economy, the growth rates of banking in the two centers were above 20 percent. This expansion in Singapore and Hong Kong, as can be seen by contrasting it with the bottom lines in the table, was markedly faster than in Europe, North America, and Japan.

In 1970 in Bahrain, neither the Bahrain Monetary Agency nor Offshore Banking Units—entities specially created to conduct international banking—even existed. The Bahrain Monetary Agency was established in late 1973; in late 1975 it invited international banks to establish Offshore Banking Units (OBUs). By December 1983 the OBUs in Bahrain had US$ 63 billion of total assets on their books.

In the Bahamas during 1970–76, banks' claims on foreign residents grew at nearly a 50 percent annual rate. Bahamian growth in the late 1970s and early 1980s was much slower, in part as many banks shifted their Caribbean emphasis to the Cayman Islands. Even so, by the end of 1981 the foreign assets of banking offices in the Bahamas had risen to nearly US$ 150 billion (falling back to some US$ 130 billion in late 1983). Recently available figures for the Cayman Islands indicate that the total assets of banks there (not only the branches of U.S. banks but also banking offices owned by parent banking organizations in other foreign countries) were US$ 131 billion at the end of 1983. Extremely rapid growth for some or all of the period 1970–83 was also experienced by Panama and the Netherlands Antilles.

Seen from some perspectives, Luxembourg should not be labeled an offshore center. In many respects, however, banks with head offices in Germany and other industrial countries did regard Luxembourg in the 1970s as offering benefits similar to those in other offshore centers. Between 1970 and 1976, bank balance sheets and the (dominant) international parts of the balance sheets both increased at annual rates of some 47 percent. Quite rapid growth persisted through 1981; bank assets after 1981 declined by a small amount.

Throughout recent economic history, financial intermediation generally and banking in particular have grown relatively faster than output of goods and services. For developing countries, this faster growth of financial intermediation might be expected to be still more pronounced than for industrial countries at an advanced stage of development. Nevertheless, for most if not all of the individual political units shown in Table 5.1 the rapid growth in banking cannot plausibly be ascribed to the secular trends identified by Goldsmith and Gurley-Shaw —at least not to such trends *within* their national economies.

Instead, a major part of the explanation lies in a different direction.

Financial intermediation is more "footloose" than most other economic activites. It can shift locations with less difficulty and without incurring prohibitively large costs. The many innovations in electronic communications and data processing have probably enhanced this differential mobility. Even more than for industry in general, therefore, the scope exists for an individual locality or nation to try to lure banking activity within its borders by imposing less stringent regulation, taxation, and supervision than that prevailing elsewhere. When framing their policies, the governments of the offshore banking centers have been very much aware of this "relocation" possiblity. And almost surely, a major part of the rapid expansion of banking in most offshore centers is attributable to the differential location incentives created by governmental policies.

Viewed from a cosmopolitan world perspective, the regulatory, tax, and supervisory incentives designed to attract banking activity to offshore centers can be described—provocatively—as a "competition in laxity." Similarly, one may ask whether the largest nations in the world could be indefinitely satisfied with an ever higher proportion of their citizens' banking transactions being conducted from offices located in the offshore centers. Even if one resists the temptation to be provocative, the growing importance of offshore banking centers raises several questions that merit analysis in a systemic, global context.

Global Public-Policy Problems in International Financial Intermediation

It is a striking fact that virtually all nations discriminate in favor of banking activities conducted in foreign currencies, especially when the banks' customers are nonresidents. Until recently the United States was an exception to this generalization. With the authorization of International Banking Facilities (IBFs) as of December 1981, however, the United States reversed its position and went along with the global trend (see Key 1982). Japan has recently considered regulatory changes designed to enhance such favorable discrimination (Institute for Financial Affairs 1983; Sakakibara and Kondoh 1984). Differential regulatory, tax, and supervisory incentives that favor international banking are strongest of all in the offshore banking centers.

For these regulatory issues, each nation or political unit in effect regards itself as individually "small" in relation to the rest of the world. It regulates intensively only those aspects of financial intermediation that are perceived as most directly affecting its own economy. It then adopts a hands-off policy, or in any event a less stringent regulatory posture, with respect to the remaining (international) activities of financial institutions located within its borders.

Implicitly if not explicitly, the attitude is to let every other nation cope with its own problems as best it can. No nation has developed a systemic, global view about the regulation, taxation, and supervision of financial intermediaries.

In such a world environment, no nation can effectively act on its own to deal with any adverse consequences attributable to this situation. Unilateral tightening of supervision and regulation by a single nation, for intermediary offices within its borders or for intermediary offices located abroad controlled by national residents, might merely induce a transfer away from its intermediary offices to those of other nations.

If action of some sort is called for, only collective action is likely to be successful. Yet international cooperation in these circumstances is another example of a collective good. Like other collective goods, the supply of international regulatory cooperation is likely to fall short of what would be mutually beneficial because each nation, acting rationally on an individual basis, ignores the potential benefits of the greater cooperation for others. Each nation's tendency to assume that it is small enough to ignore the consequences of its actions for the rest of the world is an integral part of the collective problem. As is well known, such situations can produce a suboptimal outcome for all nations collectively. The larger the group of nations involved, furthermore, the higher is the probability that some nations will act as "free riders" and hence the less likely it is that the group of nations will further their common interests.[14] Only the exercise of political leadership by some national governments and the gradual evolution of international political institutions can correct this inherent bias against cooperative responses to systemic, global problems.

Some Examples

To see the general issue in clearer perspective, consider two examples. The first is indicative of the problems that supervisory authorities can encounter in their prudential oversight of individual intermediaries. When examining the branch or subsidiary in country A of a multinational bank, suppose the country-A supervisors discover some loans

---

[14] To the extent that a collective good is supplied, all who value it tend to benefit whether or not they contribute to the cost of supplying it. Hence a disproportionately large share of the costs tends to be borne by a few, "less small" participants in the collective action. For discussion of the analytical issues, see Olson (1971) and Barry and Hardin (1982).

that, in their judgment, are of questionable quality. Perhaps the supervisors even have reliable information demonstrating that the borrowers in question are poor credit risks. Alternatively, suppose the supervisors learn that the branch or subsidiary in A has made loans to a single customer that amount to a disproportionately large proportion of the office's total balance sheet. The A-country supervisors might be especially concerned if the borrowing customers are residents of country A, but they would have grounds for concern even if the customers were residents of other countries.

To redress these perceived problems, the supervisors in A may be able to require tha bank to make adjustments in the balance sheet *of its country-A office*. But the supervisors in A may not be able to prevent the A-office of the bank from transferring the bad loans or the imprudently large loans with a single customer to the balance sheets of offices of the bank in country B or country C. The A supervisors will have, at best, incomplete information about the banking organization's operations in B and C. The supervisors in B and C will be at an analogous disadvantage with respect to the bank's operations in A. Given their information, for example, the B and C supervisors may have no basis for questioning the soundness of the loans transferred into their jurisdiction from A even though the loans may in fact be unsound and had been judged so correctly by the supervisors in A. (The likelihood of the A supervisors having superior information is higher, other things being equal, if the ultimate borrowers are residents of A.) If country C happens to attach a higher priority to attracting banking business within its borders than to supervision of that business, moreover, the C supervisors may in any case be reluctant to ask uncomfortable questions. A multinational bank with offices in many national jurisdictions thus could conceivably play one nation's supervisory authorities off against others, effectively escaping in its worldwide operations from the constraints imposed by any one of them.

This class of problems would arise most urgently for financial intermediaries that were irresponsibly or fraudulently managed. Yet even when fraud or outright irresponsibility are absent, differences in judgments are inevitable among banks and supervisors about what constitutes a "bad" loan or "imprudently large lending," not least because conditions can unexpectedly change after loan agreements are made. In the absence of considerable communication of information among national supervisory authorities, such differences tend—in the case of multinational banks—to be effectively resolved in the banks' favor. What is more, cooperation in supervision tends to be no more effective than the least strong link in the chain. In the preceding example, if the supervisors in country C have the least adequate information or ask the fewest questions, the bad loans will be transferred from the bank's in A to its offices in C. Extensive communication and cooperation between the supervisors in A and B will not be sufficient to generate a satisfactory outcome.

Taxation policies are a second area in which important examples of international externalities arise. Suppose one country abolishes withholding taxes on interest payments to foreign residents and accords preferential tax treatment to profits earned by banking offices within its borders when those profits are generated by lending to foreigners.[15] Suppose the tax incentives then induce multinational banks to shift some activity to that country away from other countries where the activity would otherwise have been booked. Then suppose that, observing this experience, numerous other countries decide to abolish withholding taxes on interest payments to foreigners and to accord preferential tax treatment to profits on lending to foreigners.[16]

Suppose this trend were to lead eventually to a worldwide adoption of the preferential tax policies. The inadvertent outcome of the sequence of independent national actions could be an effective loss, for all governments, of tax revenues on their *own* residents' profits and interest incomes.

I have stated this example in an extreme form. In practice, only some nations have taken such tax actions. I am not well enough informed to generalize confidently about actual national experiences. Nor am I competent to venture a judgment about a hypothetical "optimal" standard for withholding taxes and the tax treatment of bank profits (more precisely, a hypothetical set of guidelines for the world as a whole that could be adopted by national tax authorities if all of them were prepared to cooperate in designing the guidelines). Yet it is not implausible to conjecture that the net result of independent changes in national tax policies can be—indeed, at times has been—inadvertently harmful to the interests of many nations.[17]

---

[15] For example, Singapore took these actions in the late 1960s and early 1970s, and extended the preferential tax treatment to various other types of "offshore" income and profits during the later 1970s and 1980s.

[16] Many of the offshore banking centers accord preferential tax treatment to bank profits and do not withhold tax on interest payments to foreigners. In 1984 the United States abolished withholding taxes on interest paid to foreigners on U.S. Treasury securities. In 1984–85 Japan was said to be considering analogous steps in conjunction with proposals for "offshore" banking facilities in Japan.

[17] There may be a possible analogy here with the experience of state governments within the United States. After a few state governments extended fiscal incentives

Nascent Cooperative Efforts by National Governments

In the last decade international collective-goods problems of the type just identified have received increasing, but still modest, attention from national governments.

The most important forum for catalyzing consultations and cooperation among banking supervisory authorities is the so-called Basle or Cooke Committee, meeting under the auspices of the Bank for International Settlements. (BIS). The Committee grew out of the concerns generated by the Herstatt and Franklin National Bank crises in 1974. Prior to the formation of this Committee in 1975, consultations among the national authorities were infrequent and primarily bilateral. The Committee now meets regularly, usually three or four times a year, and has made significant progress on several fronts.[18]

One of the Committee's achievements has been the drafting of a "Concordat" on the Supervision of Banks' Foreign Establishments clarifying several aspects of the division of responsibilities among national supervisory authorities. The first version of the Concordat was agreed in December 1975. A somewhat modified version was prepared during 1983.[19]

Another achievement of the Committee was an agreement on the principle that banks' international business should be monitored on a consolidated basis. After some delays, most countries represented on the Committee took steps to implement the principle. In conjunction with another BIS standing committee, the Cooke Committee has also encouraged the collection of improved data for international banking. Examples include statistics on the maturity composition of banks' international assets and liabilities and on the country distribution of banks' lending.

Through the efforts of the Basle Committee, supervisory authorities from countries not represented at BIS meetings were invited to a

---

to induce firms to relocate plants within their states, other state governments emulated the policies. Arguably, the eventual result after several decades was only a small change in the geographical location of industry but significant revenue losses for all of the state governments.

[18] W.P. Cooke, the Head of Banking Supervision at the Bank of England, is the current chairman of the Committee; it was chaired in the initial years by George Blunden, another official of the Bank of England. The formal title of the group is the Committee on Banking Regulations and Supervisory Practices. For published accounts of the Committee's activities, see Bank of England (1981); Cooke (1983); and Johnson with Abrams (1983, Appendix I).

[19] The text of the revised version was published in IMF (1983). The initial version was reprinted in IMF (1981).

broader international conference held in London in 1979. Similar conferences were held in Washington in 1981 and in Italy in 1984. An associated development was the formation of an Offshore Group of Banking Supervisors (a first meeting was held in October 1980) and a Commission of Latin American and Caribbean Banking Supervisory and Inspection Organizations (a first meeting was held in July 1981). The members of the Offshore Group have accepted the principles of the Basle Committee's Concordat. As best one can tell, these latter two groups have been very much less active than the Basle Committee itself.

Public statements about the work of the Basle Committee assert that it has responsibility only for supervisory and some regulatory issues. In particular, it is insisted that the Committee has no mandate to discuss the international aspects of lender-of-last-resort assistance. The international aspects of "monetary control" issues are likewise said to be beyond the Committee's jurisdiction.[20]

In principle, there is no logically defensible way to separate the narrower supervision issues from the broader questions of lender-of-last-resort assistance and regulations that have a bearing on monetary control. Eventually, therefore, the mandate of the Basle Committee will need to be formally broadened or other channels will need to be used for intergovernmental discussion and cooperation on these issues.

The European Community has created several institutions for discussing supervisory problems within the EEC. The "Groupe de Contact," whose members are the banking supervisors of the Community countries, has met periodically since 1969. The Banking Advisory Committee is a steering group set up under the First Banking Coordination Directive of 1977 with responsibilities for the planning and coordination of bank regulation. An example of the work of these groups was the Directive on the Supervision of Credit Institutions on a Consolidated Basis (reprinted in IMF, 1983).

The Organization of Economic Cooperation and Development has

---

[20] The following quotation summarizes the official position on the non-responsibilities of the Basle Committee for lender-of-last-resort issues: the Concordat "sets out guidelines covering the responsibilities of the different supervisory authorities for the ongoing supervision of banks where those banks operate in more than one national jurisdiction. It is not, and was never intended to be, an agreement about responsibilities for the provision of lender of last resort facilities to the international banking system, and there should not necessarily be considered to be any automatic link between acceptance of responsibility for ongoing supervision and the assumption of a lender of last resort role" (Bank of England, 1981, p. 240).

also sponsored studies of these issues in recent years, conducted by an Expert Group on Banking responsible to the Committee on Financial Markets. Several publications resulting from this effort are now available (see, for example, Pecchioli 1983; Bingham 1985).

The International Monetary Fund has participated only indirectly in these nascent efforts to provide some prudential oversight of international financial intermediation. National governments, and the Fund staff itself, have presumed that collective action on these subjects would, if needed, be undertaken outside the Fund.

Two developments in the early 1980s suggest that the traditional lack of Fund participation in this area might undergo a reevaluation. The first development was a growing commitment of Fund staff resources to the analysis of international financial markets. As one manifestation of this analysis, the Exchange and Trade Relations Department began publishing an annual survey of developments and prospects in international banking and bond markets. The Fund's Bureau of Statistics, in cooperation with the BIS, likewise augmented its efforts to collect and interpret data for these markets. The enhanced concern in 1982–84 about the debt situation of developing countries gave a further stimulus to this increased commitment of staff resources.[21]

The second development, potentially of great significance, occurred in conjunction with the Fund's 1982–84 lending to developing nations caught up in debt-servicing crises. In a major departure from previous experience, the Fund became actively involved in negotiations between a debtor country and its commercial-bank creditors. For example, the IMF played a decisive role in resolving the debt-management crises in 1982 and 1983 of Mexico, Brazil, and several other Latin American nations. In effect, the IMF became a "financial orchestrator" helping a country to negotiate a combined financing and adjustment program satisfactory to the country and all its creditors. In cases where commercial banks were reluctant to maintain or increase their lending, the IMF made its own lending contingent on the continued participation of the banks. Such "concerted lending," described as "bailing in" rather than "bailing out" the commercial banks, brought the IMF into much closer proximity with private financial intermediaries than at any earlier time in its history. It also raised some important questions about future relationships between the Fund and private financial institutions.

---

[21] For the most recent annual survey, see Watson and others (1984). The Bureau of Statistics' new data for international banking are described on pp. 58–60 of this paper; see also the *IMF Survey* for March 18, 1985, pp. 81, 89–92.

IV. Broad Choices for the Evolution of Government Policies

There is no reason to believe that we have seen the end of the shirnking of effective economic distances between nations attributable to nonpolicy technological innovations in communications and transportation and the associated changes in tastes that they induce. Probably, therefore, assets denominated in different currencies and issued in different locations will continue to become gradually better substitutes.

Governments themselves will be under continuing pressure to adjust their domestic regulation and supervision of financial intermediation. The impetus for headlong deregulation may recently have lost steam in the United States and several other industrial countries. Nonetheless, many further changes induced by shifts in regulation can be expected in the financial structures of national economies. These in turn will generate significant side effects for cross-border and cross-currency intermediation.

Governments seem likely to face conflicting pressures about the remaining separation fences around national financial markets. Some governments may face strong demands to raise their fences (see below). At the same time, however, the trend toward discrimination in favor of financial transactions conducted in foreign currencies and with foreign residents seems likely to continue. Some governments, in other words, will probably continue to try to lure financial intermediaries to relocate business in their jurisdictions by extending additional regulatory and tax incentives.

If these broad speculations about nonpolicy innovations and policy adjustments are correct, the net effect over the next decade will be a further strengthening of the interconnectedness of financial markets. This evolution will in turn pose still greater challenges to those countries whose regulatory, tax, and supervisory environments are more stringent than the world average.

Passive Drift in the Short Run

Should we be content with this further drift toward a unified world capital market? Is the drift sustainable? Will national governments understand and accept its consequences?

The current posture of many governments is best described as passive. Some seem inattentive or even somnolent. Policies change in response to developments, but for the most part the policies are not designed to direct or manage the evolution. The nations with the most stringent regulations experience an erosion of their environments, but the erosion is gradual and not highly visible to the general public. Similar propositions apply to general macroeconomic policies: the autonomy of any one country's policy actions declines over time, but not in a dramatic way that calls attention to the persistent trend.

For the short and medium run, therefore, a continuation of this passive drift seems the most likely course for government policies. This short and medium run could easily last through the rest of the 1980s.

Over a longer run, however, this passive course could prove to be unsustainable—for political reasons. It may take a major economic or financial crisis to catalyze a widespread awareness of the underlying trends. Once the trends have been widely recognized, however, public reactions may force governments to confront the difficult choices. At some point, I conjecture, the large middle ground of public opinion that is now relatively oblivious to these issues will divide and support one of two other broad courses. For brevity, they may be labeled dis-integration and enhanced multilateral decisionmaking.

Dis-Integration

In the areas of regulation, taxation, and supervision for financial intermediaries, the course of dis-integration would entail the rebuilding of separation fences. By deliberate choice, governments would choose to try to inhibit the free flow of funds between national reservoirs.

More broadly, one can imagine governments pulling back from the implications of interdependence across the whole range of economic policies. For monetary policies, for example, central banks would seek ways to regain some of the differential impact on home ultimate targets that had gotten dissipated through financial interdependence. The nonpolicy factors bringing nations closer together cannot be effectively controlled by governments. Thus the only feasible way to recapture lost automomy—to reverse market integration and to reduce the substitutability among assets denominated in different currencies and issued in different nations—is to establish stronger barriers or frictions at national borders.

Dis-integration could occur in a disorderly way. Within each nation influential private groups, the communications media, and the national government itself could espouse a narrow definition of national (and private) interests. Through a sequence of decentralized and noncooperative decisions, national governments could revert to "protectionist" policies designed to promote their own residents' interests at the expense of foreigners. If carried out in this way, dis-integration counld be yet another illustration of the classic dilemma of collective action where members of a group inadvertently behave in a manner prejudicial to a common interest.

In principle, however, the course of dis-integration could be cooperatively managed. Conceived in that way, dis-integration can plausibly be portrayed in a positive rather than negative light—as a constructive effort to permit nations to experience divergent macroeconomic and financial conditions suited to their own particular needs and circumstances. Intergovernmental cooperation that self-consciously managed a mutually agreed sequence of national actions could prevent the dis-integration from going too far or collapsing into self-defeating anarchy.

James Tobin, for example, has put forward a thoughtful proposal designed to foster managed dis-integration. He suggests that governments impose an internationally uniform transfer tax on transactions across currencies, thereby diminishing the substitutability of assets denominated in different currencies.[22] This proposal, and others with similar intent, deserve more serious analysis and debate than they typically receive.

Although attractive in principle, the course of cooperatively managed dis-integration seems to me likely to prove infeasible or excessively costly in practice. To rebuild separation fences between national financial markets in a way that yields a large gain in autonomy for as small a sacrifice as possible of the benefits of interdependence would be an extraordinarily difficult task. The politically easy way to re-erect separation fences—catering to localized and individually differentiated demands for protection—would probably be much more costly.

For many countries, moreover, there may be no administratively feasible way to maintain an effective separation fence. So many pipes and pumping stations now connect national reservoirs—and so many new channels could be established in response to controls on existing channels—that governments simply may not have the capacity to prevent international movements of funds. To change the analogy, recapturing lost autonomy might be an exercise like trying to squeeze toothpaste back into its tube.

To be sure, high levels of overt conflict among nations could create a political climate in which severe measures to erect separation fences could be successful. A little war here or there would be a marvelous shot in the arm for exchange controls. But dis-integration achieved in that way would certainly not be cooperatively managed. It would represent disintegration in the more common sense of that word,

---

[22] Tobin first made the proposal in 1974 and subsequently elaborated it in 1978. The proposal is reprinted in Tobin (1982, chap. 20).

namely a destruction rather than a pulling back that is controlled and mutually agreed.

Enhanced Multilateral Decisionmaking

Difficult though it will prove to be, therefore, a course of strengthening the ability of national governments to cooperate through enhanced procedures of multilateral decisionmaking seems the more likely prospect for the last years of this century and the first decades of the next. Rather than pulling back from financial interdependence, this posture would actively try to adapt to it, and manage it better.

What would this broad choice imply for the area of regulation, supervision, and taxation? National governments would have to grope toward a world environment for financial intermediation that exhibits less divergence and more cooperation among countries. The first steps in this process would be the development of some agreed principles that would foster less heterogeneity in national regulations, tax treatments, and supervisory procedures. Such "world standard" principles need not imply uniformity in national policies. But they would constrain national behavior relative to the "anything goes" presumption that is now the formal state of affairs. The Concordat of the Cooke Committee can be interpreted as a first hesitant step along these lines.

Agreement on some world principles would have the corollary effect of halting the drift toward discrimination in favor of financial intermediaries' transactions with foreign residents in foreign currencies. And it would doubtless imply that nations should gradually implement the world principles. Countries with high-tax and stringently-regulated environments would thus remain under some pressure to reduce their taxes and regulations. But there would also be resistance to a competition in laxity that, unresisted, could drive regulation, supervision, and taxation toward a least common denominator for the world as a whole. Countries whose environments were much less stringent than average would have to tighten their policies toward the emerging set of world standards.

How could a set of world standards be formulated? Merely taking an unweighted average of existing national standards has no compelling logic to recommend it (economically or politically). Insisting that smaller countries conform to the existing standards of the most powerful nations has a political logic, but not one with appeal to those who must conform. Ideally, one would like to see world standards based on objective criteria—or criteria as objectively formulated as possible. Wherever it proved infeasible to maintain heterogeneity in regulations across countries, criteria would need to be developed to judge whether high-tax and stringently-regulated environments were inappropriately restrictive or whether low-tax and lightly-regulated environments were inappropriately permissive. Much groundwork would have to be laid at the analytical level before it would be reasonable to schedule intergovernmental discussions about the possibility of such world standards.

What would enhanced multilateral decisionmaking mean more generally—for example, for nations' macroeconomic policies?

The lack of an agreed analytical framework for assessing the crossborder interactions among nations' economies is a fundamental obstacle to joint discussions of macroeconomic policies. Enormous uncertainty exists about how policy actions and nonpolicy shocks originating in one country influence economic developments in other countries. At the present time, governments thus do not have an analytically sound basis to coordinate their decisions—even if they were politically disposed to do so.

An adequate analytical framework for evaluating the effects of external forces on the domestic economy does not exist even for any individual nation. Worse still, neither governments, international institutions, nor academic economists have an analytical framework capable of modeling the *interactions* among individual national economies in an internally consistent, systemic fashion. Yet some degree of consensus among objective analysts about the direction and quantitative size of such interactions is a necessary—albeit far from sufficient—condition for significant progress in facilitating coordination of national macroeconomic policies.

What Is "Cooperation"?

Cooperation among national governments as I envisage it here has a limited and precise meaning. Cooperation occurs when several governments take into account the interactions between their economies and polities and as a result mutually adjust their national policies or jointly undertake an "international" policy. The essential ingredient in cooperation is the existence of an agreement among the governments to behave differently than they would have behaved in the absence of the agreement. To be durable, agreements need to be binding and enforceable. In contrast, noncooperative decisions are characterized by an unwillingness to enter into binding commitments. Each government adapts its decisions to what it observes or expects others to do, but without constraints on its own independence of action and without assurances of constraints on the actions of others.

This concept of cooperation is not a synonym for amity, harmony, or altruism. Cooperation is merely a self-interested mutual adjustment of behavior. In particular, cooperation does not imply that national governments have identical or compatible goals. It implies nothing about goals. The goals of national governments are plainly different and often incompatible. Yet the potential for cooperation may be greatest when goals are inconsistent and discord is high.

Heightened cooperation in the sense of self-interested mutual agreements will of course be difficult to achieve, even with better awareness of the need for it. It will have to be conducted like porcupines make love—very cautiously. Without it, however, there may be no satisfactory evolution of the world economy and financial system. Managed dis-integration would require a large dose of it. It will be the very essence of enhanced multilateral decisionmaking.

References

Bagehot, Walter. 1873. *Lombard Street*. London: Kegan, Paul and Co.; reprinted by John Murray, 1924.

Bank of England. 1981. Developments in Cooperation among Banking Supervisory Authorities. *Quarterly Bulletin*.

Barry, Brian and Russell Hardin, eds. 1982. *Rational Man and Irrational Society?: An Introduction and Sourcebook*. Beverly Hills: Sage Publications.

Bingham, T.R.G. 1985. *Banking and Monetary Policy*. Paris: OECD.

Bryant, Ralph C. 1980. *Money and Monetary Policy in Interdependent Nations*. Washington, D.C.: The Brookings Institution.

Clark, Robert Charles. 1976. The Soundness of Financial Intermediaries. *Yale Law Journal* 86.

Cooke, W.P. 1983. The International Banking Scene: A Supervisory Perspective. Bank of England *Quarterly Bulletin*.

Raymond W. Goldsmith. 1969. *Financial Structure and Development*. New Haven, Connecticut: Yale University Press.

Gurley, John S., and Edward S. Shaw. 1957. The Growth of Debt and Money in the United States, 1800–1950: A Suggested Interpretation. *Review of Economics and Statistics* 39:250–262.

———. 1960. *Money in a Theory of Finance*. Washington, D.C.: The Brookings Institution.

Guttentag, Jack M., and Richard J. Herring. 1983. The Lender of Last Resort Function in an International Context. Princeton Essay in International Finance No. 151. Princeton: International Finance Section, Department of Economics, Princeton University.

Harberger, Arnold C. 1980. Vignettes on the World Capital Market. *American Economic Review, Papers and Proceedings* 70:331–337.

Herring, Richard J., and Jack M. Guttentag. 1984. Credit Rationing and Financial Disorder. *Journal of Finance* 39:1359–1382.

Hester, Donald D. 1981. Innovations and Monetary Control. *Brookings Papers on Economic Activity* 1:141–189.

Hirsch, Fred. 1977. The Bagehot Problem. *Manchester School* 45:24–55.

Institute for Financial Affairs Inc. 1983. *World Financial Centres* (Report of the Offshore Banking Survey Mission. Tokyo.

International Monetary Fund. 1981. *International Capital Markets: Recent Developments and Short-term Prospects, 1981.* IMF Occasional Paper No. 7.

International Monetary Fund. 1983. *International Capital Markets, Developments and Prospects, 1983.* IMF Occasional Paper No. 23.

Johnson, G.G., with Richard K. Abrams. 1983. Appendix I on International Coordination of Bank Supervision. *Aspects of the International Banking Safety Net.* IMF Occasional Paper No. 17. Washington, D.C.: International Monetary Fund.

Kareken, John H. 1981. Deregulating Commercial Banks: The Watchword Should Be Caution. *Quarterly Review.* Minneapolis, Minnesota: Federal Reserve Bank of Minneapolis.

————. 1984. Bank Regulation and the Effectiveness of Open Market Operations. *Brookings Papers on Economic Activity* 2:405–444.

Key, Sydney J. 1982. International Banking Facilities. *Federal Reserve Bulletin* 68:565–577.

Keynes, John Maynard. 1980. In Moggridge, Donald, ed., *Collected Writings* 25 and 26. Cambridge: Cambridge University Press and Macmillan.

Kindleberger, Charles P. 1978. *Manias, Panics, and Crashes: A History of Financial Crises.* New York: Basic Books.

————, and Jean Pierre Laffargue. 1982. *Financial Crises: Theory, History and Policy.* Cambridge: Cambridge University Press.

LeRoy, Stephen F., and Richard D. Porter. 1981. The Present Value Relation: Tests Based on Variance Bounds. *Econometrica* 49:555–574.

McKinnon, Ronald I. 1973. *Money and Capital in Economic Development.* Washington, D.C.: The Brookings Institution.

Olson, Mancur. 1971. *The Logic of Collective Action: Public Goods and the Theory of Groups.* 2nd ed. Cambridge, Mass.: Harvard University Press.

Pecchioli, Rinaldo. 1983. *The Internationalization of Banking.* Paris: Organization for Economic Cooperation and Development.

Sakakibara, Eisuke, and Akira Kondoh. 1984. *Study on the Internationalization of Tokyo's Money Market.* Policy Studies Series No. 1. Tokyo: Japan Center for International Finance.

Shaw, Edward S. 1973. *Financial Deepening in Economic Development.* Oxford: Oxford University Press.

Shiller, Robert J. 1979. The Volatility of Long-Term Interest Rates and the Expectations Models of the Term Structure. *Journal of Political Economy* 87:1190–1219.

————. 1981. Do Stock Prices Move Too Much to Be Justified by Subsequent Changes in Dividends? *American Economic Review* 71:421–436.

————. 1984. Stock Prices and Social Dynamics. *Brookings Papers on Economic Activity* 2:457–498.

Tobin, James. 1963. Commercial Banks as Creators of "Money." In Carson, Deane, ed., *Banking and Monetary Studies*. New York: Richard D. Irwin.

————. 1982. *Essays in Economics: Theory and Policy*, Vol. 3 of collected papers. MIT Press.

————. 1984. On the Efficiency of the Financial System. Fred Hirsch Memorial Lecture. *Lloyds Bank Review*.

————, and William C. Brainard. 1963. Financial Intermediaries and the Effectiveness of Monetary Controls. *American Economic Review, Papers and Proceedings* 53: 383–400.

Watson, Maxwell, and others. 1984. *International Capital Markets: Developments and Prospects, 1984*. International Monetary Fund, IMF Occasional Paper No. 31.

Wojnilower, Albert M. 1980. The Central Role of Credit Crunches in Recent Financial History. *Brookings Papers on Economic Activity* 2:277–326.

6

Financial Reform in the United States and the Financial System of the Future

James L. Pierce

Growing public disenchantment in the United States with government regulation resulted recently in the transportation, depository-institution, and communications industries becoming less regulated. Deregulation primarily involved elimination of government-enforced price-fixing and other anticompetitive practices.

Public sentiment for reducing the regulatory constraints on depository institutions was reinforced by technological and economic factors that produced wide-scale circumvention of regulations concerning interest rate ceilings and the separation of "banking" from other financial activities. Deregulation, in part, has involved recognition of reality and is an attempt to allow conventional depository institutions to compete in the marketplace.

The purpose of this paper is to analyze the causes and effects of financial reform in the United States with the objective of gaining perspective concerning evolution to the financial system of the future. It is argued that the nature of government regulation and supervision of financial institutions must change to assure continued financial stability and efficiency.

What Deregulation Has Occurred?

There is no single date or event that marks the beginning of deregulation of depository institutions. Much was accomplished long before the financial reform legislation of the 1980s. Many early instances involved interpretation of existing law by the banking regulators. For example, banks were allowed to market large denomination certificates of deposit (CDs) and operate loan production offices across state lines. This effectively eliminated interstate "branching" restrictions for their wholesale operations. In 1969, the interest rate ceiling for CDs was suspended, allowing banks to compete freely for funds in national and regional money markets. There were even some rulings that weakened interstate restrictions for the retail side of bank operations. For example, banking organizations were allowed to engage in consumer lending across state lines.

Other interpretations of existing laws allowed banks to enter a number of activities lowering the barrier between banking and other financial activities. Among these are "mutual funds" provided by bank trust departments, credit-life insurance, discount stock brokerage, investment advising services, as well as assistance in the direct placement of corporate securities and in arranging mergers and acquisitions.

Some deregulation of retail (consumer) liabilities of depository institutions also occurred as a result of regulatory *fiat*. For example, in 1976, the Federal Reserve authorized automatic transfer accounts that, in effect, allowed households to earn interest on their demand deposit balances. An interest rate ceiling was imposed on these accounts, however. Furthermore, in 1978, the interest rate on six-month consumer time accounts at depository institutions was allowed to fluctuate with market interest rates.

Legislative moves to deregulate actually began in 1974 when, as an "experiment," Congress authorized federally insured depository institutions in the New England states to offer interest-bearing negotiable order of withdrawal (NOW) accounts.[1] While the interest rate was subject to a binding ceiling, this was an important reversal of previous banking law because it eliminated for households in those states the prohibition against paying interest on transactions accounts. Over time, depository institutions in states adjacent to New England were also allowed to offer NOW accounts.

Attempts by the regulators and by Congress to allow depository institutions to meet the competition from money market mutual funds and other sources by deregulating some interest rate ceilings for some retail accounts were not effective. Depository institutions lost large quantities of funds to competitors in 1979 when market interest rates rose to spectacular levels.

Congress essentially gave up on regulating deposit interest rates by passing the Depository Institutions Deregulation Act of 1980. This law allowed NOW accounts for all federally insured depository institutions nationwide and eliminated all deposit interest rate ceilings by

---

[1] This enabled federally insured institutions in New England to compete against state-insured institutions that were allowed to offer these interest-bearing accounts.

mid-1980.[2] By allowing thrift institutions to offer transactions accounts, the law significantly blurred the distinction between banks and thrifts. The distinction was blurred further by reducing the forced specialization of thrifts in housing finance. Thrift institutions were allowed to devote significant portions of their asset portfolios to consumer loans and corporate debt. Commercial banks did not receive any new investment powers.

These moves to deregulate depository institutions was followed by the highest and most volatile interest rates, and the deepest recession, in the post-World War II history of the United States. Interest rate ceilings for many accounts prevented depository institutions from competing effectively for funds. Money market mutual funds and sweep accounts drained huge quantities of funds from depository institutions by offering transactions accounts paying market interest rates. Furthermore, thrift institutions were caught in a bind of funding existing fixed-rate mortgage loans with increasingly costly short-term liabilities whose interest rates moved with the market. Interest rates for longer-term liabilities had not been decontrolled. Bank failures rose, and the failure rate among thrift institutions approached epidemic proportions.

Congress responded with the Garn-St Germain Act of 1982, which accelerated the pace of deregulation. Interest rate ceilings were immediately eliminated on NOW accounts (subject to a minimum balance requirement) and a hybrid "money market" account was authorized that was competitive with money market mutual fund and sweep accounts. This new account has no reserve requirement and no interest rate ceilings, but allows only six transactions per month, of which a maximum of three can be by check. Despite the limitation on the number of transactions, the new money market accounts are insured and are preferred by many households to uninsured money market mutual fund and sweep accounts. There was a large shift of funds from these uninsured accounts into the new accounts at depository institutions.

The Garn-St Germain Act further reduced the distinction between banks and thrift institutions by allowing thrifts to do direct commercial lending and by expanding their power to grant consumer loans. The law also allowed thrift institutions to offer demand deposit accounts to businesses that establish a loan relationship. With this new law, government-imposed differences between banks and thrift institutions have been virtually eliminated. Differences that occur in the future will

---

[2] The prohibition against paying interest on accounts defined by law as demand deposit accounts is technically not an interest rate ceiling; legislation has not eliminated the prohibition.

largely be the result of freely chosen specialization and not of governmental *fiat*. Some thrifts probably will come to resemble commercial banks while others will remain largely in housing finance. Today, it is common to talk about "depository institutions" rather than to make a distinction between banks and thrifts; the difference is becoming too blurred to be meaningful.

Finally, the Garn-St Germain Act gave the regulators authority to allow acquisitions of troubled or failing institutions across state lines. This has produced some large interstate mergers, significantly weakening the conventional prohibition against interstate acquisitions.

State governments also have moved to deregulate depository institutions. Federal restrictions on interstate branching and acquisitions do not apply when such operations are allowed by the affected states. Recently, several states have entered into regional agreements that allow banking operations across their boundaries.[3] Some state governments also have expanded the allowable activities of depository institutions they charter relative to the powers of federally chartered institutions. For example, securities underwriting and general insurance operations are allowable in some cases.

Since passage of the Garn-St Germain Act, the regulators have actively pursued deregulation of deposit interest rates. Today, interest rate ceilings have been totally eliminated for virtually all kinds of time accounts. The only retail transactions accounts with interest rate ceilings are small-denomination NOW accounts. While depository institutions are still prohibited from paying interest on demand deposit accounts, the prohibition has been so thoroughly undermined that its effects are small. Holders of demand deposit balances earn interest indirectly through repurchase agreements, offshore bookings, and compensating balance requirements that move negatively with market interest rates. Furthermore, businesses can hold money market accounts at depository institutions.

In summary, interest rate ceilings are virtually nonexistent in the United States today. Thrift institutions can become like banks, with depository institutions allowed greater flexibility to offer new products and to expand geographically. Government-imposed price-fixing has been drastically reduced and forced specialization has been diminished.

Why Did Deregulation Occur?

While many of the reasons for deregulation are well known, it is

---

[3] The constitutionality of these agreements is currently being attacked in the courts.

useful to summarize the major factors because they provide clues to the future development of the financial system in the United States. In total, a combination of technological innovations and economic factors created forces that made deregulation inevitable.

Many regulatory restrictions on the activities of depository institutions in the United States have involved attempts to force specialization either by product or by geography. Commercial banks were expected to issue demand deposit accounts and lend to business. They were the custodians of the nation's checking account money and they were the "transmission belt" for monetary policy.[4] Under this approach, the "safety and soundness" of banks was crucial to the stability of the monetary system. Concern over bank safety and soundness led to a variety of measures that attempted to enhance bank profitability by limiting competition among them. This explains interest rate ceilings, for example. Furthermore, for a variety of social and political reasons, bank activities were circumscribed either by geographic boundaries or in terms of function. Thus, banks were prohibited from interstate branching, and they were prohibited from certain activities such as direct underwriting of domestic corporate securities or from holding equity positions in nonbanking corporations. Thus, banking was to stay away from commerce and certain kinds of finance, and it was to respect state boundaries. These restrictions were considered important for limiting the power of banks, for keeping banking focused on its essential business, and for keeping banking profitable.

Thrift institutions had another function. They were to provide long-term housing finance while also offering a safe and attractive return for consumer savings. Over time this latter function took a back seat to the provision of housing finance. Thrift institutions were required by law and regulation to devote virtually all of their resources and energies to providing housing finance.[5] Unlike commercial banks, the liabilities of thrift institutions did not come under interest rate ceilings until 1966. At that time, competition from banks, which had obtained an increase in ceiling rates, caused concern about the profitability of thrifts in an environment of rising interest rates. Ceiling rates were established for thrifts that were somewhat higher than those for banks, allowing thrifts to compete (or outcompete) banks while eliminating price competition among themselves. The imposition of interest rate ceilings and provision of a differential for thrifts were

[4] For a modern-day defense of this "traditional" role of banking see Corrigan 1982. For a criticism of the Corrigan view see Pierce 1985.

[5] This was more true of savings and loan associations than of mutual savings banks.

considered essential if thrift institutions were to finance housing.

While ceilings constrained interest-rate costs per unit of deposit account, they produced large fluctuations in the quantity of funds in accounts at depository institutions. When market interest rates rose above ceiling rates, thrift institutions lost funds. When market interest rates fell below the ceilings there were large inflows. These outflows and inflows produced sympathetic fluctuations in the supply of credit for housing. Mortgage interest rates rose sharply when market interest rates rose above deposit ceiling rates, and they fell rapidly when market interest rates declined. Fluctuations in the supply and cost of housing credit made the housing sector of the economy particularly sensitive to movements in market interest rates. It was fashionable in the late 1960s and early 1970s to describe housing expenditures as countercyclical; falling during the late phases of cyclical expansion and rising during recession. This housing expenditure behavior was due, in part, to the segmentation of the mortgage-thrift sector of the financial system from other financial markets. Economic incentives and technical innovations were to weaken this segmentation.

Before turning to a brief account of these incentives and innovations, it is useful to examine how banks responded to interest rate ceilings. Large banks simply developed instruments that were directly competitive with securities traded in the money market. Their size and reputations allowed these banks to sell certificates of deposits in the money market. They could manage their liabilities by issuing CDs when ordinary account balances fell and reducing new issues when these account balances rose. Certificates of deposit were deposits in name only; they were (and are) money market securities. When the banking regulators attempted to limit liability management by imposing interest rate ceilings on CDs, large banks responded by issuing other liabilities such as Euro-dollar debt and commercial paper that was not covered by ceilings. The regulators gave up and suspended interest rate ceilings for CDs.

The development of liability management illustrates an important form of interaction between regulators and the regulated. Because regulation constrains behavior, it produces economic incentives to circumvent it; the ensuing circumvention produces new regulations; and so on. This dynamic process is not new, but it has accelerated with the rapid advance of technology. In fact, without the continuing developments in computer, accounting, and communications technology that integrated the national money market and linked it to international markets, the explosion in managed liabilities could not have occurred.

Interest rate ceilings did not work for large banks. They had too many alternative sources of funds through domestic and international financial markets for interest rate ceilings for their ordinary deposit accounts to be effective. Smaller banks were closer to the situation of thrift institutions because they lacked access to the money market. Interest rate ceilings were a binding constraint for them.

In the early 1970s, a situation existed in the United States where interest rate ceilings were binding for ordinary savings and time account liabilities at banks and thrifts. Large depositors were not significantly affected because they could acquire money market instruments. Smaller depositors did not have access to the money market. Thus, smaller depositors were largely locked into accounts with interest rate ceilings at depository institutions. The financial markets were segmented on the basis of large versus small depositors. Large depositors could escape most and often all of the effect of interest rate ceilings; small depositors could not.

This situation produced a powerful incentive for financial firms whose liabilities were not subject to government-imposed interest rate ceilings to provide instruments to smaller depositors that provided a market rate of return while affording high liquidity and safety. The incentive could be exploited because of advances in computer, communications, and accounting technology. These advances made money market mutual funds and sweep accounts feasible. Transactions and accounting costs had become so low that these firms could offer to the public a market return and very high liquidity. Money market mutual funds and sweep accounts pool the funds of many customers to purchase short-maturity, large-denomination instruments in the money market, such as Treasury bills, commercial paper, and bank CDs. Because of the short maturity and ready marketability of the assets they hold, and the use of advanced technology, these institutions can promise to repay their customers on demand, allowing them to write checks, and even wire funds, against zero-balance accounts established at agent banks. These accounts bettered the accounts offered by depository institutions in interest return, but they were inferior in terms of risk. Deposit insurance allows depository institutions to promise payment at par. Money market mutual funds and sweep accounts lack federal insurance and cannot guarantee payment at par. Risk is limited, however, by investing the funds in U.S. government securities and high-grade paper issued by both financial and nonfinancial firms.

Decontrol of deposit interest rates became inevitable because market segmentation disappeared. If depository institutions were to provide intermediary services to the general public, they had to be able to offer a competitive return on their liabilities. Furthermore, if thrift institutions were to remain viable in a world of nonsegmented financial markets, they had to have the power to offer transactions accounts and to hold more diversified portfolios. They had to become more like banks.

The substantial integration of financial markets during the 1970s occurred in areas of the financial system that are less regulated than depository institutions. This had to be the case because it was lack of regulation that allowed these firms to offer attractive products to the public and eventually to destroy interest rate ceilings.

The mortgage market was another major area in which financial markets became better integrated. Historically, most of the mortgage loans in the U.S. were originated and held by thrift institutions and to a lesser degree by banks. There was no active secondary market for these instruments. A number of government programs helped develop a secondary market in mortgage loans. Government agencies purchase loans from depository institutions and resell them in one form or another to ultimate holders such as insurance companies and pension funds. With the development of these programs mortgage banks emerged that specialize in originating (underwriting) mortgage loans that are sold to either governmental or private purchasers. Furthermore, large depository institutions began to offer their own securities backed by mortgage loans.

These developments had the direct effect of providing depository institutions with greater liquidity. They also effectively eliminated the segmentation between the mortgage market and markets for other long-term investments. Yields on both new and old mortgage loans began to move closely in tandem with yields on corporate bonds and other long-term assets. The integration of the mortgage market with the markets for other long-term instruments weakened the counter-cyclical role of housing finance.

Developments outside of depository institutions did not stop with money market mutual funds, sweep accounts, and the mortgage market. Perhaps even more important for the future of the U.S. financial system, financial conglomerates were formed that have greater flexibility and powers than banks. These conglomerates are not considered under the law to be banks or bank holding companies and as a result escape many of the legal and regulatory restrictions imposed on banks. The financial conglomerates have grown rapidly, and their continued growth has important implications for the U.S. financial system.

Today, retailing firms such as Sears Roebuck and securities firms such as Merrill Lynch offer a variety of financial services under one roof, including real estate brokerage and finance, insurance of various sorts, depository services, mutual funds, and securities brokerage and underwriting. These firms are fast becoming financial supermarkets providing virtually all financial services in one place. The savings to the public of these supermarkets are potentially very large. Their existence and prospects of continued growth suggest that whatever segmentation that currently exists in financial markets will be further reduced.

The vehicles used by the financial conglomerates to offer a full range of financial services differ. Some own thrift institutions and offer insured depository services through them.[6] Others own "nonbank banks" that offer either insured demand deposit accounts or commercial lending, but not both.[7] Whatever the vehicle, these conglomerates have broken down the barriers between banking and commerce, and between banking and certain financial sectors such as corporate securities underwriting and insurance. Because the activities of the conglomerates fall outside bank regulatory jurisdictions, they are not bound by geographic restrictions and other limitations on their powers.

Not surprisingly, large banks have begun an active campaign to allow them the same powers as financial conglomerates, on the grounds that they need a "level playing field" to compete with the conglomerates.

The growth of financial conglomerates and the prospect of further deregulation of depository institutions to allow effective competition raises a number of public policy issues concerning financial stability, the role of federal insurance, the role of federal regulation of financial institutions, and control of financial power. The ways in which the government responds to these issues will have an important effect on the future development of the financial system. There are fundamental economic and technological factors at work that will make further integration of financial markets inevitable. These forces must be recognized and accepted if an effective, productive, and long-lasting regulatory structure is to be developed.

Current Attitudes Concerning Financial Regulation

Currently in the United States the climate for further deregulation

[6] Thrift institutions are not covered by the restrictions of the Bank Holding Company Act concerning activities of affiliates and parent organizations.

[7] The Bank Holding Company Act defines a bank as an institution that offers demand deposit accounts *and* grants commercial loans. An institution that engages in only one of these activities is called a "nonbank bank," and is exempt from bank holding company restrictions.

and for reform of the regulatory structure is not favorable. Public perception of instability of the depository system has clouded the basic issues that are involved. There is currently more public concern about the viability of the depository system than at any time since the 1930s. Failure of scores of small and medium-sized institutions, disclosure of a staggering volume of highly questionable domestic and foreign loans held by large banks, emergency assistance for and eventual federal takeover of Continental Illinois, and emergency measures to save the nation's largest thirft institution have generated fears that the whole system could topple. As evidence of the increased fragility of the system, failure of a thrift institution in the state of Ohio that did not have federal insurance not only touched off runs at other institutions in that state, but also produced deposit losses at an institution in California and apparently even affected foreign exchange markets.

It is common among the popular media, politicians, and the public in general to lay the blame for these problems on deregulation. This has destroyed interest in further deregulation and in reforming the regulatory agencies. Currently, there is growing support for re-regulation.

It would be a mistake to lay most of the blame for the problems of depository institutions on deregulation. Declining (dollar) energy prices, a high exchange rate for the dollar, and weak worldwide demand made many good loans turn bad. Despite their new powers and the growing use of variable-rate mortgage loans, thrift institutions have been slow to adjust, with many failing along the way. Furthermore, several giants of the banking industry and many smaller institutions made management blunders of heroic proportions, substituting rapid growth in their loan portfolios for good sense. In most instances, poor management was unrelated to deregulation. Several failures have involved fraud. Deregulation has had an effect, however, as rising costs of liabilities and heightened competition for loans put a squeeze on profitability. Some institutions could not survive in a less regulated world.

The Financial System of the Future

Despite the current retrenchment, there is little doubt that depository institutions will become less regulated in the long run. Technological advances will continue to break down the segmentation of markets and force depository institutions to offer a wider range of services if they are to be competitive with other market participants.

Huge changes have already occurred. The costs of buying and selling assets and of transferring funds, both domestically and internationally, have been greatly reduced. Virtually all assets traded on organized markets can be bought and sold in a few minutes, with the funds available to the seller either the same day or overnight. Not only has this greatly increased asset liquidity; it also means that many kinds of firms can enter the transactions account business, once the exclusive preserve of banks.

The revolution has not stopped at the nation's boundaries. New electronic payment technologies have integrated U.S. financial markets with those in the rest of the world. Satellites and computers allow almost instantaneous transactions between geographically distant places in the world. As a consequence, depository institutions can raise funds overseas at a moment's notice, and U.S. residents can make payments in the U.S. with funds booked overseas.

Relatively little has been written on the implications of existing advances in transactions technologies for monetary stability, monetary policy, or regulation.[8] There is even less on the implications of future developments. Many discussions of futuristic "banking" dwell on the effects of debit cards or mini computers used to make direct payments from buyer to seller. For reasons to be discussed below, there are strong reasons for believing that advances in this area will be slow in the United States. The major advances have been, and probably will continue to be, in the area of asset transactions and provision of financial services. As mentioned before, advances in computer, communications, and accounting technologies have allowed firms to package and sell bundles of securities and other assets to households and firms. Costs are so low that even small accounts are profitable. Mutual funds (securities pooling) have proliferated and have already been extended to such areas as mortgage-backed securities, foreign assets, futures markets, and blocks of real assets. Brokers and investment advisors have done a remarkable job of explaining and selling these services to ordinary households and firms. With each advance in this area, liquidity of individual agents' assets is increased, with nominal price certainty often protected by hedging strategies. Not only will there be fuller integration of financial markets, but also better integration of financial and real markets.

One important implication of the revolution in computing, information processing, and communications is that the distinction between banking and many other financial activities will be effectively elimi-

---

[8] A partial list includes Benston 1983; Eisenbeis 1983; Ford 1985: Hester 1981; Kane 1983; Pierce 1985; Phillips 1983; Rosenblum and Pavel 1984.

nated. Depository institutions will be replaced by financial-services firms similar in many ways to the financial conglomerates that already exist. These financial supermarkets will offer all of the conventional banking services along with insurance, mutual funds, real estate services, securities brokerage and underwriting, and access to commodity, futures, and foreign asset markets, as well as types of services not yet foreseen. It appears virtually inevitable that the barriers between banking and other sectors of the economy will be broken down. Banking in the United States will more closely resemble banking in many other industrialized countries. While specialization will probably continue to varying degrees, it will be the result of economic incentives and talents rather than governmental *fiat*.

In the distant future, firms are likely to conduct transactions with their customers electronically, eventually eliminating, for the most part, the need for money. There are many technological, economic, and organizational impediments to electronic "banking" that will slow its development. Truly low-cost home terminals that are reliable and easily operated are difficult to develop. Furthermore, public resistance to computer use is likely to be a continuing problem. Widespread use of computers in schools will ultimately break down some resistance, but it will also illustrate the frailties of computers. More importantly, in a country with tens of thousands of financial institutions and millions of firms, it is exceedingly difficult to obtain the cooperation and trust needed to build communications and payments systems. Problems of reliability of the systems, of establishing liabilities for errors and malfunctions, are difficult to solve. The problems are not in principle insurmountable, but it is likely that a very long time will be required to achieve the institutional and organizational changes needed to have a full electronic funds transfer (EFT) system.[9] Added to these problems are those associated with antitrust laws that may well inhibit development of national networks.

Finally, and perhaps most important, revolutionary changes in the ways that financial-services firms charge for transactions and services will be required before EFT becomes reality. Currently, for example, many depository institutions do not charge for transactions account activity. The only advantages to the public of EFT are saved postage and added convenience. If users had to pay the long-run marginal cost of financial transactions, EFT often would have an added cost advantage. Furthermore, credit card compaines grant automatic 30–day credit interest-free, and they do not charge a fee per transaction.

[9] An excellent discussion of these issues is provided by Phillips 1983.

As long as these practices are followed, it will be difficult if not impossible to induce households to use debit cards and direct computer access extensively for transactions. Credit cards will dominate in many instances. Given the competitive environment in the United States, it is unlikely that charging systems for transactions services for various media will be put on a rational basis in the foreseeable future. Until this occurs, EFT cannot flourish.[10]

Full-fledged EFT is not a crucial ingredient in the financial and monetary system of the future. Gains in asset "liquidification" and market integration can and will continue without it. These gains can be of great benefit to the public in terms of resource savings, but they also pose potential problems for public policy in the U.S.

There are two separate but closely related problems that should be addressed before the financial evolution of the U.S. goes much further. The first problem involves the execution of monetary policy. This topic will be touched upon only briefly here because it is the subject of other papers at this conference. The second problem involves establishing a regulatory structure that assures financial stability while allowing the financial system to evolve naturally.

Monetary Policy

The integration of financial markets that has occurred over the last two decades and the deregulation that followed have resulted in markets being cleared more by price and less by quantity adjustments. The financial system of the future will be even more fully integrated both domestically and internationally. Interest rate elasticities of demand and supply will have an even greater role in allocating credit and real resources. This is a substantial change from the 1970s and earlier, when interest rate ceilings affected the economy in the short run through producing large adjustments in the quantity of credit. Short-run interest rate fluctuations are likely to be larger than in the past. Furthermore, the increasing use of money that pays a market-determined interest rate will probably make the "LM curve" steeper, intensifying short-term interest rate fluctuations.

Monetary policy can continue to function in this world, but the quantity of money will be completely endogenous and, therefore, subject to even less close control in the short run. In a world in which many assets are virtually perfectly liquid, it is impossible to have a meaningful definition of money. Attempts to control the growth of

---

[10] For a more detailed discussion, see Pierce 1979.

some collection of liquid assets arbitrarily defined as money will simply encourage the use of other assets that are near-perfect substitutes. Furthermore, it appears that reserve requirements will become even less effective than they are today. Money and credit measures will provide useful information as economic indicators but will die a well-deserved death as targets of policy.

A problem for monetary policy is to adjust to a less regulated and more integrated financial system.[11] There is likely to be continuing uncertainty concerning how to actively facilitate stabilization and about how private markets will respond to policy changes. It appears that for years to come the case for a relatively stable and predictable policy stance will be even more compelling than heretofore.

Markets are so interconnected and the flow of funds so flexible that U.S. monetary policy influences all domestic financial markets. In order to affect the U.S. financial system, the Federal Reserve ends up influencing and being influenced by foreign financial markets. This has far-reaching consequences for domestic interest rates and credit, exchange rates, and foreign relations.

Monetary policy and financial regulation are interrelated because each seeks to promote monetary and financial stability. If either becomes less effective in its pursuit of stability, the burden on the other is increased.

A New Regulatory Structure for the United States

Since the mid-1930s the Federal Reserve has contributed greatly to monetary stability by freely converting demand deposit balances into currency (offsetting the decline in total bank reserves through open market operations) and by standing as lender of last resort to banks. The potential for instability has been increasing recently, however, and is likely to continue to increase unless changes are made in the nation's regulatory structure. This is occurring, in part, because an important part of monetary and financial functions are performed by institutions (financial conglomerates) outside the "club." These institutions offer monetary liabilities for which there is no federal insurance, they are subject to relatively little supervision and regulation, and they lack direct access to the Federal Reserve. They offer assets to the public that on the micro level are as liquid as money. The liquidity disappears at the macro level, however, as long as these institutions remain outside the club.

---

[11] It is surprising that more problems have not developed already; see Pierce 1984.

The regulatory structure for U.S. financial institutions has not changed substantially since the mid-1930s despite a revolution in the financial and monetary systems. Depository institutions are still closely supervised and regulated by their own set of regulators. Other financial firms that offer many services similar to those of depository institutions are less heavily regulated by a different set of regulators.

There is ample evidence that the existing regulatory structure for depository institutions is not working well. It is difficult to escape the impression that the regulators are overwhelmed by the problems they face. Certainly there is ample evidence that they have not done a good job in limiting risk-taking by depository institutions. Rather than anticipating problems stemming from overcommitment to foreign, energy, or real estate loans, or from too rapid growth of certain institutions, the regulators seem to be the last ones to know that an institution is in trouble. In a desperate attempt to keep Continental Illinois Bank afloat, the Federal Deposit Insurance Corporation (FDIC) offered a blanket guarantee of all the liabilities of the bank and its holding company, including liabilities of foreign branches and subsidiaries.[12] Furthermore, the regulators have stated that the largest banks in the country will not be allowed to fail. This offering of a blanket, but amorphous, guarantee of all the liabilities issued by the largest institutions reduces even further the market discipline provided by lenders at risk, because the risk has been shifted to the federal government. The guarantee of nonfailure confers virtual "public utility" status on the largest banks with all the ramifications for future regulatory sanctions. This is a large step in the wrong direction.

In the current chaotic environment, it may be tempting to attempt to turn back the clock and restrict bank activities in an effort to return banking to a simpler time when problems were less complex and seemingly more manageable. This would be unlikely to succeed, and if it did, financial activity would be shifted to less regulated and less stable elements of the financial system. It is not desirable to attempt to force depository institutions to keep out of new areas either in terms of products or in geographic terms. This will simply encourage rapid growth of financial conglomerates. Depository institutions will respond by trying to develop ways around regulatory impediments. If they are successful, little will be accomplished except wasting resources in finding ways around regulations. If regulations are successful in keeping depository institutions out of new areas, the depositories will still

---

[12] The law requires only that the first $100,000 of domestic deposit accounts be insured for each customer.

waste resources in attempting to circumvent regulation. Furthermore, less regulated financial conglomerates will provide new services, but without competition from depository institutions. Over time depository institutions will shrink in importance.

Financial markets and institutions must be allowed to change and evolve with new technology and changing needs of the public. The trick is to allow change to occur while maintaining monetary stability and fighting abuses of financial power. Government supervision and some kinds of regulation must remain. The nature and form of the regulation and supervision must change, however.

A critical goal of regulation and insurance is to promote financial stability and protect the public's means of payment. This objective involves all institutions that provide means of payment to the public. All issuers of transactions accounts should be regulated uniformly irrespective of whether they are the Bank of America, Sears Roebuck, or Merrill Lynch. Furthermore, all transactions accounts should have federal insurance irrespective of size and type of either issuer or holder. Transactions accounts are part of the nation's monetary system and should be safe.

All the activities of financial-service firms need not be regulated and insured to the same degree. Much can be accomplished by requiring corporate structures for activities supported by insured transactions-accounts that are separate from other financial activities within a holding company or financial conglomerate.[13] The separately capitalized entity offering transactions accounts would be heavily regulated to limit risk and would have to hold safe assets, operating much like a mutual fund.[14] Other activities within the holding company or conglomerate would be conducted by separate corporations whose liabilities would not be insured and for which there would be no reserve requirements. These separate corporations would require little regulation beyond that applicable to any conventional firm in the United States. Their transactions with the transactions-account corporation would be highly restricted to protect transactions accounts. It is necessary to stop trying to insure and regulate everything and to stop trying to avoid "bank" failures no matter what. The transactions account function should be protected, but poorly managed conglomerates or holding companies should pay the economic price of their mismanagement.

---

[13] A compelling case for using "corporate separateness" as a regulatory tool is provided by Chase and Waage 1983.

[14] Here, the ability to vary capital requirements with risk would be particularly productive.

Market discipline provided by creditors who are at risk is a powerful tool that limits risk-taking, and it is a tool that regulators should be supporting and cultivating.

There are many ways to improve market discipline. The most commonly mentioned technique is to require greater disclosure while assuring creditors that their funds truly are at risk. Another promising approach is to require credit ratings and lines of credit for institutions offering CDs and other managed liabilities.

Credit ratings and lines of credit have provided impressive stability and market discipline in the U.S. commercial paper market. Issuers of commercial paper are normally required to have standby lines of credit with depository institutions. The size and terms of the credit lines are influenced by the performance and financial strength of the issuers, and, therefore, limit their risk-taking. The existence of credit lines protects holders of commercial paper and makes the market less prone to panics. Credit lines became standard practice following the panic created by failure of the Penn Central Railroad and help explain why the market has displayed considerable stability since that time. Issuers of CDs and other kinds of managed liabilities do not "back" their debt by credit lines.

The current situation in the markets for CDs and other managed liabilities encourages abrupt (discontinuous) drops in the liability bases of some institutions when there are "flights to quality." A market in lines of credit would smooth the adjustments for affected institutions, while imposing discipline in the longer run. Credit lines for managed liabilities would have the same function as in the commercial paper market. Institutions granting the lines would have a self-interest in monitoring the activities of these customers and in exercising the same kind of discipline as on participants in the commercial paper market and others.

Credit lines also create a safety net to protect institutions that encounter temporary liquidity problems associated with inability to rollover their liabilities. This is functionally a very different kind of safety net than the one that was created *ex post* for Continental Illinois. Here the purpose is not to keep otherwise sunken institutions afloat, but to keep otherwise seaworthy institutions from being sunk by a liquidity storm. The lines of credit would involve obligations to grant loans with maturities of, say, 30 to 180 days and would, therefore, be a more secure source of funds than is available in the federal funds or Euromarkets.

The market for lines of credit has the potential of replacing a substantial amount of regulation with more effective and efficient private discipline. The kinds of problems encountered by some institutions in rolling over their CDs and other managed liabilities in the mid-1970s and the problems of the mid-1980s would have been eased by a market for lines of credit. If the market had been in place, it is likely that market discipline would have prevented the rapid growth and inappropriate risk-taking that got certain institutions into trouble and triggered liquidity problems for others. Even if the liquidity strains had developed, they would have been handled by use of lines of credit. Heavy intervention by the regulators and calls for tighter government controls on depository institutions could have been reduced, if not eliminated.

It is important to stress that the line of credit market is not intended to replace the Federal Reserve's discount window, but rather to reserve the discount window for situations that private markets cannot handle. The discount window and open market operations must always be available as the ultimate sources of liquidity to the economy. While market discipline and private liquidity can make important contributions, there are potential situations when they are not sufficient. The line of credit market increases stability by providing market diversification; it is a market in risk. It cannot protect against nondiversifiable (macro) risk. For example, if a large number of CD issuers are affected simultaneously, as might occur if there were massive defaults on foreign loans or during a flight to currency, the central bank must provide the liquidity. Short of these emergencies, however, private markets can make important contributions, while lessening government regulation.

The requirement that firms issuing CDs obtain and publish credit ratings is also an attempt to emulate the commercial paper market. Credit ratings provide another source of market discipline and they will help establish risk premiums.

Extension of federal insurance to transactions account liabilities irrespective of size is recognition that these liabilities are an important source of instability for which no market solution is apparent. Transactions accounts are true "hot money."[15] There is little reason to believe that personal time accounts can provide a meaningful form of market discipline either. Since rapid loss of these accounts could trigger a liquidity crisis for depository institutions during flights to quality, it is probably best to insure them irrespective of size or type of issuer. The personal-nonpersonal account distinction in the United States is valuable because it is apparently impossible for market participants to find a way to extend insurance indirectly to nonpersonal accounts.

[15] See Diamond and Dybvig 1983.

Personal time accounts would join transactions accounts in supporting the activities of the low risk and tightly-regulated corporations within holding companies and conglomerates.

In order for meaningful and productive regulatory reform to be achieved, it will be necessary to reassign responsibilities while revamping and consolidating the numerous federal regulatory agencies that currently abound. This restructuring is long overdue and is an important element in achieving a stable and innovative financial system for the future.

References

Benston, George. ed. 1983. *Financial Services: The Changing Institutions and Government Policy*. Englewood Cliffs: Prentice Hall.

Chase, Samuel, and Waage, D. 1983. Corporate Separateness as a Tool of Bank Regulation. Washington, D.C: Samuel Chase and Company.

Corrigan, E. Gerald. 1982. Are Banks Special? *Annual Report*. Federal Reserve Bank of Minneapolis: 1–24.

Diamond, D.W. and Dybvig, P.H. 1983. Bank Runs, Deposit Insurance and Liquidity. *Journal of Political Economy:* June.

Eisenbeis, Robert. 1983. How Should Bank Holding Companies be Regulated? *Economic Review*. Federal Reserve Bank of Atlanta, January.

Ford, William. 1983. Banking's New Competition: Myths and Realities. *Economic Review*. Federal Reserve Bank of Atlanta, January.

Hester, Donald. 1981. Innovations and Monetary Control. *Brookings Papers on Economic Activity:* 1.

Kane, Edward. 1983. Strategic Planning in a World of Deregulation and Rapid Technological Change. Ohio State University Working Paper. August.

Pierce, James L. 1984. Did Financial Innovation Hurt the Great Monetarist Experiment? *American Economic Review*. May.

———. 1985. An Essay on the Expansion of Banking Powers. In Ingo, Walter, ed., *Deregulating Wall Street*. New York: John Wiley & Sons.

Phillips, Almarin. 1983. Changing Technology and Future Financial Activity. University of Pennsylvania Working Paper. May.

Rosenblum, Harvey and Pavel, Christine. 1984. Financial Services in Transion: The Effects of Nonbank Competitors. Federal Reserve Bank of Chicago.

Comments

Jim S. Mallyon

There is, of course, much I agree with in the stimulating and thought-provoking papers presented by Jim Pierce and Ralph Bryant. We must thank them for them.

I will not comment on most of the many points of agreement. Rather, where I agree with them, I will confine my comments to some points which, because of their importance and the fact that not everyone agrees with them, bear repeating. I will, however, mainly focus on some points of disagreement.

Mr. Pierce identifies in his paper the forces he sees as driving deregulation. They include strong competitive market pressures, technological innovation, and a variety of social and political forces. I believe the same forces can be found in many countries. They certainly have been at work in Australia. I note that both authors feel that deregulation may be slowing in the U.S.A. I also get a feeling that in the international area, Ralph Bryant appears to pine for increased regulation to promote macro economic and financial conditions that diverge between countries. He does come to the view that such a course is not likely to be feasible. He talks of the difficulties of getting toothpaste back into the tube. I wonder, if one achieves that, why it would not ooze out again. I see no reason why competitive market forces and technological change will not continue to see developments that have business move around regulatory barriers. I also believe that competition and technological change will lead to further deregulation over time although the actual timing could depend on other short-run considerations.

When Jim Pierce looks at future development of financial markets that he regards as sensible he makes the following points:

(i) There is a need to recognize that the fundamental economic and technological factors at work will make further integration of financial markets inevitable. These will, amongst other things, work against regulations in both domestic and foreign capital markets.

(ii) There is a need, as has already been suggested during discussions here, for there to be some—I emphasize some—official oversight over at least some financial institutions in the interests of financial stability. I will mention some qualifications to the general proposition which I, of course, agree with—in a moment.

(iii) There is a need to allow some financial institutions to fail. I believe without some such failures one will not have an efficient financial system. Of course, how they depart the scene is important for general stability of the financial system. It also seems to me that differences in attitudes in various countries about the question of whether institutions should fail would be one difficulty in achieving the international lender-of-last-resort arrangements suggested as necessary by Ralph Bryant.

Nor do I have any trouble with the concern expressed by Bryant that supervision of world capital markets is an area for further development by central banks and that in the meantime unregulated capital will continue to grow. It is a question of whether the extent of present regulation is as narrow as suggested by Bryant.

I would at this point like to mention my qualification to support for prudential controls in the interests of financial stability. I fear that prudential supervision could become an overly strong growth factor for regulation in the coming years. It is unfortunately only too easy to impose particular requirements in the name of stability. We all agree there should be some requirements. The crucial question is the assessment of the appropriate detail. I think there is a rich field for analysis here. I hope academics quickly focus on this aspect of the subject and come to the assistance of those who feel a light hand is appropriate.

I am not so sure of the general applicability of some other suggestions Mr. Pierce makes about future financial developments and the appropriate regulatory framework for the U.S. Indeed, as I reflect on it, I wonder whether the advantage he and Jim Tobin attribute to regulation of all transaction accounts comes about because in the U.S. it would mean a reduction in the range of deposit insurance and regulation. In the Australian environment it would mean an increase in regulation. Thus, it might be a second-best solution for the U.S. For Australia, it would in my mind be a retrograde step compared to the present situation.

I particularly wonder about the suggestions that all issuers of transaction accounts should be regulated uniformly and the suggested device of requiring separate corporate structures for activities supported by insured transaction accounts. It seems to me that we might simply again be trying to define what in the past we unsuccessfully tried to define as banking. Beyond that I find it difficult to believe that one can identify the transaction accounts that are to be the focus of regulation. We all know that these days financial institutions are offering financial packages involving linkages between transaction accounts on which no, low, or lower interest is paid and other accounts on which higher rates are paid. The simple question is where would one draw the line? The answer, of course, is not simple.

I also wonder why regulations imposed on these accounts will not lead to the emergence of near-competitors? It seems to me we have been around this area before and the experience has given us some clear case-studies to draw on.

That said, it seems to me that there is perhaps a more important question as to whether the focus of regulation on the public's means of payments should be on the balances at the end of the line, so to speak (and how they are invested), or rather on the stability of the organizations financially involved in the process of effecting payment. When we contemplate EFTs, it is not even clear that all participants will be financial institutions.

Again, I wonder about both the effectiveness and appropriateness of seeking to regulate only one segment of a financial company or conglomerate. I presume Ralph Bryant, with his concern to cover the worldwide operations of banks, would also question the effectiveness of controls on only part of a financial institution's business. As to the appropriateness, a crucial issue is whether there is interaction between the standing of the regulated segments and other areas of the conglomerate.

I wonder whether a better base for the prudential regulation would be to establish oversight of the total operations of those financial institutions regarded as being at the low-risk end of the spectrum of financial institutions. That does not preclude their undertaking risky business but would ensure they had a balance sheet (capital, liquidity, etc.) which was consistent with their overall low risk status. That view possibly comes easily to me because of the narrow definition of bank that has been long held in Australia. I must point out that experience has shown how hard it is to meaningfully separate the business of associated companies. At the end of the day the accountants establish separate positions, but frequently they hardly describe a meaningful separation of behavior from the point of view of either the financial institutions or their customers.

I will limit myself to three other brief comments.

First, I agree with Mr. Pierce that in the U.S. environment with wide-ranging deposit insurance arrangements, it is difficult to have other than a wide-ranging definition of money. I am not certain that under a different institutional structure markets might not establish a narrower workable concept of money. That gets us back to whether the regulations make that concept stable or whether over time regulations cause the emergence of close substitutes. It may be a question of whether controls are market-oriented or not. If they are not, over time I believe one will have to use very broad definitions.

Second, on the question of targets, I might mention that in Australia some conditional forecasts/targets were recently abandoned. That was for the simple reason that with deregulation and the shifting of business to banks and banks onto balance sheets they had become meaningless. One interesting development is that market analysts have complained they no longer have evidence of what policy the authorities are following. Let me simply say it may be they have been short-circuiting the market analysis you would expect of them and replacing it by watching movements in a single number. I suggest what needs to be changed is clear, and it is not substituting another single number for them to watch.

Third, could I conclude by noting a small point Ralph Bryant made. He mentions that Australia is one country considering regulations aimed at discriminating in favor of banking activities conducted in foreign currencies. He notes a commissioned paper by Professor Hewson which was published in 1982. I might simply note that since that paper was available the environment in Australia has become less favorable to such special action. After all, we have floated the Australian dollar, completely disbanded exchange control, admitted 17 new banks with substantial or total foreign ownership, and set up an open season for foreign institutions to rearrange or establish a position in our money market sector.

Comments

Joseph Bisignano

The papers I have been asked to comment on are broad in nature and involve many fundamental questions in monetary and financial economics. I think it best to state at the outset what I think is their primary subject matter. The first key issue is what distinguishes a "deposit" from a non-deposit liability in a financial institution. I focus on this because a fundamental concern of these papers is which liabilities of depository institutions ought to have insurance attributes and which ought not to. The answer often centers around reasons to insure the payments medium, and methods of doing so, and reasons not to insure other liabilities of depository institutions. I would broaden the concern to that of the optimal provision of means of payment and the desired availability of a "riskless asset" available to store wealth in financial form. Implicit in the judgment to insure certain liabilities is the claim that they possess public goods characteristics. Failure of some financial institutions is argued to result in external effects beyond the direct wealth effects on the individual deposit holders.

A second concern of these papers is whether less regulated financial markets and increased availability of domestic and international financial services, allowing contracting over a wider number of states of nature and over all future dates, increases the likelihood of domestic and international financial instability. At a conceptual level this concern focuses on the notion of "equilibrium" in financial markets. At the practical level it involves the determination of the necessary degree of prudential supervision and/or the "optimal" degree of equity capitalization of financial institutions. Lurking behind this second concern is the question of the degree to which private institutions which create goods with potentially large externalities should be allowed to freely determine their "risk exposure"—that is, the output level for certain liabilities.

Third, the two papers are also concerned with the problems that financial innovation and deregulation pose for monetary control. For reasons of space, I will focus primarily on the first two issues. My comments first will be conceptual in nature, and then specific to some of the normative comments of the papers.

These papers are asking a fundamental question of public policy: how can greater financial innovation and deregulation increase potential financial market instability and in what way should government provide supervision and insurance to minimize the externalities caused by instability? To provide some framework for discussion, I appeal to two fundamental notions of efficiency in financial markets which, not surprisingly, formed part of James Tobin's Fred Hirsch Memorial Lecture in his discussion of the efficiency of the financial system.[1] The first is the notion of efficiency in the Arrow-Debreu sense (what Tobin calls full insurance efficiency), which consists of a world of competitive markets for goods and services defined over all states of nature and for all future periods. In arguing that deregulation and innovation in financial markets move the competitive world closer to an Arrow-Debreu world with numerous contingent futures markets, we should recall two theoretical problems with such appeal. First, imperfect or incomplete information may result in competitive markets having no equilibrium, as described some years ago by Rothschild and Stiglitz.[2] Secondly, contingent markets may not exist when the states of nature depend on the behavior of the agents in the financial systems, as described by Radner and Hahn.[3]

The second notion I appeal to is that of valuation efficiency, the ability of a market to assess "accurately" the present value of uncertain future payment streams. The difficulty of empirically establishing the latter in existing financial markets—for example, recent work by Robert Shiller and others on testing the expectations theory of the term structures of interest rates—gives rise by itself to skepticism over the merits of believing that financial markets can be unambiguously improved in a competitive sense by permitting greater freedom for the development of new financial contracts and greater competition in the provision of

[1] James Tobin, "On the Efficiency of the Financial System," *Lloyds Bank Review* (July 1984).

[2] Michael Rothschild and Joseph Stiglitz, "Equilibrium in Competitive Insurance Markets: An Essay on the Economics of Imperfect Information," *Quarterly Journal of Economics* (1976).

[3] See Frank Hahn, *Equilibrium and Macroeconomics*, chapter 2, MIT Press, Cambridge, Mass., (1984), and R. Radner, "Competitive Equilibrium Under Uncertainty," *Econometrica* (1972).

financial liabilities that act as means of payment.[4] In short, without assurance of greater efficiency in valuation, claims for improved efficiency of competitive financial equilibrium may be overstated.

Two practical problems stand in the way of moving toward a satisfaction of these market efficiency criteria, disclosure, and enforceability of contracts. Thomas Cargill has reported, for example, that Japan has no substantial financial disclosure requirements or private credit rating agencies. For other countries, the quality of available financial information may be worse than no information. It is also questionable whether international contracts like those involved in our current international debt crises are legally enforceable, in the same sense that domestic contracts are enforceable. This latter point has recently been emphasized by Niehans.[5] Thus, there are plenty of theoretical and practical reasons to caution against unrestrained enthusiasm for promoting further financial innovation and deregulation.

Given these theoretical and practical reservations, what broad issues need to be addressed in a debate over the desirable degree of financial innovation and deregulation? I can think of three: separability, enforceability, and the moral hazard problem.

By the separability problem, I mean the division of certain parts of a financial institution into insured and regulated blocs. There are particular services—for example, Pierce mentions payments or transactions services—which one may describe as "fundamental," and thus requiring government insurance and regulation. How to divide large financial institutions into independent insured and non-insured blocs and to convey to the marketplace that these blocs are fundamentally separate for insurance purposes is difficult, particularly within the structure of the bank holding company structure in the United States. Pierce appeals to the concept of "corporate separateness" as a regulatory tool, in which certain financial activities of a holding company or financial conglomerate would be undertaken by separate corporations whose

---

[4] See Robert J. Shiller, "The Volatility of Long-term Interest Rates and Expectations Models of the Term Structure," *Journal of Political Economy* (December 1979) and Kenneth J. Singleton, "Expectations Models of the Term Structure and Implied Variance Bounds," *Journal of Political Economy* (December 1980). It should be mentioned, however, that the finding that asset price volatility is greater than that implied by "conventional" expectations models of security valuation may be due to their assumption of the risk neutrality of investors. To understand how risk aversion may lead to an increase in the dispersion of asset prices, see Stephen F. LeRoy and C. J. LaCivita, "Risk Aversion and the Dispersion of Asset Prices," *Journal of Business* (October 1981).

[5] Jurg Niehans, "International Debt with Unenforceable Claims," *Economic Review*, Federal Reserve Bank of San Francisco (Winter 1985).

liabilities would *not* have insurance or reserve requirements, while another separate corporation would have insured and reservable liabilities.[6]

In my opinion, Pierce overemphasizes the need to insure the integrity of the "payments mechanism" and de-emphasizes the importance of intermediation services provided by the banking industry in promoting economic growth and stability. With the gradual breakdown in the prohibition of banks offering new lines of financial services, the move towards "universal banking" in the United States will test the feasibility of the notion of corporate separateness. To date, a degree of corporate separateness in banking in the United States has been imposed by law and regulation. In particular, the Glass-Steagall Act of 1933 prevents banks from undertaking most underwriting activities. But also the Banking and Bank Holding Company Acts attempt to delineate a bank, and the latter empower the Federal Reserve to determine "permissible" holding company lines of commerce.

A move towards "universal banking," for example, as it exists in Germany, could create a serious information (signal) extraction problem for the private market, since the ability of an institution to engage in traditional banking business, together with underwriting and the ownership of non-banks, creates, if not potential "conflicts of interest," at least uncertainty over the major interests of the conglomerate's management. This was a central question raised by the Gessler Report, which investigated the benefits and weaknesses of universal banking in Germany.[7] This is as well a problem for the insurers, regulators, and government bodies vested with serving the public interest.

The second issue of "enforceability" of claims is legal in nature and deals with the recourse to legal enforceability of financial claims in case of default. This issue is of some weight in the international lending area as it affects the economic nature of contracts, alters accurate risk-return assessments, and increases the risks which central banks are exposed to in insuring the stability of their "independent" financial

---

[6] "According to the separateness doctrine, if two or more corporations are affiliated (i.e., have common ownership) the fact that one encounters difficulties does not imply a legal obligation on the part of the other to come to the rescue. Using the separateness approach, it ought to be possible to permit corporations engaged in other activities to own banks as well, without requiring the regulators to attempt to oversee non-bank activities in the manner that banking activities are supervised." Samuel Chase and Donn L. Waage, "Corporate Separateness as a Tool of Bank Regulation," Samuel Chase and Company, Washington, D.C., (1983).

[7] Hans-Jacob Krummel, "German Universal Banking Scrutinized: Some Remarks Concerning the Gessler Report," *Journal of Banking and Finance* (March 1980).

systems. The need for greater cooperation among supervisory authorities as a result is obvious.[8]

The issues of corporate separateness and enforceability are important largely because of the well-known "moral hazard problem"—the divergence between private marginal cost and marginal social cost caused by public insurance programs that lead to inefficient allocations of resources. Public insurance of private financial deposit liabilities is said to increase the incentive of insured financial institutions to assume (consume) greater risk in order to seek a greater expected return. This problem confronts all government insurance programs which do not use market criteria to set insurance premiums. Financial institutions have the incentive to "leverage their insurance," in a sense implicitly extending the insurance umbrella provided by government over all of the liabilities of the institution. I interpret this problem as the reason that Pierce, for example, wishes to separate the institutions into insured and noninsured liability blocs, so that the noninsured blocs do not create a moral hazard problem for the regulatory authority.

Pierce is of the opinion, I believe, that separating the transactions account services of financial institutions and insuring them fully gets away from the moral hazard problem. Bryant attributes the moral hazard dilemma to be the prudential oversight reason for the supervision and regulation of financial intermediaries. Is it simply the prevention of bank runs which should concern us? Pierce apparently thinks this to be the case. If so, a regime of 100 percent reserve requirements would appear to solve the problem. I doubt, however, whether insuring the convertibility of sight deposits into currency helps us out of the problem, particularly the international problem Bryant is addressing. It is the entire function of financial intermediation which is at risk.

The potential breakdown of the financial intermediation function threatens the stability of trade in real goods, which relies on the ability to use saving as a means of transferring wealth through time, and on the ability to use borrowing to expand one's intertemporal budget constraint.[9] The payments system concern is to my mind a convenient rug

[8] On the need for greater international cooperation in banking supervision, see Chapter IV of *The Internationalization of Banking: The Policy Issues*, OECD, Paris (1983).

[9] An interesting recent treatment of the theoretical structure of financial intermediation and its role in economic growth may be seen in Robert M. Townsend, "Financial Structure and Economic Activity," *The American Economic Review* (December 1983). Ben S. Bernanke examines the role of the breakdown of financial intermediation in contributing to the severity and length of the Great Depression in "Nonmonetary Effects of the Financial Crisis in the Propagation of the Great Depression," *American Economic Review* (June 1983).

under which we often sweep intermediation problems which often are less amenable to easy characterization or solution. How to ensure the health of the domestic and international market in financial intermediation, where the present value of future claims is difficult to evaluate, where equity bases are highly leveraged, and where public policy has both the desire to foster greater efficiency in the exchange of future claims and the desire to minimize the externalities on the financial system caused by the default of these claims, is more at the heart of current concern over recent financial innovation and deregulation.

Both papers seem to imply that greater "efficiency" in the provision of financial services necessarily increases market risk. At least, neither paper suggests that risk might be reduced with greater financial deregulation and innovation. In fact, behind some of the analysis I thought I saw the long-time controversy over the stabilizing or destabilizing properties of speculation. A major thread running through both papers is the suggestion that governments have been slow to realize the possibility of major financial crisis caused by financial innovation, deregulation, and internationalization.

But I do not see why greater efficiency in the provision of financial services *necessarily* leads to a greater likelihood of financial instability. Bryant warns of the "passive drift" of government policies, suggesting that it "may take a major economic or financial crisis to catalyze a widespread awareness of underlying trends." Pierce states that "the potential for instability has been increasing recently." But are these risks of instability really the result of financial innovation and deregulation? The case for this is not clearly drawn. I would argue that much of the "potential for instability" is the result of increased government protection via the increase in explicit deposit insurance and the implicit insurance given large depositors by the regulatory authorities. Another characterization might be that both Pierce and Bryant are struggling with the issue of how to ensure a more complete Arrow-Debreu competitive equilibrium in financial markets when in recent years financial markets do not seem to have earned a good track record in valuing future claims, as measured by current valuation theories.

Let us move to the issue of monetary control. Governments determine the quantity of fiat debt. Central banks determine the quantity of fiat debt held by the public that will be interest-bearing vs. non-interest-bearing, the latter acting as means of payment. Financial deregulation and innovation may alter government's potential inflation tax revenue from its monopoly over money creation if the private market creates instruments which reduce the demand for non-interest-bearing fiat debt, the monetary base.

Financial innovation and deregulation thus may create problems for monetary control. Some central banks have resisted moves to deregulate their financial markets for precisely this reason. Whether deregulation and innovation have been a problem for monetary authorities is an empirical issue, involving, among other things, the stability of the demand for base money and the private nonbank sector's demand for both narrowly and broadly defined balances. On the surface, it has led to reduced emphasis, even abandonment in some cases, of central bank targeting of monetary aggregates.

Canada may be a textbook example of how financial deregulation and innovation have changed the direction of short-run monetary policy. The principal innovation in Canada in recent years has been the introduction by chartered banks of daily interest checkable savings accounts. Their introduction drew funds both from savings and personal checking accounts. While the introduction of checkable savings accounts in Canada led to little growth in Canadian M1 between mid-1981 and late 1982, it later led to increases in this aggregate outstripping the growth in nominal spending between late 1982 and mid-1983, largely in response to declines in interest rates.[10] The shift out of personal checking accounts continued into 1984, resulting in a wide divergence between two alternative measures of the "narrow" monetary aggregate in Canada, M1 and M1A, where the latter aggregate includes daily interest checkable savings deposits and nonpersonal notice deposits at banks. As a consequence, Canada has abandoned the targeting of narrow monetary aggregates.

While there are certainly good examples of how deregulation and innovation have recently affected money demand in particular countries, I would caution against wholesale application of this conjecture. Financial deregulation and innovation have taken place recently in an environment of worldwide declines in inflation rates among major industrial countries. The significant and related declines in interest rates in the United States in 1982 and 1984 led to major increases in growth rates of the narrow monetary aggregate M1. This has led some to argue that the United States has been subject to "unexplainable" shifts in velocity. While the velocity behavior in the United States may have been unanticipated, it is not entirely unexplainable. Much of it can be statistically captured by the interest rate induced increase in the demand to hold nominal money balances. Nor is the U.S. velocity behavior unique. As Figure 1 of the paper by Yumoto, Shima, Koike,

---

[10] See *Bank of Canda Review* (December 1983 and January 1985), "Monetary Aggregates: Some Recent Developments."

and Taguchi clearly shows, six of the seven major industrial economies have seen major reversals in their trend M1 velocity behavior since 1980. I would argue that this behavior is more likely due to the disinflation of the 1980s than to financial deregulation and innovation.

While deregulation does seem to have been responsible for some increase in the short-run interest elasticity of money demand in the United States, it can be anticipated that over the longer run—once stock adjustments to the availablity of the new instruments are complete and transactions balances yield interest returns which move with market rates—the demand for money is likely to be *less* interest-elastic. If the "own yield" on transactions balances moves directly with market rates, the differential will stabilize, causing the textbook "LM schedule" to be more vertical. One result will be that random shocks to the "real side" of the economy will be absorbed more by movements in interest rates than by changes in nominal income. In the short run, however, it is true that money demand functions may be "destabilized" by the introduction of new transactions instruments which combine both savings and payments attributes.

My last point on the issue of monetary control is a caution that the difficulty encountered with "monetary control" may not all stem from the demand side of the money equation. Money supply, specifically the behavior of the monetary authorities, has been influenced in some cases by the atypical behavior of real interest rates and the U.S. dollar exchange rate since 1980. The supply of monetary base during this period has been sufficiently jostled by shifts in central bank objectives in recent years to caution against repeated employment of the argument that financial innovation and deregulation have destabilized money demand relationships. The "identification problem" should not be lost sight of.

My comments have ranged far and wide, I hope reflecting more the breadth of the two papers than my tendency to be discursive. I end with one short note: let's be practical. Is the only fundamental concern with the effects of deregulation and innovation in the United States that of ensuring the stability of the payments mechanism? I don't think it is. There seems to be public interest in the private provision of a government-insured savings vehicle. Moreover, there is public concern with the externalities and adjustment costs involved in the potential for failure of large private institutions, be they banks, saving institutions, or auto companies. I believe there to be a public demand for the government to provide insurance for nondiversifiable risk, much of which is caused by our own or other governments' policies. What appears clear is that a major difference exists between countries, and their central banks, in the manner in which they "socialize" the costs of non-diversifiable macro risks, with some countries preferring to spread the costs of these nondiversifiable risks over the entire economy rather than having them concentrated in any one sector alone. In this sense, the U.S. treatment of the failure of the Continental Illinois Bank was a major shift in government policy towards financial intermediation failure.

CHAPTER 22

Comments

Shōichi Rōyama

I would like to start my comment by relating briefly an experience I had earlier this month. I had an opportunity to visit a small bank in a region of the U.S. The president of the bank was very proud of his traditional bank management. He was very careful to preserve good relations with his customers. For instance, he welcomed his guests in his small president's office decorated with family photos, his diploma, and so on. According to him, his customers rewarded him with a good profit for his hard work from early in the morning to late in the evening. This example—a tiny example perhaps—shows that customer relations are one important element of the financial market, which is quite different from the textbook market models such as the Walrasian market. Let me call this textbook market an open market where, in stark contrast to the customers' market, price is the only concern of the participants. I believe that the customers' market and the open market are two typical forms of market organization in the financial world.

The wide-ranging paper by Dr. Bryant states that worldwide integration of domestic open markets is now under way. I quite agree with this observation and its policy implications as shown in his paper. However, the same statement can hardly be applied to the customers' market.

What is the likely impact of the internationally developing open market on the domestic customers' market, or the traditional market? The relations between the two types of market may provide the most important key in considering the future structures of a financial system in individual countries, or in the world as a whole.

The main concern of this third session is to investigate the process of financial innovations and to depict a vision of the financial system in the future. I believe the financial system is moving much more toward an open market system from a customers' system.

Mr. Yumoto et al. and Mr. Greenwood yesterday provided excellent surveys of the ongoing process of change in individual countries and in the world. I believe that it is our task now to sum up the case studies and construct a general analysis of financial innovations in order to form an idea about desirable financial reform, and to clarify a vision of the future financial system.

The causes of the transition of the financial system from the traditional customers'-market-dominated system to an open-market-dominated system were pointed out yesterday. However, I would like to emphasize that we should pay attention to the diffusion process of financial innovations as well as their causes.

As almost all the participants at this conference may agree, financial innovations are the product of private entities led by their own self-interests. In other words, there has to be some incentive in the existing financial system to introduce new products, new techniques, new organizations, and so on. The incentive for such financial innovation is, needless to say, profits, particularly profits which are expected to continue for many years.

The large discrepancy among rates of return on assets in the existing markets will provide a profit opportunity for innovators. This aspect was emphasized in the papers presented yesterday, and also in Professor Pierce's paper presented this morning. I do not want to discuss the reason for the large discrepancy. Instead, I would like to emphasize that in order for innovations to be caused, the discrepancy should be large relative to the cost of such innovations. In this connection, I believe that it is important that the information revolution in recent years has contributed to the considerable reduction of the cost of innovation.

In short, financial innovations have been introduced because the innovators expect to earn a net profit under new economic and technological circumstances.

This statement, however, must be followed by the question of whether the large discrepancy among rates of return on various assets on the one hand and the declining cost of innovations on the other is both the necessary and sufficient condition for financial innovations to emerge.

I believe that it is only the necessary condition. From my viewpoint, there exist the following sufficient conditions for the success and wide diffusion of innovations:

    1) There should exist deep and wide-open financial markets such as the secondary market for government bonds or the TB market.

    2) There should be competition in the financial services industry.

3) There should be an abundant supply of managerial resources in the financial service industry.

Judging from the paper by Professor Pierce, these sufficient conditions have been satisfied historically in the U.S. financial system, and thus, as far as the U.S. is concerned, there is no necessity to pay the matter any special attention. However, in Japan and, I believe, in most other countries, some of these sufficient conditions are either not fulfilled or have just started to be fulfilled. Very recently, owing particularly to the internationalization of financial systems, the first condition has been realized. However, the situation with regard to the second and third conditions differ from country to country. This leads to the differences we can observe in the process of financial innovation. By "process" I mean here to include not only the cause but also the diffusion of financial innovations.

Such a consideration provides us a variety of policy implications.

The first is the impact of government deficit. Yesterday afternoon, Dr. McClam emphasized this point. I would like to endorse his view in the following way. In some countries, like Japan, government deficits are financed by the issuance of marketable government bonds, not by borrowing from the bank. The first sufficient condition for financial innovations was fulfilled by the emergence and development of the secondary market for these bonds. This pattern has been typical in Japan since 1975, when massive government deficit was financed by government bonds. In other countries, increased accessibility to the international open markets might have played a more important role than the emergence of a domestic open market. In short, government deficits and internationalization have played key roles in the degree of satisfaction of the sufficient conditions for financial innovation.

Second, anti-trust or competition policy applied to the financial services industry plays a key role in the financial innovation process. Some countries may not have any competition regulation which applies to the financial service industry; others do have it. Japan has a very systematic anti-trust policy. However, the banking industry is in almost cases under exemption. I believe that the different policy attitude with regard to competition has a great bearing on the differences in the financial innovation process.

Third, managerial resource problems in the financial service industry and how they are dealt with is a quite important issue, particularly for the future development of the financial system. This may be one of the problems of human resource development policy. The internationalization of financial services can be explained from the point of view of managerial resource problems in this industry in the following way: the internationalization of banks or other financial institutions means a kind of export or import of managerial resources from one country to the other. Such movement of managerial resources should be considered more carefully and should be analyzed.

Let me conclude my comment in this way. The future shape of the financial system under financial innovations will differ from country to country, even though there will be considerable progress in the worldwide integration of financial markets, especially in the field of wholesale, open market transactions, as Dr. Bryant emphasized in his paper.

However, the conduct of government policies such as interest-rate regulation, government deficit, foreign exchange control, and competition policy, as well as human resource development and other policies, will determine how dominant the open market price mechanisms will be in the working of the whole financial system in the future.

Comments

Stephen Potter

It seemed to me that, as the representative of the OECD, I would be best employed in seeking to realize a comparative advantage on the "international" side. As Professor Pierce's paper touches only peripherally on international aspects, most of what I have to say therefore relates to Dr. Bryant's paper.

If I may say so, that paper has all the strengths one associates with Ralph Bryant. It is careful, it is comprehensive, and it is clear. I found it helpful in sorting out ideas. Where I was disappointed—and this no doubt reflects my own professional deformation—was right at the end of the paper when, having said what appeared to me sensible things about multilateral decision-making in respect of regulation, supervision, and taxation, the author seems rather at a loss when he comes to macroeconomic policies, and merely regrets the lack of an agreed analytical framework for assessing international economic linkages.

It is certainly true that an agreed framework is lacking, though (if I may insert something of a *cri de coeur* at this point) this is not for want of trying! Even so, it would perhaps have been possible to say something in this paper about how the trends towards greater international interconnectedness on the financial side have affected the way economies interact internationally, and the implications that follow for the constraints and possibilities for macroeconomic policy.

To begin with, the exchange rate does indeed seem to be determined in an asset market. This is something that is merely asserted in much of today's literature. But it is instructive to look at this question in the light of Bryant's discussion of the extent to which financial flows lead or follow international trade, or have nothing to do with it. It has become one of the stylized facts of international finance that daily transactions in the foreign exchange markets amount to $100 billion or more. This can be taken to be essentially the daily churning of the $2.7

trillion—perhaps by now close to $3 trillion—of banking assets. Meanwhile, world trade on a daily basis amounts to less than $10 billion. Clearly the overwhelming influence in the market in the short run comes from purely financial transactions.

If we look at a longer period, say a year, the $3 trillion stock of banking assets does not look so enormous in relation to trade flows of $2 trillion, but it still completely dwarfs trade or current account imbalances, large as some of these have now become.

The dominance of financial transactions in exchange rate determination is by now of course part of conventional wisdom. Yet it is a fairly recent phenomenon. Up to 1979, it was still true to say, for example, that broad movements in the Japanese yen were quite well explained by movements in the current account, though this was admittedly already less true of other major currencies.

Most people would presumably still expect the exchange rate to be determined by purchasing power parity or the current account over the longer run, but with a less and less precise idea any more what that may mean. In the past year or so, exchange rates have been seen to go in the "wrong" direction in relation to current account imbalances that were already large and rising.

Increased capital mobility has, almost by definition, made it easier to finance current account positions. Since 1973, the average absolute size of current account surpluses and deficits, in relation to nations' GNP, has been larger than before. This is partly explained by the OPEC surpluses and oil-related deficits, but seems more generally to reflect the greater ease of financing.

It would seem, then, that although greater financial integration tends to strengthen the international transmission of interest rates, the pressure towards convergent business cycle developments, via the current account, is weakened. This of course pre-supposes that the countries concerned are not close to their creditworthiness limits. And it is not clear how such limits might themselves be affected by greater freedom of capital movements.

The pressure from the market to adjust current account positions may be still weaker, or even non-existent for a prolonged period, for a country that is operating an unbalanced mix of monetary and fiscal policy—if, that is, the Mundell-Fleming (or should we now say Feldstein-Volcker?) conditions apply, such that expansionary fiscal policy with unchanged money growth yields an *appreciation* of the currency.

Most countries other than the United States have normally assumed that fiscal expansion, even if it is not accommodated, would lead to currency *de*preciation. But increasing capital mobility could at some point be expected to turn this result around, with the effect of higher interest rates dominating the worsening of the current account. For what it is worth, simulation runs with the latest experimental version of OECD's international linkage model give an appreciation in the case of Japan and Germany as well as for the United States. Many financial commentators seem to assume that the same would be true in practice for the United Kingdom.

But whether or not this is so does not seem to detract from the more general conclusion that with the internationalization of banking and the general reduction of obstacles to capital flows the pressure to adjust the current account can be rather slight for a considerable period. Indeed, for considerable periods, and of course within limits, it might be thought that the current account could be forgotten about. But a *persistent* current deficit inevitably involves accumulation of net foreign debt, and adjustment pressures may suddenly become acute as a "credit-worthiness" limit, which is impossible to determine in advance, is reached. This is what happened in Latin America. And it is what could happen to the United States.

The rather pedestrian conclusion I draw from this is that moves on regulation, supervision, and taxation need to be accompanied by increased efforts at what is known in the jargon as "multilateral surveillance" of macroeconomic policies. Clearly the system has quite a lot of "give" in it, and our knowledge is deficient, so that any attempt to "fine-tune" policy cooperation would be vain. What would be involved, rather, is the exercise of "peer pressure" among different countries' policymakers, with a view to effecting "preventive" modifications of policies designed to bring economies back on to more sustainable paths *before* they run into trouble. And such a surveillance process would, it seems, need to cover the fiscal-monetary mix.

Implications for Monetary Policy

7

Monetary Policy under Financial Innovation and Deregulation

Robert E. Hall

I. Introduction

No monetary policy is immune from the destabilizing effect of financial change. In this paper, I look first at a simple model of an open economy, subject to the three types of shocks that are relevant for stabilization: financial shocks, spending shocks, and price shocks. I argue that, of the three, the financial shocks are by far the largest concern for monetary policy. The basis of the argument is the proposition that controlling the growth of nominal GNP is a sensible compromise between the goals of price stability and output stability. Spending and price shocks are shown to have little impact upon nominal GNP, even though they have important effects separately on real GNP and the price level.

Although financial shocks are the predominant source of fluctuations in nominal GNP and therefore the source of the most trouble in monetary policy, it is less clear that monetary policy should actively try to offset financial shocks. I show that the shocks are relatively difficult to predict. Over the past two decades of U.S. history, most of the shocks have occurred during financial panics, most often preceding recessions. The most important exception was a large stimulative shock that occurred the year after the most significant financial deregulation.

The paper concludes by pointing out a further move toward financial liberalization that could have significant effect in reducing the magnitude of financial shocks. If the central bank paid near-market interest rates on reserves, and expanded the stock of reserves to meet the resulting increased demand, the incidence of destabilizing panics would fall. With an economy saturated in reserves, a policy of constant growth of the monetary base could be expected to provide a reasonably smooth evolution of nominal GNP.

2. A Model of the Impacts of Financial, Spending, and Price Shocks

In this section I will work out a model of an open economy with gradually adjusting prices, subject to random shocks in financial markets, in aggregate spending, and in the price level. The model combines the IS-LM model of income determination in the short run with a price adjustment equation. The latter takes account of both aggregate demand effects on prices and the effects of changes in the exchange rate.

I will characterize the financial side of the economy in terms of the LM curve:

$$y = \mu r + m - p + \varepsilon \tag{2.1}$$

Here y is the log of real GNP, r is the interest rate, m is the log of the monetary base, p is the log of the price level, and ε is a random disturbance. The LM curve describes the combinations of output, interest rates, and prices that equate the supply and demand for the monetary base. In this and the subsequent equations, the variables are expressed as deviations from trend. Moreover, the economy is viewed as starting in the immediately preceding year on the trend path of all variables. That is, the LM curve shows the combinations of the changes in real GNP, interest rates, and price levels that equate the demand for the monetary base to the trend increase in the supply. The random shift in the LM curve, ε, will have a major role in the ensuing discussion. Both changes in financial regulations and shifts in consumer preferences among monetary assets will be reflected in ε.

The model characterizes the spending side of the economy in terms of the IS curve:

$$y = -\alpha r + \eta \tag{2.2}$$

The IS curve describes the combinations of real GNP and the interest rate that equate the demand and supply of goods and services. Spending is perturbed by a random shift, η. Again, y stands for the growth of real GNP and r for the change in the interest rate. Although spending is presumably controlled by the real interest rate, I will assume that no important changes occur in expected inflation from one year to the next.

The third equation describes the process of price adjustment:

$$p = \phi y - \delta r + \nu \tag{2.3}$$

The rate of increase, p, of the price level is positively related to real GNP, y, negatively related to the interest rate, r, and is perturbed by a shock, ν. The first term is the standard Phillips curve relation of inflation to the excess demand for goods and services. The second term is the reduced form of the relationship described by Rudiger Dornbusch (1976) for an economy with a floating exchange rate and gradually adjusting prices: an event which raises the interest rate also causes appreciation of the currency, which lowers the price of tradable goods and so lowers the overall price level. The disturbance, ν, incorporates all sources of variation in the price level apart from the excess demand and tradables effects captured by the other terms. It includes both spontaneous domestic inflation shocks, such as bursts of trade union militance, and influences from the world economy not related to changes in the domestic interest rate, such as oil price increases and jumps in the exchange rate.

Let me start the discussion of the properties of the model by considering the case of unresponsive prices: $\phi = \delta = 0$. In this case, the price level next year is determined just by the random price shift, ν. The solution of the model is

$$y = \theta m + \theta \varepsilon + (1 - \theta)\eta - \theta \nu \tag{2.4}$$

$$p = \nu \tag{2.5}$$

The sum of these two equations is the equation for the change in nominal GNP (since the variables are logs):

$$y + p = \theta m + \theta \varepsilon + (1 - \theta)(\eta + \nu) \tag{2.6}$$

All of the relevant properties of the economy are described by the parameter θ. In terms of the original parameters, it is

$$\theta = \frac{1}{1 + \mu/\alpha} \tag{2.7}$$

If money demand is fairly unresponsive to the interest rate (μ is small) or spending is fairly sensitive to the interest rate (α is large), then θ is close to one. In this case, the spending disturbance, η, is relatively unimportant for real GNP. The financial disturbance, ε, and the price disturbance, ν, affect real GNP with nearly unit elasitcity. However, because the price disturbance, ν, affects real GNP with elasticity -1, and affects the price level with elasticity of $+1$, that disturbance has little effect on nominal GNP. The only disturbance that is important for nominal GNP is the financial disturbance, ε. To the extent that monetary policy is concerned with keeping nominal GNP growth on target, the only important issue is the financial disturbance. The spending disturbance has little impact on real or nominal GNP. The price disturbance has a strong effect on real GNP and prices, but in opposite directions.

A modern open economy with financial deregulation has a θ close to one, I will argue. First, money demand is relatively inelastic with respect to the interest rate. Banks are free to pay close to market rates on all deposits. Non-interest-bearing currency is a relatively small part of the total money stock. When interest rates rise, the public does not substitute away from money vigorously because their earnings on money rise more or less in parallel with interest rates. Second, spending is sensitive to interest rates. In addition to the response of total investment to the interest rate, the division of spending between domestic and foreign sources is effectively highly sensitive to the interest rate. A small increase in the domestic interest rate brings appreciation in the currency and a less competitive position in tradables. In other words, in an open economy without trade barriers or capital controls, fluctuations in domestic spending cause corresponding fluctuations in the current account rather than in GNP.

The fixed-price analysis is too simple for two reasons. First, changes in the domestic economy bring changes in the exchange rate, with consequent changes in the price of tradables and thus in the overall price level. Second, wage rates and prices of nontradables are somewhat responsive to the degree of excess demand or supply. The solution to the model with these two factors, captured by the coefficients ϕ and δ respectively, is

$$y = \theta\gamma\left(m + \varepsilon + \frac{\delta + \mu}{\alpha}\eta - \nu\right) \tag{2.8}$$

$$p = \theta(1 - \gamma)(m + \varepsilon)$$
$$+ \left[\theta(1 - \gamma)\frac{\delta + \mu}{\alpha} - \frac{\delta}{\alpha}\right]\eta + [1 - \theta(1 - \gamma)]\nu \tag{2.9}$$

Here θ is a derived parameter that describes the overall effect of a disturbance:

$$\theta = \frac{1 + \phi + \delta/\alpha}{1 + \phi + \mu/\alpha + \delta/\alpha} \tag{2.10}$$

As in the case of fixed prices, θ is close to one if money demand is insensitive to the interest rate (μ close to zero) or if spending is highly sensitive to the interest rate [α large]. But θ will also be close to one if prices are highly flexible, either because ϕ is large or because δ is large.

The derived parameter γ controls the distribution of effects of shocks between real GNP and the price level. It is

$$\gamma = \frac{1}{1 + \phi + \delta/\alpha} \tag{2.11}$$

Note that γ is one when the price level is unresponsive [ϕ and δ are zero) and approaches zero when either or both of those coefficients become large.

The positive impact of a financial disturbance, ε, on real GNP depends on the product of θ and γ. That product is at its highest level of 1 in an economy with rigid prices and either interest-inelastic money demand or highly interest-elastic aggregate demand. The impact of ε on the price level is at its highest level, also 1, in the same economy with completely flexible prices. The influence of the spending shock, η, on real GNP is described by $\theta\gamma(\delta/\alpha + \mu/\alpha)$. If spending is highly interest-elastic (α is large), spending shocks have little effect on real GNP-they are dissipated in modest changes in the interest rate. However, unlike the earlier case of price rigidity, with flexible prices, it is not sufficient that money demand be interest-inelastic ($\mu = 0$) in order that the spending shock not affect real GNP. If δ/α is not too small, that is, if the decline in prices associated with the higher interest rate from a positive spending disturbance is reasonably large, then real GNP will respond through a different channel: A shock raises the interest rate, appreciates the currency, lowers the price level, and shifts the LM curve to the right. Again, this mechanism is important only if the interest-elasticity of spending, described by α, is not too high. In particular, if the higher value of the currency brings a large increase in the current account deficit, then α is high and the effect through this channel is small.

The negative effect of a price shock, ν, on real GNP is controlled by the same coefficient, $\theta\gamma$, as in the case of a financial shock. Again, an economy with a rigid price level and a horizontal IS curve or a vertical LM curve will be most sensitive to this type of shock.

With regard to the price level, a financial disturbance, ε, affects the price level over the first year according to $\theta(1 - \gamma)$. This expression has its maximum value of one in the case of an economy with perfectly flexible prices and horizontal IS or vertical LM curves. For the spending shock, η, there are two conflicting effects. First, to the extent that the shock raises output, aggregate demand rises and the price adjustment process raises the price level. The elasticity for this effect is $\theta(1 - \gamma) (\delta/\alpha + \mu/\alpha)$. Second, the interest-rate response appreciates the currency and depresses the price level; the elasticity governing this relation is $-\delta/\alpha$. In an economy with weak price adjustment for nontradables (low ϕ) or interest-inelastic money demand (low μ), together with some degree of sensitivity of prices to the interest rate through the exchange rate (δ positive), the relationship will be negative. A spending shock will depress the price level.

The impact of a price shock, ν, on the price level is described by the expression $1 - \theta(1 - \gamma)$. The impact is always positive, but is smaller in an economy where price shocks have large real effects (high θ) and where prices are flexible (low γ).

If monetary policymakers are specifically concerned with nominal GNP, they will need to make use of the sum of the earlier expressions for y and p:

$$y + p = \theta m + \theta \varepsilon + [\theta(\delta/\alpha + \mu/\alpha) - \delta/\alpha]\eta + (1 - \theta)\nu \qquad (2.12)$$

Note that the price-flexibility coefficient, γ, does not appear in this expression. It controls the division of the effects of the disturbances between real GNP and the price level, and is irrelevant when the two variables are added together. The impact of a financial shock, ε, on nominal GNP is described by θ. In an economy with either interest-inelastic money demand (μ close to zero) or highly interest-elastic spending (α high), θ will be close to one and the impact of ε on nominal GNP will be almost unit-elastic.

The effect of a spending shock, η, on nominal GNP is described by the coefficient $\theta(\delta/\alpha + \mu/\alpha) - \delta/\alpha$. Recall that the spending shock unambiguously raises real GNP but may decrease the price level. If the negative effect on the price level is strong enough, nominal GNP may fall in the face of a positive spending shock. This will happen if δ exceeds α, that is, if the negative effect on the price level (in percentage points) of an increase in the interest rate exceeds the negative effect (also in percentage points) on real GNP in the IS curve of an increase in the interest rate. As this appears to be an unlikely case, I will assume that the effect of a spending shock on nominal GNP is at least slightly positive. The effect of a price shock, ν, on nominal GNP is controlled by the simple expression $1 - \theta$. In a high-θ economy with a flat IS curve and a steep LM curve, price shocks will have little effect on nominal GNP. Although a price shock has an adverse effect on the economy by lowering real GNP with an elasticity $\theta\gamma$, the elasticity of the price level with respect to the shock is $1 - \theta(1 - \gamma)$, so the net effect is an elasticity of $1 - \theta$. Note that the degree of price flexibility has relatively little role in determining the effect of a price shock on nominal GNP, even though it is very important in distributing the effect of the shock between real GNP and the price level.

3. Implications of Innovation and Deregulation

Changing financial markets and institutions have two roles in the model I have just presented. First, individual steps in the process of financial change appear as individual financial shocks, ε. For example, if deregulation permits the sudden growth of transaction accounts with low reserve requirements, a positive ε will occur. For a given interest rate, a higher level of real GNP will be consistent with the equality of supply and demand for the monetary base. As I indicated at the beginning of the last section, I am assuming at this stage that the central bank does not adjust the base to try to offset the change in the demand schedule for the base.

The second important influence of financial liberalization is in changing the slopes of the crucial schedules. There are good reasons to believe that recent changes in many countries have tended to raise the value of θ in each of them. Let me repeat the definition of θ and the coefficients that go into it:

$$\theta = \frac{1 + \phi + \delta/\alpha}{1 + \phi + \delta/\alpha + \mu/\alpha} \tag{3.1}$$

ϕ: response of price level to demand (elasticity)
δ: response of price level to interest rate (semi-elasticity)
α: response of spending to interest rate (semi-elasticity)
μ: response of base demand to interest rate (semi-elasticity)

Payment of interest on demand deposits and the lowering of reserve requirements diminishes μ and raises θ closer to 1. The demand for the monetary base arises in part from the demand for reserves, and that demand derives in turn from the demand for those monetary instruments subject to reserve requirements. With low reserve requirements and competitive interest rates on reservable accounts, the demand for reserves is not very responsive to market rates. Account holders have little incentive to shift into other forms of wealth when interest rates rise. However, as long as reserves do not pay market rates themselves, rates paid by banks on reservable accounts will not vary exactly with market interest rates and μ must be a little bit positive. Further, no major nation, so far as I know, has pushed liberalization to the point of allowing private, interest-bearing currency that might displace the non-interest-bearing government currency. In theory, μ should also be somewhat positive because the public should substitute away from currency in times of higher interest rates. Empirical evidence on this last point is weak.

Where liberalization has increased the openness of the economy, the critical parameter θ has increased on that account as well. An open economy has a higher α than a closed one because a higher interest rate attracts resources from trading partners. The IS curve of a highly open economy is flat. A large decline in production, y, can occur when the interest rate rises only slightly because investors and consumers will satisfy their wants with imported products and domestic producers will export less. Capital and import controls thwart this process; as they are dismantled, the value of α rises. To a certain extent, the same liberalization will raise δ and make the domestic price level more sensitive to the interest rate. However, the net effect of increases in α and δ is almost certainly to raise θ.

At the end point of liberalization, the LM curve will be vertical and μ will be zero. In such an economy, θ will be one and the expression for the relation between the shocks on the economy and nominal GNP is very simple:

$$y + p = m + \varepsilon \tag{3.2}$$

That is, the only disturbance that influences nominal GNP is the financial disturbance. Spending shifts and price shocks do not affect nominal GNP even though they both affect real GNP and the price level. Let me emphasize this point in a

> *Proposition.* In a fully deregulated economy where monetary policy is concerned with nominal GNP, the *only* types of disturbances that need be considered are financial. Spending and price shocks are irrelevant.

4. The Logic of Nominal GNP Targeting

I have written elsewhere at length on nominal GNP targeting and its generalizations (Hall 1984). Let me quickly summarize the case here. Consider the rather general problem of conducting stabilization policy in an economy subject to the disturbances considered in Section 2 of this paper: financial, spending, and price shocks. The goal of policy is to minimize a weighted average of the variances of the departures of output and inflation from their target values. The general solution can be characterized as choosing a policy that stabilizes $Ay + p$. A is a coefficient that depends on the relative social cost of output as against inflation fluctuations. A very strict policy that kept inflation close to zero at all times would have a small A; a policy that aimed mainly for full employment would have a large A. Nominal GNP targeting corresponds to the value $A = 1$; it is intermediate between a hawkish anti-inflation policy and a dovish full-employment policy.

5. Conducting Monetary Policy

Next I will consider the problems of conducting monetary policy in the face of financial and other shocks. I will assume that monetary actions taken in one year have little effect until the next year, so that the problem of this year's policy is to set in motion a policy that will achieve a desired effect under next year's conditions. I further assume that the goals of policy can be expressed as achieving a predetermined level of nominal GNP next year.

I will write the solution to the model as

$$(y + p = \theta m + \theta \varepsilon + \phi \eta + (1 - \theta) \nu \tag{5.1}$$

Recall that the monetary base enters with the same coefficient, θ, as does the financial shock, ε. In a modern economy, I would expect θ to be close to one, so the monetary base is a powerful determinant of nominal GNP one year hence. I have also substituted the new coefficient, ϕ, for the more complicated expression governing the response of nominal GNP to the spending shock, η. I would expect ϕ to be close to zero. As before, the price shock, ν, has a coefficient of $1 - \theta$, which would also be close to zero under the conditions I have in mind.

If the target of monetary policy is to achieve a level of nominal GNP, g, and if policymakers could anticipate the shocks perfectly, then the appropriate level of the monetary base is:

$$m = -\varepsilon + \frac{1}{\theta} [g - \phi \eta - (1 - \theta) \nu] \tag{5.2}$$

Independent of any parameters, monetary policy should fully offset the financial shock, ε. The other shocks should be offset by coefficients ϕ/θ and $[1 - \theta]/\theta$, which will be small.

Of course, policymakers will not know the values of the forthcoming shocks and will not be able to achieve the nominal GNP target exactly. Instead, they will make use of forecasts of the shocks. Because spending and price shocks are not easy to forecast a year in advance, and because those shocks receive little weight in the policy formula anyway, it is probably appropriate to drop them from the formula. The simpler formula is

$$m = -\varepsilon + \frac{1}{\theta} g \tag{5.3}$$

Now ε is interpreted as the best available forecast for the financial shift over the forthcoming year. The monetary policy rule is, in words, *expand the monetary base by the desired growth in nominal GNP, adjusted for the elasticity of nominal GNP with respect to the base, less the expected financial shift.*

In the steady state, the desired growth of nominal GNP is likely to be the same from year to year—it will be the natural growth rate of real output. The rule recommends that the growth of the monetary base be equal to that constant, natural rate plus an adjustment for expected financial shifts. The rule recommended by monetarists is the same except that they propose to ignore the financial shifts. How different are the two recommendations?

The answer rests on a single issue, the predictability of the financial shifts. Figure 1 shows a measure of the shifts that have occurred in the United States since 1962. It plots the GNP velocity of the monetary base, that is, the ratio of nominal GNP to the monetary base (as adjusted by the Federal Reserve Board for changes in reserve requirements). Velocity has risen along a steady trend, as the public has gradually substituted away from currency and reservable deposits as methods for carrying out transactions. The upward trend is interrupted occasionally by declines in velocity, usually associated with recessions or financial crises. The first one in the figure occurred in 1966. Similar declines in velocity occurred in 1970, 1974, and 1980, each coinciding with a recession. Then velocity jumped upward in a completely unprecedented way in 1981, largely as a result of major regulatory changes enacted in 1980. The recession of 1982, which brought the economy to a lower level of real output, compared to potential, than in any recession since the great depression, was accompanied by a dramatic decline in velocity.

The experience summarized in Figure 7.1 makes it plain that the most recurrent pattern of financial shocks are those that precede recessions or coincide with periods of financial stress. When panic hits the financial system, the public tries to shed less liquid assets and move into currency and reservable accounts. Base velocity declines as a result. But the single biggest shock to velocity was the upward spurt following deregulation in 1980.

Macroeconomic forecasters have not been notably successful in predicting the financial crises that periodically grip the U.S. and other economies. However, the velocity shifts of Figure 7.1 are somewhat predictable. For example, a regression with the annual change in velocity as the dependent variable and the lagged change in velocity and the lagged 6-month Treasury bill interest rate as predictors explains about

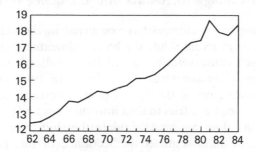

Figure 7.1
Velocity of the U.S. Monetary Base, 1962–84

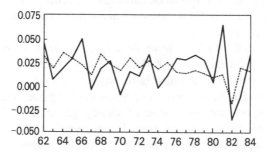

Figure 7.2
Actual Change in Base Velocity (Solid Line) and Predicted Change (Dotted Line), United States, 1962–84

25 percent of the variance in the dependent variable. Figure 7.2 shows the explanatory success of the simple regression.

The regression does not incorporate any information available a year in advance about financial deregulation. In 1980, observers were aware that important financial change was in the works, but it is not clear that they could have predicted that a sharp jump in base velocity was about to occur.

As a general matter, it is far from clear that the financial shocks, ε, that are much the most important consideration in the theory of monetary stabilization, are sufficiently forecastable as to make the activist policy of equation 5.3 materially different from the monetarist policy of ignoring ε and simply raising the base by a constant percent each year. However, it is abundantly clear that εs have been an important influence on the U.S. economy in past decades, especially in the early 1980s.

6. *Financial Change to Reduce the Incidence of Shocks*

Although important changes have occurred in the U.S. and other financial systems in recent years, the basic vulnerability of the systems to panics which cause velocity to fall has remained unchanged. In percentage terms, the contraction of velocity in 1982 was the worst of the two-decade span of the figures in the previous section. Panics are times when the public tries to shift into currency and reserves. When the central bank does not accommodate the shift, recession follows, through the mechanism outlined in Section 2 of this paper. In the United States, precisely this observation led to the creation of the Federal Reserve, whose instructions were to expand the base as necessary to head off panics. However, the Federal Reserve, just as central banks in many other countries, has to be cautious in accommodation. History shows it is all too easy for a series of accommodations to turn into a policy of chronic inflation.

Elsewhere (Hall, 1983), I have described a program of monetary change that would avoid the conflict between accommodation and inflation. The essence of the idea is to pay interest on reserves at close to market rates. Paying interest on reserves has long been recommended by economists on microeconomic efficiency grounds. Holders of reserves needlessly economize on their balances when interest rates are high. At the optimum, the opportunity cost of holding reserves as against other financial instruments would be essentially zero. Milton Friedman (1969) advocated a policy of chronic deflation in which nominal interest rates would be close to zero as one way to attain the optimum where the economy is saturated in reserves. But paying the market rate on reserves is an alternative route to the same end without the inconvenience of continuing change in the price level.

The macroeconomic case for interest-bearing reserves is less familiar. Obviously, the demand for reserves would be far higher than it is today if they bore interest. If the central bank pays interest on reserves, it has to provide a much higher volume of reserves. Just paying interest without expansion of the quantity would be a significantly deflationary move. In the United States, if the Federal Reserve began a policy of paying interest on reserves at the three-month Treasury bill rate less 20 basis points, it might find it necessary to expand reserves from $40 billion to $300 billion.

Were a significant fraction of the outstanding national debt in the form of interest-bearing reserves, it stands to reason that the incidence of financial shocks would be reduced. Today, a panic in the United States causes investors to question the safety of trillions of dollars of financial instruments other than base money, and to try to move into only about $200 billion in the monetary base. If the base were close to $500 billion instead, the financial shift in percentage terms would be far smaller. Saturation in reserves would bring increased financial stability as well as microeconomic efficiency.

A switch to near market rates of interest on reserves together with a large increase in the volume of reserves would not change the central bank's basic responsibility for stabilization. But it would make it far easier, because the ε shocks would be much smaller. A policy of constant growth of the monetary base would give better price and output stability under reserve saturation than under a restricted monetary base.

References

Dornbusch. Rudiger 1976. Expectations and Exchange Rate Dynamics, *Journal of Political Economy*, vol. 84, December, pp. 1161–1176.

Friedman Milton. 1969. The Optimum Quantity of Money, Chapter 1 in *The Optimum Quantity of Money and Other Essays*. Chicago: Aldine, 1969, pp. 1–68.

Hall Robert E. 1984. Monetary Strategy with an Elastic Price Standard, in *Price Stability and Public Policy*, Federal Reserve Bank of Kansas City.

———. 1983. Optimal Fiduciary Monetary Systems, *Journal of Monetary Economics*, vol. 12, pp. 33–50, July.

8

Monetary Policy in an Evolutionary Disequilibrium

Donald D. Hester

Macroeconomic theory has been used to justify prescriptions for monetary policy that differ widely in form and substance. These prescriptions arise from analyzing equilibrium properties of a variety of different models that invoke different assumptions and concern different variables. The assumptions and sets of variables are unchanging in each instance. The prescriptions do not derive from models that incorporate systemic (structural) change. The primary activity of financial intermediaries is to devise and market packages of services that allow their clients to reach goals expeditiously. Intermediaries are inherently innovators.

In this paper I argue that conventional prescriptions about monetary policy are seriously incomplete because their proposers fail to confront indisputable evidence of rapid institutional and technical change in financial markets and a proliferation of ever closer substitutes for "money." New assets and institutions change all but pathological Walrasian equilibria, both instantaneously and in the long run. When attributes of new assets and the characteristics of new institutions are unpredictable, equilibrium paths become amorphous. The effects from employing policy prescriptions that are based on an analysis of how a change in a monetary aggregate or interest rate affects equilibrium in some hypothetical model become correspondingly unpredictable. Theoretical predictions are always conditional claims; the assumptions are supposed to be satisfied.

Innovation and change are major determinants of the human condition, but their occurrence does not render meaningless canons of good behavior or theorems about efficient allocations of resources in economics. Financial innovation is an investment activity that modifies modes of behavior and technology, and it induces changes in the allocation of individual and regulatory resources. The object of this paper is to analyze how the unpredictable occurrence of innovations modifies financial behavior by firms and individuals and the implementation of monetary policy.

The first section is an introduction that defines monetary policy and financial innovation and interprets them abstractly. The second section contains an assessment of the causes and consequences of unanticipated changes and deregulation on behavior by participants in domestic financial markets, by participants in international financial markets, and on the observable characteristics of financial markets. The third section consists of a discussion of a number of important technical and regulatory aspects of financial markets, which require attention if desirable properties of financial markets are to be retained. The concluding section includes an analysis of the limits of the effectiveness of monetary policy and proposes several operating principles as guides for the conduct of monetary policy.

I. Introduction

A monetary policy may be defined as a time sequence of monetary base (outside money) obligations of a sovereign political body. There is no consensus among economists about what information set or sequence of sets is useful for designing a monetary policy. At the risk of oversimplifying, a constant monetary growth rule for an arbitrary aggregate, say, M1, is based on a very primitive information set, the value of M1 at some earlier date and a parameter whose value was established once and for all time. Necessary conditions for implementing such a rule are that a relation exist between the monetary base and M1 and that other conditions such as the size of federal deficits or the public's demand for currency allow an arbitrary path for M1 to be feasible. Pegging a nominal interest rate requires a similarly primitive information set, an arbitrary number defined on the set of reals and the one-time choice of an asset which is to bear the announced rate. Necessary conditions for implementing this second rule are that a correspondence exist between the rate and the base and that the public be willing to hold the asset when it pays the announced rate.

Both rules and all others that come to mind are abjectly decadent exercises in numerology, in the absence of a fully specified economic model. To be fully specified, a model at a minimum must represent a set of agents; the information that they have; their goals; technical restrictions on productivity, accumulation, and exchange; sets of assets, goods, and services; and the prices at which they are valued. In the context of such models, as is well known, it is possible to construct examples where either rule yields desirable or mischievous results in terms of variables that are arguments of some social welfare function.

When such models have content, values of their variables are restricted, at least in probability to certain ranges and the models can be used to make predictions. An innovation changes one or more of the agents, assets, goods, services, and technical relations. This, in turn, modifies prices and the information possessed by agents with the effect that the content of models and their predictions are changed. An innovation may make following either of the simple rules a prescription for disaster.

For example, suppose an innovation causes a new medium of exchange to emerge that dominates the traditonal measure of M1, demand deposits and currency, because it bears interest. A rule of maintaining a constant rate of growth of the traditonal measure would condemn an economy to escalating inflation as the public switched to the new interest bearing medium. Analogously, a rule of pegging the treasury bill rate at, say, 4%, could prove infeasible if an innovation was a close substitute for a bill. A central bank might have to buy large quantities of bills to maintain the rate, which would result in a large increase in the monetary base.

The very possibility of financial innovation is a strong reason for having discretionary monetary policy rather than inflexibly adhering to some arbitrary rule. Discretion may mean no more than coarse tuning of target path growth rates or simply redefining, from time to time, what it is that is to grow at a constant rate. The U.S. Federal Reserve has used both tactics in recent years. Indeed, the number of components that comprise monetary aggregates has grown a good deal faster than the aggregates themselves.

The strategy for incorporating an innovation in the specification of a control problem and for modifying monetary policy depends on the nature of the innovation. There are two broad classes of innovation. First, if an innovation introduces a new service, agent, asset, or good, there is little that can be said without a series of somewhat arbitrary assumptions. The new element will not appear in existing data sets. Often a new element can reasonably be assumed to be a close substitute for an existing component—e.g. NOW (negotiable order of withdrawal) accounts are a close substitute for demand deposit accounts. In such cases it is obviously sensible to redefine monetary aggregates so as to combine nearly identical quantities. If there is no uniquely close existing substitute for a new element, modifying policy is far more challenging. One tack is to ignore the innovation until forecasts go awry and/ or until it has been in existence long enough to generate some data—

typically time series evidence. This conservative approach is probably safe because most innovations start on a small scale and have few macro consequences for several years. However, when they do become quantitatively important, time series are likely to be too short to provide much guidance. Theory will be the major guide to model respecification and policy revision.

Second, if instead of providing a new element, an innovation modifies the technical relations that exist among objects and agents in the market, a rather different approach is required. There will be no new element that declares an innovation has occurred. To detect the presence of innovation it would be necessary to draw rather large samples as in quality control models. Drift together with balance sheet identities should suggest how filtering techniques may be applied to achieve goals.

Innovations occur for diverse reasons, which is why they are so difficult to analyze. In part they are analogous to mutations in nature. They occur because a creative agent has preceived that an improvement is possible. Most mutations and human perceptions of possible improvements prove to be nonviable; they do not permanently change the system. Many potential financial market innovations are probably never tested, because new financial instruments or techniques must be widely understood if they are to be successful. Educating the public and marketing such ideas are costly, and the probability that a rival will choose to free ride is high. This institutional inertia is likely to be an important part of the seeming time invariance in the demand function for money which Goldfeld (1973) reported.

An important reason for innovations in the economics literature is that they are induced by changes in factor prices—e.g. Fellner (1956, pp. 52–53). In the United States and in other "capitalist" economies real wage rates and the financial sector's share of total employment have risen rather steadily over the postwar period.[1] The recent high rate of financial innovation may be little more than a lagged response that was induced by changing factor costs. If, on the other hand, as Friedman (1959) has suggested, money and financial services are luxuries, the shift in employment toward finance need not indicate induced innovation. The construction of a general equilibrium framework necessary to distinguish between these alternative explanations is beyond the scope of the present paper.

[1] Between 1950 and 1980, U.S. wage and salary workers employed in finance, real estate, and insurance increased from four to six percent of total employment. [Source: *Economic Report of the President*, 1983, p. 205.] For information about financial employment in other countries, see Krohn (1984).

A third explanation for recent financial innovation is that banks and other financial institutions are largely data processing agents and technical progress in data processing is very rapid. Financial institutions can complete existing processing and validating tasks with increasing speed and accuracy and are increasingly able to offer and control new services and assets. Financial software is readily transferable among institutions, and innovators have been quick to license new services and establish franchising. The cost of diffusion of an innovation must have fallen greatly.

A fourth source of innovation are the artificial barriers to flows of goods, funds, and services that different nations and their monetary authorities have erected. While not exactly mercantilists, the Kennedy and Johnson administrations in the U.S. went to some lengths to defend against withdrawals of gold. Measures such as the interest equalization tax and the voluntary credit restraint program created pressure for the establishment of offshore subsidiaries and branches by U.S. banks and nonfinancial corporations.

Regulation Q and other barriers to paying interest to savers had similar effects in the U.S. and elsewhere. Measures to increase arbitrarily the minimum denominations of government securities created a demand for the services of money market mutual funds. Further examples are differences in the reserve requirements that are imposed on essentially identical liabilities, both intra- and internationally. Obstructions create incentives for change! Similarly, a lack of coordination of policy among participants in a fixed exchange rate system created arbitrage opportunities that could be realized through artificial financial transactions and underinvoicing.[2]

A fifth reason for innovation is the existence of differences in the effectiveness of surveillance by bank regulators and protections for depositors in different markets. Surveillance, guarantees, and deposit insurance are designed to protect the public from externalities that obtain when financial institutions fail, and should be sharply distinguished from macro policies that are discussed in the preceding paragraph. When externalities exist, financial markets do not yield Pareto efficient outcomes. When macro policies are required, markets are nonexistent or do not clear. Neither situation is desirable, but valid prescriptions rarely result from lumping together dissimilar illnesses.

Examples of innovations that seek to deceive or evade regulations

---

[2] There is a great similarity between such transactions and "dry exchange" which Florentine Renaissance financial institutions used to evade bans on charging interest. See de Roover (1974, Ch. 4).

are repurchase agreements that would seem to be fully collateralized and thus safe, but are not; lending more than regulations would allow a bank through both a bank and artfully created subsidiaries of its holding company; downstreaming capital so that a bank's net worth exceeds that of the holding company that owns it; and introducing accounting games that misrepresent a bank's safety or commitments. Internationally, banks have tended to book loans and liabilities in locations that minimize surveillance, by playing regulations in different countries off against one another. It does not require an activity analysis algorithm to see that a bank may overextend itself relative to every country's safety standard by choosing carefully where to book assets and liabilities. In the event of a default, the central bank where a bank's head office is located may or may not accept responsibility for protecting creditors. Ponzi games may develop. These are global extensions of the "competition in laxity" Arthur Burns criticized in 1974.

A final and perhaps the most important reason for financial innovation is associated with the continuity of relationships between financial institutions like banks and their customers. Bank credit is tailored to the requirements of specific borrowers and profits are dependent upon trust and repeated dealings. Bankers will leap windmills to provide services to profitable accounts. Monetary policies that seek to curtail credit flows to such clients are met with all modes of evasive actions, as the U.S. Federal Reserve learned between 1966 and 1970 and witnessed subsequently. Sharp unanticipated changes in the posture of monetary policy (the sorts which devotees of rational expectations say are most likely to succeed) are very likely to generate innovations. This is true whether or not artificial barriers are present.

II. Probable Causes and Consequences of Unregulated Change and Deregulation

In this section an interpretation of the probable causes and consequences of innovation and deregulation is proposed that includes the behavior of firms, individuals, and monetary authorites. The discussion is organized according to whether transactions and services are provided within a sovereign country and in currency units of that country or elsewhere in that country's or some other country's currency. This distinction is employed because of the present clear difference in the effectiveness of regulation at home and abroad. Evidence in support of the proposed interpretation is presented in the form of examples drawn from the experiences of the United States and other countries.

A. Domestic Financial Markets

An innovation by a domestic financial institution unambiguously expands the set of opportunities for that firm; it can do something in addition to what it could do. Similarly, deregulation that relaxes rules that apply to an institution expands its set of opportunities. The effects are less clear for an industry of such firms, hereafter an intermediary. In competitive markets a new process or asset may expand or contract the set of activities that break even. Casual empiricism suggests that innovations expand offerings in financial markets, and in the present paper that is a maintained hypothesis. Financial intermediaries that tailor credit to the needs of their borrowing customers are, in any case, not perfectly competitive.

When larger numbers of assets and services are available to clients of financial intermediaries, superficially it would seem that clients cannot be worse off. This inference is generally invalid, however, because a change alters the nature and pricing of existing services; some customers may gain and others lose depending upon what services they use. Hakansson (1982) has studied this question and reports conditions under which an innovation is welfare improving—essentially that everyone can consume the same services as before and that some consume more. His restrictive conditions are not likely to be satisfied in practice. What is clear is that rationally innovating financial institutions will only innovate if they perceive profit flows will be enhanced. Other firms in the same industry may forgo adopting the innovation or may adopt it grudgingly to defend their turf. Innovations must be viewed at the firm level. Deregulation, on the other hand, is best viewed at the industry level. Only in highly concentrated industries would conclusions from studying the two processes tend to converge. In this paper it is assumed that intermediaries are sufficiently concentrated that they can be viewed as if they are a single firm.[3] I shall also assume that there is only one depository intermediary as well. Conclusions will not be seriously qualified by this assumption so long as markets are well defined and segregated.

With these assumptions, innovations will occur and deregulation

---

[3] This is, of course, an extraordinarily strong assumption. However, in most countries domestic commercial banks are few in number and are highly concentrated. The assumption is grossly inaccurate for the United States where forces for financial market deregulation and innovation are most in evidence. To attempt to analyze the dynamics of imperfect competition within the U.S. banking market is beyond the scope of this paper. The issue is addressed below when offshore banking is addressed.

be desired by an intermediary only if the intermediary's expected profits are enhanced. An innovation that unconditionally expands cash flow is obviously desirable. Similarly, an innovation that deters entry into an intermediary's market by firms in another industry may be attractive. As in all capital market decisions, the choice hangs on the rate of return that can be realized on the resources required to adopt the innovation.

Deterrence and "turf protection" appear to be the principal motives for most financial innovations by banks. Attempted entry into asset and liability markets dominated by banks appears to underlie most financial innovations by non-banks. The inducement for entry has been prospective high and rising profits that banks realize when market interest rates rise in an uncertain world—cf. Saloner (1982). Until inflexible interest rate ceilings are removed from deposit liabilities of banks, increases in market interest rates imply prospective increases in bank profits that attract entrants. The presence of cash reserve requirements that apply to banks, but not others, also induce entrants when interest rates are high, because the reserve requirement handicap of banks is correspondingly high. The problem may also arise if an intermediary has a portfolio with low (high) fixed interest rate assets (liabilities) and is surprised by a sudden increase (decrease) in market rates. A predator with a potential entry innovation can exploit such situations.

An interesting feature of this process is that financial innovations are induced by high or changing nominal rather than real interest rates. Bank profits and their attractiveness to potentially innovating entrants are a function of the difference between the rate that banks earn on loans and securities and the rates that banks must pay for deposits and other liabilities. It matters little to innovators that prices are constant over time or rising at 10 percent per year.

By adopting a cost-increasing (profit-diminishing) innovation, banks reduce the probability of entry by rivals. Banks have other barriers to entry as well. They attempt to establish "full service" relationships and have very low profit margins on activities where entry is easy; they also have formidable credentials in terms of government and regulatory agency certifications and deposit insurance. Profit enhancing or reducing regulation can always be imposed by monetary or other political authorities. The power to regulate is, within limits, the power to coerce and allocate funds. The limit to such power is the probability of entry of unregulated firms—often through innovation. The extent of and determinants of how this power is applied are implicitly treated in much that follows.

By assumption, successful innovations and deregulation expand the set of services and offerings in loan and deposit markets; these in turn facilitate the holding of physical capital and capital formation. New instruments and services afford borrowers and lenders more opportunities to tailor portfolios to individual requirements and often allow greater flexibility in responding to or protecting oneself from unanticipated shocks. Almost tautologically they are expansionary in the sense of Brainard and Tobin (1963), because they lower the required rate of return from holding capital.[4] How much an innovation reduces the required rate of return initially or in the long run is analytically intractable—essentially an exercise in constructing counterfactual experiments. The answer depends upon the nature of the innovation, its rate of diffusion, and the timing of subsequent innovations which it may cause.

Because innovations tend to occur at times when nominal interest rates are high or rising, they weaken the effectiveness of restrictive monetary policy. The weakening takes three forms. First, an innovation increases uncertainty about the magnitudes of all policy instrument multipliers. Second, the expansionary effects of innovation mean that any dose of restrictive medicine must be stronger once an innovation is perceived to have occurred, if a desired degree of restraint is to be achieved.

Third, once adopted, innovations probably are irreversible. It is very costly to introduce a new product or service, but not too costly to continue an existing offering. Since successful innovations infringe on monopoly rents of a depository intermediary either by driving up its own costs or by having another industry provide close substitutes, innovations almost surely reduce depository intermediary profits— especially after nominal market interest rates decline. Reduced profits mean that smaller amounts of retained earnings will be available internally to replenish bank capital and that the opportunity cost of raising banks capital funds externally will rise. The depository intermediary will become increasingly fragile as its capital account weakens and this may limit the magnitude of feasible discretionary policy actions. This third form of weakening can be avoided if regulators enforce high

---

[4] It is possible that an innovation is such a breakthrough that it allows savers to reduce the size of their portfolios. When the portfolio demand for assets falls, then presumably the required rate of return on capital would rise. In this paper such a strongly asset-saving innovation is assumed not to occur. The defense for the assumption are the fact that an adopted innovation increases income and the strong empirical evidence that the wealth elasticity of income considerably exceeds unity (Projector and Weiss 1966).

minimum levels of capital or if the intermediary becomes more adept at risk management.

The monopoly rents being eroded away by innovations are largely artificial rents that were created by regulations and barriers to entry. They are tolerated and often welcomed by government officials because they serve to enhance the solvency and stability of depository institutions. Entry by non-banks is rational because abnormal profits exist and can be expropriated, so to speak, by boring in with innovations. Regulators and lawmakers appear to resist these incursions on occasion, but deterence seems to be politically costly for them.

The erosion process poses a potentially nasty dilemma for macro policy makers as well. Suppose someone should want some monetary aggregate, say, M2, to grow at, say, 7 percent per annum. For simplicity, assume that the aggregate consists solely of the deposits of some hypothetical intermediary. Finally, suppose for precautionary reasons that regulators require that the intermediary's capital be at least 6 percent of deposits. To maintain this minimum safety margin, the intermediary's net worth must also expand by at least 7 percent per annum. With sufficient erosion of profits through innovation, the two goals may not be simultaneously achievable. Subscribers to new equity issues are not likely to invest in an intermediary, if the odds are slight that they could earn dividends.[5] A tradeoff may thus exist between maintaining an intermediary's stability and achieving an aggregate's targeted rate of growth.

The tradeoff could be avoided either by choosing a sufficiently low monetary aggregate growth rate or by surreptitiously relaxing the leverage constraint. The latter can be achieved through fancy bookkeeping or by allowing an intermediary to issue subordinated debt or establish subsidiaries that are controlled through the device of a holding company. In recent years in many countries, monetary aggregate target growth rates are falling and bank-related subsidiaries have been expanding.

   i. *Examples of financial innovation within the U.S.* In the United States profits from banking became conspicuously high in the 1950s when interest rates in financial markets rose and rates of return on bank liabilities such as demand, savings, and time deposits did not.[6] Entry into banking markets by large nonfinancial corporations occurred both

---

   [5] Foley and Hellwig's (1975) "stand alone" principle implies that they would also not invest with the expectation of selling out to another group of investors in the secondary market.

   [6] A more extensive discussion of the postwar history of U.S. financial innovation is available in Hester (1981, pp. 146–168).

through relatively rapidly growing trade credit and the rapid expansion of the market for commercial paper. Thrift institutions' market share of consumer savings also expanded rapidly. Banks eventually responded by introducing negotiable certificates of deposit and by matching high interest rates that thrift institutions had been paying on savings deposits. Both of these responses served to reduce the profits of banks. Bank costs were also driven up by a steadily rising rate of turnover of corporate demand deposits. Techniques for corporate cash management improved steadily as information processing capabilities expanded and as the opportunity cost of holding idle demand deposits rose with interest rates.

After the introduction of negotiable certificates of deposit, there were no conspicuous innovations until 1966, although there was slow, steady progress. Interest rates fluctuated in a narrow band during this period. However, a new wave of dramatic innovations accompanied the rising interest rates that were precipitated by the U.S. involvement in Vietnam. With the imposition of arbitrary interest rate ceilings on time and savings deposits, reserve requirements on borrowed liabilities, and restrictions on foreign investments that occurred between 1966 and 1970, a new profitable window of opportunity was opened for firms that were not banks. Banks went through congeneric transformations that temporarily allowed them to operate as nonbanks through subsidiaries of the new one-bank holding company. Also, they shifted a large fraction of their banking for large corporations to overseas branches where business could go on more or less as usual. These innovations together with an emergent market for repurchase agreements successfully deterred nonfinancial corporations from entering traditional markets for banking services, but sharply reduced banking industry profitability. The profits of subsidiaries of banks were not so severely affected, and offshore tax advantages blunted some of the private sector cost of this second series of deterrent actions. The deterrence was abetted by the timely default of the Penn Central Railroad in the commercial paper market. Risk of default in the commercial paper market served to remind participants why it was sometimes attractive to make use of banks as intermediaries![7]

[7] Mortgage loan markets in the U.S. had been seriously crippled by the simultaneous occurrence of rising interest rates in security markets and newly imposed ceilings on interest rates that thrift associations could pay depositors. Private enterprise was slow to take advantage of this opportunity. Political pressures mounted and the government responded by creating three new mortgage programs, FNMA, GNMA, and FHLMC. These government credit market innovations were to increasingly dominate single family mortgage markets and blunt the contractionary effec-

With the collapse of the Penn Central and the large number of preceding innovations, the Federal Reserve began to change its strategy. Interest rate ceilings were progressively removed from large denomination time deposits, certificates of deposit, and bank-related commercial paper. This action greatly reduced the incentive to create offshore facilities, although the volume of funds at offshore banks continued to expand rapidly because reserve requirements could be avoided and it was reasonably apparent that the U.S. dollar was about to depreciate. The Federal Reserve could not both be a lender of last resort in the commercial paper market crisis and bid up interest rates to protect the dollar. The situation was resolved with President Nixon's speech of August 15, 1971, which introduced a new set of barriers to market flows. Interferences in financial markets would slightly abet a new wave of innovations.

Time and savings accounts having less than $100,000 were still subject to low interest rate ceilings. These accounts were extraordinarily profitable for banks and thrifts, because nominal interest rates on assets were high and rising over the years 1972–74. The potential for profit through innovation was recognized by the creators of money market mutual funds in 1972, who were partially responding to a sharp and contrived increase in the minimum denomination of U.S. Treasury bills to $10,000. The NOW account was also introduced that year by thrift institutions in New England. Both innovations were able to capture a share of the high profits that banks were earning by raising funds through interest free demand deposits and inconvenient passbook savings accounts. Large corporations increasingly held transactions balances in the form of overnight repurchase agreements. These changes in practice were reflected in concurrent rises in the turnover rate of demand deposits.

This skirmishing with potential and actual entrants by banks was again reasonably successful in preserving banking markets, but dear in terms of bank profits. Retained earnings fell and the ratio of net worth to bank assets fell sharply between 1965 and 1974 at the largest U.S. banks.[8] Interest rates became increasingly volatile after 1970, perhaps because of the Federal Reserve's abandonment of interest

---

tiveness of rising interest rates in housing markets for the next fifteen years.

[8] In an attempt to preserve their profits, banks responded to this growing competition by establishing real estate investment trusts with whom they unsuccessfully tried to place a large volume of real estate loans. The loans were often bearing low fixed interest rates. REITs experienced large losses that were subsequently absorbed by managing banks, particularly between 1973 and 1977, to avoid lawsuits by other investors in the trusts.

ceilings on large denomination time deposits. In 1975 a new innovation, the financial instrument futures market, appeared which allowed interest rate risks to be shared and shed. This innovation may partly substitute for increased financial leverage in the portfolios of depository intermediaries. However, its introduction is not costless for it substitutes liquidity risk for interest rate risk, because of its "marked to market" disciplinary feature.

After the severe recession of 1973–75, interest rates fell and there was little incentive to enter relatively unprofitable banking markets until 1978. In early 1978 short-term interest rates began to rise and again individuals and institutions sought to share in the prospectively high profits that banks might realize with high nominal interest rates. Money market mutual funds began to grow. As a response, the banking regulators permitted banks and thrifts to offer six-month, minimum denomination $10,000 money market certificate accounts in June 1978. Interest rates continued to rise and increasingly money market mutual funds, nonfinancial corporations, and foreign banks grew at the expense of domestic banks and thrifts. The International Banking Act was passed in 1978 and U.S. banks began to lend very aggressively in Latin America in an attempt to secure new profitable markets. A crisis threatened in early 1980 which was first addressed by activating the Emergency Credit Control Act of 1969, and then by successively redefining monetary aggregates and passing landmark legislation in 1980 and 1982 that was designed to eliminate many remaining barriers to competition. Both the Depository Institutions Deregulation and Monetary Control Act of 1980 and the Garn-St. Germain Bill of 1982 worked to deter entry through innovation by eliminating interest rate ceilings on small denomination deposit accounts. Both measures are being phased in over an extended period; more legislation is sure to follow.

Rough empirical support for the foregoing interpretation of U.S. banks can be found in Table 8.1 where profits before and after taxes, expressed as a percentage of bank assets, are reported for different years.[9] Bank profits rose unevenly until 1960, because of rising interest rates on assets and relatively flat rates on liabilities. Then, as interest costs of liabilities rose, the ratio of member bank profits to assets fell about 15 percent by 1968. Profits declined markedly further between 1970 and 1975 as additional innovations occurred. Profits were essen-

[9] Before 1969 data are for banks that were members of the Federal Reserve System; after 1969 data are for all insured banks. The two series differ because the latter includes many small banks that tend to be more profitable than the larger member banks. The two parts of the table should be viewed separately, because the spliced time series understates the decline in profitability.

Table 8.1 Profits before and after Tax as a Percentage of Total Bank Assets

	Member Banks[a]			All Insured Banks[b]	
Year (1)	Profits Before Tax (2)	Profits After Tax (3)	Year (4)	Profits Before Tax (5)	Profits After Tax (6)
1951	1.00%	0.53%	1970	1.25%	.85%
1952	1.06	.55	1971	1.04	.81%
1953	1.15	.55	1972	.97	.76
1954	1.12	.67	1973	1.00	.75
1955	1.22	.58	1974	.94	.72
1956	1.37	.59	1975	.85	.69
1957	1.42	.65	1976	.88	.70
1958	1.32	.77	1977	.92	.71
1959	1.48	.64	1978	1.06	.76
1960	1.62	.84	1979	1.12	.80
1961	1.46	.80	1980	1.10	.79
1962	1.34	.73	1981	1.04	.76
1963	1.29	.73	1982	.91	.71
1964	1.29	.71	1983	.84	.67
1965	1.21	.70			
1966	1.28	.68			
1967	1.24	.74			
1968	1.30	.72			

[a] Source: Board of Governors of the Federal Reserve System, *Banking and Monetary Statistics 1941–1970*.

[b] Source: Board of Governors of the Federal Reserve System, *Federal Reserve Bulletin*, selected issues.

tially stagnant at a low level between 1974 and 1977; they rose briefly with interest rates until 1980 when the effects of deregulation and the new legislation began to take effect.

ii. *Domestic financial innovation in other countries.* The occurrence of financial innovations in different nations has been usefully summarized by M. A. Akhtar (1983). Therefore this subsection is not a comprehensive description, but a brief survey of the course of innovations in three nations: Japan, Italy, and the United Kingdom. In each country there are a small number of very large commercial banks which have close ties to their respective central banks. As a result domestic interbank competition is likely to be limited.

In Japan the central bank and other planning broups such as MITI have considerable influence on other industrial and commercial firms that float securities and borrow from banks. Innovations are rather easy to monitor in such circumstances and probably only occur with the prior approval of the monetary authorities. Suzuki (1984) has provided an excellent analysis of Japanese financial innovations. He reports that, with the exception of the *Gensaki* (repurchase agreement) market, they largely occurred in the last decade when Japanese economic growth slowed markedly and the era of floating exchange rates began. In a graph he shows that many nominal market interest rates rose rapidly in 1973 and 1974 and frequently reached post-1960 highs; a second set of peaks occurred in 1980. Between 1973 and 1982 he reports that the share of total final borrowings in the flow of funds accounts by deposit banks fell from about 64% to about 42%. Their share reduction was picked up by direct placements and by other financial intermediaries.

The high interest rates in 1973 and 1974 were partly a consequence of rapidly expanding outstanding government debt. In 1975 the government began to issue long-term bonds and the volume of Gensaki transactions increased rapidly. In 1978 medium-term government bonds were issued for the first time. Private sector bond mutual funds began to appear. Beginning in 1979 ceilings on interest rates banks could pay on time deposits and CDs have been progressively relaxed, and floating rate deposit accounts have been introduced. Electronic funds transfers and sweep accounts were introduced over the past decade. Competition between securities firms and banks increased, but at the end of 1982 Suzuki reports that only about 15% of the liabilities of private banking institutions were free of interest rate regulation. Therefore, financial institution deregulation in Japan is at a very early stage for households and small businesses. Large enterprises with access to international sources are a different story; they are considered below.

Does this picture support the foregoing interpretation for why innovation occurs? I suggest that it does, once allowance is made for differences in market structure. The seemingly irreversible process was initiated by the high nominal interest rates that occurred in 1973 and 1974, and was abetted, as Suzuki stresses, by "the large-scale issue of government bonds (p. 43)." In my view he underestimates the long-run effects of the early period of high nominal interest rates, but I agree with him that in Japan innovation has not severely impaired the conduct of monetary policy. In my view this is largely because deregulation and innovation have yet to occur on a broad scale.

In Italy a very different series of events occurred in the past decade. For most of the preceding thirty years, the Italian economy had been perhaps the most rapidly expanding in Europe. It entered the 1970s with serious inflation and labor market strife. When the first OPEC shock hit, as Caranza and Fazio (1983) have reported, the Bank of Italy devised a strategy of attempting to control total domestic credit as an intermediate target.

This strategy was soon imperiled by massive government deficits that were to average 10 % of gross domestic product for the next decade. The bank was faced with a choice between annihilating the private sector and sticking with its strategy, ratifying the deficits with inflation by grossly exceeding its targets, or attempting a very difficult intermediate policy of imposing arbitrary credit ceilings and compulsory deposit regulations on foreign currency purchases. For several years after the severe inflationary surges in 1974 and 1976 the Bank pursued this last course. Caranza and Fazio report that the approach was finally abandoned in 1983 because of 1) the continuing large public borrowing, 2) new forms of intermediation (innovations), and 3) increasing public estimates of future inflation. Real interest rates, say, as measured by the difference between the Treasury bill rate and the rate of inflation of consumer prices, were negative in 1974, 1976, and 1979–81.

In Italy deposits of all types bear market rates of interest and are not officially regulated by monetary authorities. Only currency and reserves bear no interest. Rigid domestic credit controls and accelerating inflation induced innovations in the forms of lending through nonbanking affiliates of banks, floating interest rate bonds, and borrowing from foreign sources. Competitive pressures from borrowers generate innovations in asset markets when the implicit price of a credit constraint is sufficiently high. In 1983 the Bank of Italy eliminated formal credit restrictions and introduced several changes that should allow it to use market oriented forms of monetary policy with greater effect. By adopting this new strategy, the bank has largely eliminated the shadow price on bank credit, and should slow the pace of financial innovation. A voluntary credit restraint program remains in effect for banks and other lenders, however, and large government deficits continue.

Italy appears to be freer of regulations than either Japan or the U.S.—especially on the liability side. Its high rate of inflation and difficulty in conducting monetary policy suggest that serious problems will be encountered as innovations continue and deregulation proceeds in the context of large government deficits.

The United Kingdom began the decade of the 1970s with an extremely structured capital market in which administered interest rates differed from the Bank Rate by traditional differentials. The inefficiencies latent in such a system had been discovered by entrepreneurs and were being eliminated by a group of rapidly growing secondary, wholesale banks and other entrants. The government responded to this erosion by introducing an ambitious deregulation program entitled "Competition and Credit Control" which de-emphasized the bank rate, encouraged liability management and market determination of interest rate differentials, and established a very loose mechanism by which the Bank of England might influence monetary aggregates and interest rates.

Almost immediately after the program was adopted, Britain's broad monetary aggregate, M3, began to grow at rates that averaged 20% per annum. When this quantity was finally controlled in 1974, the narrow aggregate, M1, began to grow at comparable rates for the next five years. Interest rates rose sharply in 1972 as the magnitude of monetary growth became apparent, and fluctuated wildly thereafter. The international value of the pound was largely immunized from this domestic turmoil, because oil prices were rising and North Sea oil was coming into production. The Bank of England began imposing special cash reserve requirements and ultimately resorted to the practice of imposing high marginal reserve requirements (the "Corset") on banks that were expanding too rapidly.

This series of new reserve requirements appeared to induce a new wave of innovations and creative accounting that involved booking transactions in the Euro-dollar and Euro-sterling markets. The Corset was abandoned in 1980, and a policy of restrictive fiscal and monetary growth was adopted by the Thatcher government. Nevertheless, in the context of continuing deregulation M1 has been growing at double-digit rates over much of the subsequent period, unemployment has been high and rising, and the pound has weakened markedly as world oil prices slumped.

While all this chaos cannot be blamed on deregulation and innovations, it is apparent that there has been great difficulty in fashioning a consistent and workable monetary policy. Both before and after the introduction of competition and credit control, financial innovations were troublesome.

This survey of four countries illustrates the great heterogeneity of monetary experiences that major countries have experienced in the last fifteen years. It serves as a warning that any conclusions about how deregulation and financial innovation affect the design and implementation of monetary policy must be understood to be tentative—subject to severe qualification in the contexts of individual countries.

B. Transnational Financial Innovation

A financial institution that is constrained by regulations or markets in its own country can sometimes profit by opening branches or subsidiaries elsewhere. External expansion unambiguously expands the set of activities that the institution can undertake, because legal arrangements among countries do not allow a country to enforce its domestic regulations on foreign soil. Opportunities to bank on foreign soil, however, do not necessarily enhance bank profits. A bank may encounter seriously inhibiting regulations in a new country, and the cost of opening and maintaining a new facility may be substantial. As in the preceding section it is assumed that a bank will operate in another country only if its expected profits are increased.

Banks can be deterred from operating in other countries by their own or foreign governments. Therefore, arranging the possibility of entry is best viewed as an industry or a national diplomatic undertaking. In either case a treaty almost surely entails reciprocity and the risk that foreign banks will to some extent compete in domestic markets. In the present discussion this possibility is assumed to be absent; banks are assumed to seek foreign locations only to conduct business with clients who have head offices in their own country.[10] The clients are allowed to establish foreign subsidiaries in order to negotiate transactions in a foreign tax or legal environment. With this assumption the possibility of establishing foreign branches or subsidiaries is analogous to deregulation within a country, and the previous discussion applies, mutatis mutandis.

Perhaps the purest example of what I have in mind is the "shell" branch of large U.S. banks, which are little more than a mailbox in another country, a storage area in a bank's computer, and a set of documents, loan agreements, and contracts drawn up under the other country's legal code. There are negligible costs to establishing and maintaining such facilities, and a bank's room for maneuver can be considerably enhanced by having one. Analogues to these shells can even be established within a country's own border, as in the case of International Banking Facilities (IBFs) in the United States. The IBF is attractive to U.S. banks because it allows them to operate under U.S. legal code and have no reserve requirements or interest rate ceilings, but potentially unattractive because it is barred from *direct* transactions with domestic clients and is subject to relatively high U.S. rates of income taxation. The last feature has been relatively unimportant in recent years because banks have been extremely successful innovators when it comes to avoiding taxes.

---

[10] Allowing domestic competition by foreign entrants necessarily reduces the attractiveness of trans-national banking to some countries' banks, but not necessarily all.

Banks in both the U.S. and other countries, of course, have entered foreign markets with many other institutional structures such as agencies, leasing corporation subsidiaries, full-service foreign branches, and foreign subsidiary banks acquired through merger. Each of these forms and other varieties of subsidiaries allow banks or their holding company parents to take advantage of differences in countries' laws and regulations and to spread across a larger number of countries than is possible through shells. Often they require substantial investments of capital. Their richness in institutional detail is beyond the scope of the present paper, but very important.

In the narrow perspective being adopted here, banks (hereafter, "banks" denotes either banks or bank holding companies, since the distinction will be irrelevant) establish these relatively costless facilities in other countries to achieve several specific goals. First, banks can reduce the burden of reserve requirements and achieve higher leverage. Reserve and capital requirements that are applied to deposits in a bank's own country are frequently inapplicable or less rigorously enforced when the deposits are booked in facilities in other countries. The implicit costs of rigorous enforcement in the case of a bank's domestic deposits are likely to be especially high when interest rates are high, which is likely to occur when monetary policy in the bank's home country is restrictive.[11] On such occasions offshore banking should be expanding rapidly, and the effectiveness of monetary policy compromised. This is especially true when deposits can be booked abroad in units of the home country's currency, such as Euro-dollars or Euro-marks, but it may also happen in another currency, if the opportunity cost of foregoing loans to good domestic customers is high enough. Both loans and deposits migrate to foreign havens.

Second, banks and their clients can avoid income and wealth taxes by booking deposits or loans in facilities located in tax havens or by laundering funds through other facilities at artificial exchange rates in the tradition of medieval and Renaissance bankers.[12] This function is important whether or not banks themselves are otherwise adept at avoiding taxes, because by artfully booking loans, deposits, and other

[11] I have in mind real short-term interest rates, such as the real federal funds rate. However, when nominal interest rates on some existing assets or liabilities are inflexible, the argument carries over as well to nominal interest rates. In the remainder of this subsection, this caveat applies repeatedly and will not be restated.

[12] Profits of branches are consolidated with those of the home office in the U.S. Internal Revenue Code. Subsidiaries' profits need not be so consolidated. I have used the term "facility" in the text to indicate a general shell form that allows a bank to take advantage of such anomalies.

assets and liabilities for clients, the clients' taxes can be reduced. An important service of intermediaries is to help multinational corporations realize profits in places where tax rates are low. This practice of banks weakens fiscal policy more than monetary policy, but is no less important than that in the preceding paragraph when seeking to stabilize a national economy.

Third, banks can avoid specific regulatory strictures by booking some loans or assets domestically and some through their foreign facilities. For example, loans to a borrowing country can be expanded beyond regulatory guidelines by having a bank book loans both at its home office and at its Swiss subsidiary. International banking consortia, of course, permit much larger volumes of loans than what some central bank may think prudent. Indeed, a bank's own Euro-dollar deposits may implicitly be financing what the bank or its central bank thinks unwise, in a world of incomplete disclosure. Attempts by some central banks or governments to impede financial flows to certain sectors or firms can be thwarted in the Euro-markets. In this even such specific monetary policies are weakened, and bubbles or Ponzi games may occur.

Fourth, even if there were no reserve or capital requirements, a bank with facilities in enough different time zones can profit by effectively extending more credit than a bank in a single location. A bank branch's books must satisfy certain regulatory and accounting standards at the end of a business day. However, in the United States and elsewhere where daylight overdrafts and day loans are commonplace, accounting controls within a business day are relatively weak. Clever large banks with branches placed strategically so that there is always a branch open could wire funds and document facsimiles from East to west and thus avoid ever facing rigid end-of-day accounting tests. In effect these weak accounting standards allow sophisticated banks to counterfeit a country's outside money. Again, in such a world, monetary policies are weakened and bubbles become possible.

Against these goals and opportunities and their resulting impetus for innovation stands the overriding goal of any bank, which is to maintain its own reputation for being safe and reliable. Banks who overextend relative to capital often are found out, and more is lost than gained, as the Continental Bank has demonstrated. A similar fate may await banks who are caught illegally transferring funds to avoid taxes. The stockholders of large U.S. multinational banks have not fared well in relation to other stockholders in recent years, in par because of extensive Latin American loans and associated perceived risks. If these "market" signals were really effective, there would probably be less cause for concern with the international expansion of banking and its high rate of innovation. The temptations flowing from high interest rates have and will lead banks astray.

I know of no complete list of transnational financial innovations. The process and progress were loosely summarized in Hester (1981, 1982), where it is reported that funds substantially flowed across U.S. borders when interest rates were high. Weekend accounting games have been nicely described by Coats (1981). However, much transnational innovation has been very recent or is generally undocumented for competitive and antiregulatory reasons. The effects of the spurt in the acquistition of specialized banking firms in London by large international banks, fluctuations in the rate of acquisition of U.S. banks by foreign interests, the introduction in 1981 of same-day clearing in CHIPS (the [New York] Clearing House International Payments System), and the linkage in futures trading between the Chicago and Singapore markets are presently unclear.

Indeed the growth in the volume of Euro-dollars and other Euro-currencies is not very meaningfully measured or interpretable because of the extraordinary volatility of exchange rates. Such problems commonly occur when one attempts to measure monetary aggregates. Are Euro-currencies held by the residents of some country to be interpreted as part of that country's liquid assets—e.g. part of M2 or M3? International statistics with which I am familiar do not report them by type of owner or by residency status.

Table 8.2 provides some evidence about the volume and number of Euro-dollar transactions and provides comparable data for transactions within the United States. The data suggest that Euro-dollars have an appreciable transactions component, and that perhaps a significant volume of corporate payments in the United States originates with overseas deposits. Between 1970 and 1980 the number of banks effecting CHIPS transactions expanded tenfold. Beginning in 1979 the number was constant for about four years and then began expanding again as the U.S. economy entered a recovery phase. The number of CHIPS transactions rose twelve-fold between 1970 and 1975, but only about trebled in the subsequent eight years. It was between 1972 and 1976 that the domestic demand for money (M1) function in the U.S. appeared to shift down (Goldfeld 1976). A partial explanation may have been the emergence of CHIPS. The ratio of the number of CHIPS transactions to the number of Federal Reserve wire transfers was about constant between 1975 and 1982.

The dollar volume of CHIPS transfers of funds rose about twenty-fold between 1970 and 1975 and about quintupled between 1975 and

Table 7.2   Measures of Transactions Activity in the U.S.

Year	Debits to Demand Deposits[a] ($ Trillions)	Demand Deposit Turnover[a] (annual rate)	Number of Wire Transfers[c] (millions)	Number of CHIPS Messages[b] (millions)	Volume of CHIPS Transfers[a] ($ trillions)	Number of CHIPS Banks[c]
	(1)	(2)	(3)	(4)	(5)	(6)
1970	10.9	77.0	7	0.5	0.5	9
1971	12.4	83.7	8	0.8	1.1	15
1972	14.8	90.7	9	2.0	4.8	15
1973	18.6	110.2	12	2.7	9.2	15
1974	22.2	128.0	15	3.5	10.7	56
1975	23.6	131.0	17	6.0	11.0	63
1976	28.9	153.5	21	7.1	13.1	69
1977	34.3[f]	129.2[f]	25	8.2	16.2	77
1978	40.3	139.4	29	9.6	20.4	80
1979	49.8	163.5	35	10.9	26.8	92
1980	63.0	202.3	43	13.2	37.1	100
1981	80.9	285.3	54	15.9	40.0	99
1982	90.9	324.2	58	18.6	53.0	99
1983	109.6	379.7	NA	20.2	60.3	117
1984	128.1[e]	436.7[e]	NA	NA	69.1[d]	NA

[a] *Source*: *Federal Reserve Bulletin*, various issues, December data at annual rates.

[b] *Source*: Annual Reports of Board of Governors of the Federal Reserve System. Data reflect double counting since both the sender and receiver are counted.

[c] *Source*: Correspondence with Mr. John P. Owens, Manager, CHIPS Participant Support.

[d] This item was imputed from 1983 annual figure and percentage change between 1983 and 1984 for first eleven months.

[e] 1984 entries are for August 1984, at an annual rate.

[f] The series on debits and deposit turnover were redefined in 1977.

1983. Between 1973 and 1981 the dollar volume of CHIPS transfers was about one-half of the mushrooming volume of debits to demand deposits. The change from two-day to same-day settlement in late 1981 probably contributed to a 30 percent rise in CHIPS transactions in 1982. The ratio of dollar volumes of CHIPS to wire transfers was higher after 1981 than previously.

Since same-day clearing is more convenient for corporations doing transactions than two-day clearing, this sharp increase again suggests that a non-negligible fraction of CHIPS transfers were being used for transactions.[13] This is especially true for large corporations since there was a sharp increase in the average size of transactions at this time. These patterns further complicate the question of how to measure M1, the transactions component of money, and how to interpret its movements. The rather incredible growth in demand deposit turnover between 1978 and 1984 suggests effects that innovations have already had upon the usefulness of M1.

Finally, in a technical sense a country's monetary policy is almost inevitably weakened when substantial amounts of international assets are denominated in its unit of account. The massive volumes of dollar-denominated assets and liabilities in the world suggest that the market for the U.S. dollar is very broad. An open market sale of, say, $1 billion is likely to have a smaller effect in the U.S. under these conditions than it would in a world where no dollars were held by foreign residents. A minor consequence is that open market operations will need to be larger absolutely relative to the U.S. monetary base in order to achieve the same effect that was obtainable in a closed economy. More serious is the fact that shocks to a country's demand for and supply of money may be relatively larger than in the closed economy case, and this may change the effectiveness of monetary policy and the choice between controlling monetary aggregates and interest rates, as Poole (1970) argued. Also potentially serious are the damages that monetary and fiscal policies may have on other countries in this world of the "dirty" float, and the potential political repercussions therefrom. By dirty float I mean a regime in which exchange rates fluctuate, but are also manipulated through central bank interventions.

III. Market Technology and Monetary Policy

Monetary policy affects economic activity by altering the values and variety of assets in portfolios. A necessary condition for open market operations that consist of swapping outside money for government securities to be effective is that money and securities are not perfect substitutes. Changes in reserve requirements, Lombard rates, or other policy stipulations can be effective only if they induce changes in desired portfolios.

Outside money—currency and deposits of nongovernmental institutions carried with a country's central bank—performs two roles in a modern economy. First, it is the medium through which transactions

---

[13] Another change in late 1981 was the opening of International Banking Facilities. The increased 1982 CHIPS volume may also be a consequence of this innovation.

are "finalized" in the sense of serving as legal tender. Second, through reserve requirements and settlement rules it is the principal vehicle through which a central bank controls the volume of inside money created by depository intermediaries.

As argued above, financial innovations and deregulation tend to increase the set of assets and liabilities in an economy. They also tend to reduce the amount of outside money that is demanded by individuals; innovations have increased the efficiency with which transactions are finalized and both innovations and deregulation have allowed a number of close substitutes for outside money to emerge. Also, as argued above, high interest rates and restrictive monetary policy appear to have induced both innovation and deregulation. The question examined in this section is how the effectiveness of monetary policy is changed when high interest rates induce irreversible increases in the number of assets and the efficiency with which transactions are cleared.

A. A Simple Macro Model

The framework is an economy in which there are a large number of heterogeneous individuals, and a small number of financial intermediaries who are threatened with entry. Individuals are price and rate takers and there is a single physical good. Initially there are n assets in the economy; the first is the stock of physical capital which is indistinguishable from the physical good. The nth asset is outside money, which is exogenously determined by the monetary authority and pays no interest; it is the numeraire. The first $n - 1$ assets have infinitesimal maturities and pay rates of return that vary over time. Uncertainty emanates from the goods market; production of the good has a random component, e, whose distribution is universally known. The labor force is taken as exogenous.

The second through n-1st assets are defined by financial contracts among individuals, the government, and intermediaries that might take the form of loans, deposits, bonds, etc. The assets are not sufficient in number to span the state space. When shocks to production occur, individuals and institutions modify their portfolios according to their own best interests. The combination of shocks and portfolio responses induces a joint distribution of rates of return for the first $n - 1$ assets. The joint distribution of asset rates of return need not be stationary over time, because the population of investors is slowly changing and because the set of assets may be expanding over time. It is convenient to assume that individuals are risk averse, have twice differentiable utility functions, and view all assets as being gross substitutes.

Initially there are $n - 1$ supply functions and n demand functions for assets that suffice with the production function to determine $n - 1$ rates of return, $n - 1$ asset stocks, the price of the physical good, and output. Consumption is determined implicitly when output and net investment are determined, since government spending, taxation, and net foreign investment are taken as exogenous. The tradeoff between changes in output and prices is not likely to be stationary over time. Nominal rates are contractually determined in a manner that reflects the marginal product of labor when the price level is unchanging.

Assets in the model are heterogeneous; none has a rate of return that is a linear combination of other rates of return. They should be thought of as being somewhat state-dependent but, as noted above, incapable of spanning the space of outcomes that is generated by random shocks to production. While bankruptcy is not allowed for obvious technical reasons, depositors and others may well receive only a fraction of their investment back in seriously depressed states. Realized rates of return can be negative!

It is assumed that the monetary authority seeks to avoid labor unrest by using open market operations to peg the price level, and thereby make workers' price expectations rational. (I surely do not claim that this is wise, although it does seem to have a real-world counterpart.) As a result, when a negative supply shock occurs monetary policy is contractionary to prevent what would otherwise be a period of rising prices, and when a positive supply shock occurs monetary policy is expansionary.[14]

The method that the monetary authority uses to determine the volume of open market operations in response to supply shocks is important, but is left vague in this discussion. I assume that everyone can observe supply shocks at the same time and that the central bank has enough assets in its portfolio to peg the price level in the absence of innovations. In a closed economy this is analogous to assuming that a government can determine its own stock of outside money and that a mapping exists and can be used at each instant to control the price level with the stock of outside money.[15] This assumption is very strong

---

[14] An analysis of the welfare consequences of such a policy is beyond the scope of the present paper. Individuals often are simultaneously recipients of labor and capital income. Suffice it to say that a policy of protecting the veracity of workers' expectations about prices is a very diffierent policy from one which attempts to shelter their consumption expenditures from shocks. Net debtors are at the mercy of net creditors when central banks respond to negative supply shocks solely by attempting to peg the price level.

[15] This assumption can obviously be weakened, but only at the cost of complicating the discussion in the next part of this paper.

and difficult to justify in a multinational context, as is evident from any number of unsuccessful attempts to peg exchange rates.

While workers' price expectations and the real value of their labor income are protected, investors are rewarded with higher interest rates when a negative supply shock occurs. Investors could render this policy infeasible if they choose to spend interest income or to invest in physical capital. In this case restrictive fiscal policy through increased taxes or reduced government spending would be the only solution. Even if investors cooperate, government deficits would rise as interest payments on debt rose and private sector net debtors would be increasingly penalized until they reduced consumption or sold physical capital to escape rising interest rates.

The story is similar when a positive shock occurs. In this instance monetary policy is expansionary and open market operations cause interest rates to decline. Debtors' interest expenditures decline and they benefit from the boon. Creditors' income declines and workers' purchasing power of labor income is unchanged. This policy also can be frustrated if spending on real goods fails to rise, but such an outcome seems improbable.

B. Introducing Financial Innovation

Now suppose that interest rates rise in response to a negative shock— perhaps a war that diverts goods from domestic markets or an arbitrarily large increase in oil prices. The probability of a financial market innovation is assumed to be an increasing function of the level of nominal interest rates. Suppose an innovation occurs that takes the form of a new asset, the $n+1$st. There will be a supply and demand for it that will be functions of all interest rates, production, wealth, and tastes. In these respects the innovation is indistinguishable from other assets. Demand functions for existing assets must be modified to incorporate the interest rate of the new asset. The assumption that all assets are gross substitutes continues to apply, and I assume that the innovation allows greater but not complete spanning of the state space.

At the moment the innovation occurs, disequilibrium prevails and interest rates move in various directions. For some time individuals may appear to violate the assumption of gross substitutability as they struggle to rebalance their portfolios. Once equilibrium is restored, life continues as before, but with the set of assets permanently larger.

In equilibrium the effects of introducing a new asset depend upon the market structure that exists among financial institutions. If all institutions within an intermediary class are price takers and there is no collusion amongst intermediaries, introduction of a new asset seems to be equivalent to establishing a new intermediary specializing in that single asset. From Brainard and Tobin (1963) it can be seen that introducing a new intermediary is unambiguously expansionary in the sense that the required rate of return on physical capital falls. Therefore, open market sales would need to be larger after an innovation occurred in order to achieve a given desired level of restraint.

If imperfect competition exists it generally is not possible to view a new innovation as if it were a new intermediary, and I am not able to conclude that innovation is expansionary. The same would apply if the innovation were protected by copyrights or patents. I believe an innovation would usually be expansionary, but one can construct counterexamples.

When the possibility of innovation exists, the task of the monetary authority is much more difficult. A central bank may still observe supply shocks, but it does not necessarily observe the occurrence of an innovation. With an innovation the mapping between outside money and prices may be non-unique or may not exist for a transition period between the two regimes. A sequence of policy moves that would peg the price level would be very hard to determine. In such circumstances transitory variations in the price level might be unavoidable, and the credibility of the authority's policy stance weakened.

If only one innovation ever occurs, the problem does not seem very serious. Once the central bank puzzles out what happened, it can return to pegging the price level with considerable precision. However, if a continuing sequence of innovations is experienced, monetary authorities may never understand the operative regime and a constant price level becomes unobtainable. This possibility cannot be excluded *a priori* because innovations, like supply shocks, to some extent occur autonomously.

In the assumed structure (and apparently in the real world) innovations are also induced by high nominal interest rates, which proxy for the strength of loan demand by the public. The task of a central bank can be eased somewhat by a policy that keeps interest rates from rising to high levels or becoming too volatile. Indeed, with the assumed specification, avoiding high and volatile interest rates is the only mechanism for avoiding a high induced rate of financial innovation.

It almost goes without saying that a necessary condition for avoiding high nominal interest rates is the avoidance of negative real rates of interest. If real interest rates are perceived to be negative by borrowers, a speculative bubble is inevitable in the absence of credit rationing. Negative real interest rates were not consistent with price stability during most of the decade beginning 1970. It is my opinion that the spate of high real interest rates which has plagued the world in recent years is partly a belated overreaction to the recognition of this problem by major central banks in the late 1970s.

C. Financial Innovations that Expedite Processing of Information

A major part of financial innovation in recent decades has been improvement in the technical efficiency (speed and reduced cost) with which transactions can be executed. I have in mind credit cards, debit cards, improved wire transfer facilities, automated payrolls and tellers, preauthorized transfers, point-of-sale terminals, etc. Except for credit cards, whose maximal summed minimum monthly payment belongs in the aggregate purporting to measure transactions media, these innovations introduced no new financial asset. Instead they are product improvements that reduce the demand for transactions media such as currency, demand deposits, and other low-interest-bearing checkable deposits. They are obvious responses to high and rising interest rates. The effects of their introduction in the U.S. are evident in column 2 of Table 8.2. In the U.S. the ratio of the ultimate transactions media—currency plus reserves on deposit at Federal Reserve Banks—to GNP has declined steadily in the past fifteen years.

In the foregoing framework, the share of outside money that is held in portfolios solely for the purpose of executing transactions has been diminishing. Such changes can be represented by a decline in the demand for non-interest-bearing cash assets or by what is equivalent, an autonomous injection of outside money. Again assuming that individuals view assets as being gross substitutes and that individuals and firms are interest rate takers, it is possible to predict the effects of this sort of financial innovation. From Brainard and Tobin (1963) it can be seen that increasing the stock of outside money unambiguously reduces the required rate of return on capital and is therefore expansionary. A central bank must reduce the rate of growth of outside money when such innovations are occurring more rapidly, if it wishes to achieve a given target level of prices.

As before, no conclusion about the effects of such innovations on GNP can be drawn when financial markets are imperfectly competitive. The effects then depend upon which agents have access to the advanced clearing technology. It seems likely that substantial redistributive effects in favor of those with access would occur at the expense of those who were excluded. That at least was the experience in the U.S. before 1981 when large corporations and their banks were manipulating Federal Reserve float.

D. Transnational Financial Innovations

Transnational financial innovations do not fit cleanly into the foregoing framework, except in the artificial form in which they were considered above. Specifically, if it is assumed that transnational innovations only directly affect the country where an intermediary is based, then conclusions follow trivially. Transnational financial innovation is analogous to introducing a new asset and/or to expediting transactions in that country; all of the foregoing conclusions apply.

Suppose instead that an intermediary enters a second country and new branches or subsidiaries do business with individuals in this country, but not in their home country. If the entrant is viable, then it must effectively be providing services or assets that were not previously available in the second country. With the usual assumptions of gross substitution and being interest rate takers, the required rate of return for capital must fall with entry. The second country's central bank must engage in a contractionary series of open market sales in order to maintain a stable price level, when entry occurs.

More interesting cases arise when the expanding intermediary operates in both the first and second countries without restriction. Suppose that its constituent firms are interest rate takers in each country and that residents in each view all assets and liabilities as being gross substitutes. How will entry affect the welfare of individuals?

Assume that the framework described at the beginning of this section applies in each country and that a flexible exchange rate regime exists. Arbitrarily the currency in the first country is taken as a numeraire. Individuals in each country can freely hold assets offered by intermediaries, irrespective of their national origin, but they can only hold assets denominated in their own country's currency. Intermediaries can, however, operate with an unbalanced book in the sense that they can use funds received in one country to acquire assets that exist in a second country. The exchange rate is determined by the requirement that the demand and supply for currencies are equated at a level where there is no net flow of currencies. In effect liabilities and assets of both countries are traded among intermediaries until each is content with its holdings. The market is assumed to be Walrasian; no trades occur until an exchange rate is quoted that results in zero excess demand.

Firms in the various intermediaries will not enter the other country unless they are better off in terms of their expected rate of return. Suppose that they do enter. More intermediaries operating in a country implies that a greater number of financial assets will be available to its residents. Individuals in each country may or may not benefit from this arrangement. As Hakannson (1982) suggests, it is not necessarily the case that the menu of assets offered by these multinational inter-mediaries spans the set of assets that were offered before capital markets were opened to foreign entrants. For example, if someone were extremely averse to exchange rate risk and none of the intermediaries ran a balanced book, he would be worse off.

In addition, as Hakannson reports, the wealth of citizens in one of the countries could decline at the time the regime is changing to admit foreign intermediaries. One cannot exclude the possibility that opening up a country's borders will raise its required rate of return on capital and, therefore, be contractionary. The reason such outcomes are possible is that various factors of production and resources are not costlessly mobile. As in welfare economics, compensation must be paid by gainers to losers to induce them to open up capital markets. It is not evident how one determines the magnitude of such compensation or makes it politically acceptable.

Assuming that countries manage to open up their capital markets to each other's intermediaries, it is clear from exercises performed with multi-country models that policy actions by one country can inflict serious damage on another. Such questions are beyond the scope of this paper; the focus here is only on the feasibility of policy from the myopic perspective of a single monetary authority.

Assuming monetary authorities continue to seek to stabilize domestic price levels, as in the closed economy case, it no longer follows that a negative supply shock should be met by a contractionary monetary policy. A negative supply shock could generate withdrawals of foreign capital as intermediaries seek to reduce their exchange rate risk exposure. Their actions could generate precipitous rises in interest rates and declines in prices. There almost always would be an optimal policy response, but its nature cannot be known without extraordinarily detailed information about behavior in the various countries.

In closing, I wish to state forcefully that it does not follow from this need for greater understanding about the way the world works that one should resort to (a) pegging interest rates, (b) adopting a constant monetary growth rate rule, or (c) closing one's border to foreign capital or intermediaries. In the last section of this paper I will argue that it is desirable to limit the variability of exchange rate fluctuations and to seek arrangements by which international shocks, both positive and negative, are shared.

E. On the Importance of Introducing and Enforcing Rigorous Clearing Standards

The rapidly rising volume of CHIPS transfers indicates that international transfers of funds have been soaring. They appear to include a transactions component that is also not readily imbedded in the framework of this section. If a transactions component exists in the sense that a country's *domestic* transactions are being financed by daily transfers from foreign countries, the demand for the country's currency and reserves will be lower than otherwise. If the country's central bank is seeking to maintain a constant domestic price level, it should compensate for the external financing of domestic transactions by making open market sales.

Many of the CHIPS transfers are transactions between nonresidents of the United States. They are in part between subsidiaries or branches of U.S. nonfinancial corporations (intermediated by banks) that are located in foreign countries. Such dollar-denominated transfers may be international trade transactions, which have been growing more rapidly than domestic economic activity during most of the past forty years.[16] They also are, in part, transactions between two entities that are both located in the same foreign country or transactions that could as well have been completed domestically between head offices in the U.S.

The latter two cases illustrate a fundamental weakness in monetary policy design that is based on controlling the volume of a country's transactions medium. In a world with extensively commingled domestic and international accounts, there is no way to know whether transactions in a country's currency units finance domestic or foreign economic activity.[17] In effect the volume of a country's transactions has been disconnected from the volume of its own transactions medium—its outside money.

Controlling the volume of transactions media to control nominal transactions in a closed economy illustrates one of the two primary rationalizations for how monetary policy can affect real economic activity and/or prices. It has a long and honorable intellectual history, and was implicit in contributions by Henry Simons and some early articles by Milton Friedman. The other rationalization is of course

[16] Space does not allow a discussion of the implications of the growing volume of international transactions for *collective* monetary policy in the world, but it is a topic that badly needs more study.

[17] The reasons for choosing to make transactions in another country were presented in the previous section.

through interest rates which may either be viewed as influencing the excess demand for investment or the excess demand for loans. It is not vulnerable to the measurement defect just noted, because of the actions of arbitrageurs and speculators. However, as will become evident in the next section, it also has a shortcoming in that the resources of arbitrageurs and speculators may be insufficient in a world of widly fluctuating exchange rates.

The probable loss of the outside money linkage is seriously damaging to the design of monetary policy in a transnational context. This loss is amplified by a similar loss that is associated with innovations discussed above in Part C of this section, and whose effects are evident in the first columns of Table 8.2. The remainder of this section proposes a series of institutional and regulatory changes that are designed to restore partially the linkage between the volume of outside money and nominal economic activity in a country. The proposed rules concern clearing of transactions and are an attempt to modernize the legal tender feature of outside money. The central bank jargon for what I am discussing is "finality" or the conditions under which financial transactions are agreed upon as being settled. The subject is appropriate for this conference because settlement rules are the anvil upon which private sector monetary policy actions are beaten into shape.

Consider first a closed economy with a modern interbank wire transfer mechanism, such as exists in the U.S. At the start of a business day a large bank in the U.S. typically must acquire a large number of securities which it had "sold" in the overnight repurchase agreement market. It simultaneously credits the deposit accounts of the firms and state and local governments that delivered the securities with "good" or immediately available funds. These customers of the bank then can pay bills and make purchases with this cash, which is legally indistinguishable from outside money. In effect, the bank has legally counterfeited transactions media which only has to be retired late in the business day when accounts must conventionally be settled. The link between transactions and the official governmental transactions medium, outside money, has been broken.

This slippage can be eliminated or at least lessened by tightening the accounting mechanism that a central bank (the Federal Reserve) uses to police its accounts. An extremely effective mechanism would be to require that no bank's account at the Federal Reserve is ever overdrawn during a day. This would constrict the volume of overnight or continuing contract repurchase agreements that a bank could accept. If a bank had too many maturing repurchase agreements, it might not have sufficient Reserve Bank balances to instantaneously execute customers' instructions. Wire transfer queues would form and daylight overdrafts would disappear.

The proposal would serve to re-establish the distinction between outside money and government securities, which is the central underpinning of open market operations. The rapid expansion of security repurchase agreements during the early 1970s was a financial market innovation that blunted the distinction. The proposal might be opposed by a country's fiscal authority, because it would increase financing costs of government debt by making securities less attractive assets. Partly offsetting this increased cost would be a greater demand for currency and reserves.

An even more effective mechanism would be to introduce real-time reserve accounting, which would require banks almost always either to hold excess reserves or to be paying interest at the Federal Reserve discount window. This would cause substantial investments in computer soft- and hardware by both banks and the Federal Reserve; it doubtless would be opposed by financial intermediaries, since nobody enjoys making "needless" outlays. It has all the charm and benefits of antipollution equipment. The computer has allowed much slippage in the link between transactions media and nominal magnitudes; technology should be symmetrically applied by regulators and regulatees.

Offshore transactions that are cleared through CHIPS are in clearing house funds. They absorb no outside money until the end of a business day when clearing house banks must settle with the Federal Reserve. Any attempt at changing the settlement process with the Federal Reserve is likely to require changes in the settlement protocols at CHIPS. Since CHIPS is now operating on a "same day" basis, CHIPS must achieve settlement before the Fed wire can shut down. If an accelerated Federal Reserve clearing schedule were adopted, CHIPS would need to clear even more rapidly than the wire. With this observation, CHIPS clearing reforms are seen to be implied by either of the foregoing proposals.

Offshore transactions that are cleared on a within-branch or within-bank basis are, of course, not subject to CHIPS rules. They would not be subject to Federal Reserve reserve requirements ordinarily. This is a difficult area in which to propose rules since a bank may in effect be allowing the establishment of intrabank loans, by transferring funds across time zones. The payoff to a bank for participating in such a system is the avoidance of reserve requirements. In this respect it is similar to the wee kend Eurodollar games that Coats (1981) analyzed. If market interest rates were paid on required reserves, the incentive to make inter-time-zone loans would be reduced. Banks run a serious risk of being caught in a Ponzi game with such loans, and probably would not participate if reserves were interest bearing.

Heretofore, regulatory agency reforms of mechanisms for clearing transactions seem to have been motivated by concerns that a failure by some institution to meet its settlement responsibilities would endanger the financial system. The failures or near-failures of the Herstatt Bank, the Drysdale Government Securities Co., the Franklin National Bank, and the Continental Illinois National Bank come to mind. Such instances induced tiering of interest rates, CHIPS to go to a same-day clearing basis, and participants in the federal funds market to develop software to limit the amounts of daylight overdrafts and overnight loans that any bank can obtain. These changes moved the systems in the direction that I am proposing and had the effect, at the time they were introduced, of constricting the flow of items that could be cleared with existing facilities. Over time these restrictive effects disappeared as facilities were improved. The changes I propose above will improve both the reliability of the system and accuracy in achieving the optimal amount of outside money.

It is no accident that concern about systemwide vulnerability to clearing failures led to improvements in the control of the effective amount of outside money. The reason outside money's legal tender feature is attractive is that it allows individuals to finalize their own transactions and thereby reduce future risks of litigation. Immediately available funds are useful only if they are in fact good. Recent attempts to privatize clearing functions that were encouraged by the U.S. Monetary Control Act of 1980 are a step in the wrong direction, if such mechanisms increase the probability of a failure to achieve settlement. The effective amount of outside money would then become less predictable. It is important to validate the integrity of private sector systems and to insure that the combined public and private network is sound.

Finally, a very simple and comprehensive institutional change is to recognize that a country's currency unit and liabilities denominated in it are that country's responsibility, wherever they are booked. If the Federal Reserve, for example, raises reserve requirements on dollar-denominated demand deposits in the U.S., the principle of symmetry suggests that dollar-denominated demand deposits booked elsewhere should also be subject to higher reserve requirements. Failure to observe this principle merely invites international currency flows and innovations that may well prove to be destabilizing. The focus should be on the liability and not where it is booked or in what country's bank it is booked.

To implement this reform, it is necessary for central banks to agree to respect and enforce each other's regulations to the extent that liabilities are denominated in each other's unit of account. A country could avoid this seeming infringement of its sovereignty by declining to allow foreign currency denominated accounts.

Countries that failed to cooperate would presumably be subject to sanctions. For example, a central bank could refuse to allow its banks to transact in the currencies of such countries or to open branches there. No doubt enforcement problems would arise if some liability were unique to a country, but denominated in currencies of other countries. Also, the scope of authority of central banks varies across countries. It might be awkward for the Bank of England to tell building societies that they must deposit 12% of their dollar-denominated checkable deposits with the Bank. I doubt that such problems would seriously disable the thrust of this proposal, but bankers can be remarkably innovative!

IV. The Practice of Monetary Policy When Induced Innovations are Possible

This concluding section contains an assessment of the gains that can be expected from pursuing different monetary policy strategies when financial innovations are possible. The goal throughout is to identify operating principles that central banks should adhere to. As was evident in the survey of the monetary experiences of Italy, Japan, the U.K., and the U.S., it is very unlikely that the same strategy should be adopted in different countries; reliable basic principles are the most that should be expected. While I believe that the technical proposals just considered have considerable merit, the regime assumed in the present section is what actually exists. The first part concerns a single closed economy, and the last a system of interconnected economies.

A. Closed Economy

As indicated in the beginning of this paper, rigid adherence to any rule is likely to be mischievous. As regimes change, the meaning of the nominal interest rate on some asset changes. It is only a relative price. The same applies to monetary aggregates such as old M1, the sum of currency and demand deposits adjusted. When NOW accounts or other checkable deposits appear, definitions must change to reflect the new regime. What is to be included in the narrow transactions aggregate must be determined in terms of theoretical arguments about substitution elasticities and plausible institutional arrangements. Econometric evidence from distant time periods is not a reliable foundation; nor is rote adherence to 6 %—whether it be an interest rate or an aggregate growth rate.

Suppose through some discretionary judgmental process, a central bank at some point in time decides to focus on some crude empirical approximation to a desired nominal interest rate and aggregate or several interest rates and aggregates. The bank will undoubtedly continue to monitor and refine their meanings with the passage of time.

At this point one properly should present an extensive discourse about whether expectations are rational and describe the information sets that different agents are using when making decisions. One should also discuss the nature of contracts and whether or not they are fully indexed with respect to prices. Rather than comply, I simply assume that information is incomplete and that markets are imperfect for reasons that have been suggested by Grossman and Stiglitz (1976). Further, I assume that private sector agents are risk-averse. A central bank is less relatively risk-averse than private sector agents and is not constrained to act profitably.[18] It can afford to be better informed and is. This allows it incompletely to control the course of the economy.

There is no reliable formal model for policymakers because of random and induced innovations that change structural equations. For institutional reasons that need no repeating here, prices and wages are partially determined by contracts that span significantly long time intervals and are not fully indexed. In the short run it is plausible that nominal interest rates can be set at any desired level by sufficiently aggressive open market operations. Therefore, even in the absence of a complete formal model, a central bank can (with some error) determine a real short-term rate of interest. In particular it can approximately set the *ex post* real federal funds rate, given some set of wage and price contracts.

The first operating principle is that real interest rates should be strictly positive, in order to avoid inflationary speculative bubbles. Because the largest nonfinancial corporations can actually borrow at interest rates that are often about fifty basis points above the federal funds rate in the commercial paper, Euro-dollar, or repurchase agreement markets, the real funds rate could be as low as -0.50% without a bubble. However, the price indices that are relevant vary considerably across firms and none of them is accurately measured. In light of

---

[18] An important provision of the Depository Institutions Deregulation and Monetary Control Act of 1980 constrains the Federal Reserve not to subsidize its check processing and other services provided to banks, so as to allow private sector competition. If the Federal Reserve's informational advantage was reduced by this provision, its ability to control nominal GNP may have been weakened.

these difficulties, a central bank would do well to keep the real short-term rate above a threshold of one or one and one-half percent.

Nominal interest rates in the marketplace and inflation rates are virtually continuous random variables that respond to a variety of shocks. At any point in time purchases of an arbitrary good are occurring at several different prices. Market prices are thus not well defined (non-unique) and generally unobservable. Similar but less severe conditions exist in markets for securities and federal funds. Arbitrageurs attempt to keep spot prices within a certain range, and speculators attempt to provide the same service intertemporally. The prices speculators, hedgers, and "sequence transactors" set in forward and futures markets reflect information and beliefs about the future, which are often vague.[19] These traders' reserves and access to credit are limited relative to the resources available to central banks.

A second operating principle is that a central bank should attempt to influence and intimidate traders by being willing to transact in certain asset markets at prices or rates that reflect its assumed informational advantages. It should intervene at times and in assets where its intentions can be clearly inferred; it should not necessarily intervene continuously or respond immediately to shocks. It is quite plausible that it may not know the source of a shock or how to respond to it.[20]

Even if central banks were no better informed than other market participants about some shock, they have a responsibility to a different clientele than other traders. Volatile rumor-dominated markets tend to discourage saving in forms that are socially beneficial, gold hoards, manorial haciendas, and a low rate of private capital formation result.[21] A third operating principle is that central banks should respond actively in capital markets where volatility threatens to inflict severe intra- or intertemporal capital market hardships. This is partly to affirm that central banks continue to have a lender-of-last-resort function in a regime with continuing innovations.

In the second section I argued that financial innovations resulted

[19] Sequence transactors are individuals who must place orders in spot markets for future delivery at prices that will be in effect at the time of delivery.

[20] I am not writing an apology for the incompetence of central banks. My view is best conveyed by an analogy. When one finds a victim of an accident who is bleeding or otherwise requires first aid, on average it is best that more informed observers attempt to provide assistance. There is no assurance that the optimal procedures will be employed.

[21] Central banks surely can be dominated by scoundrels in government, but attacking discretionary intervention for such reasons is to treat symptoms rather than causes.

from certain institutional features of banking markets. When nominal interest rates rose in asset markets, bank profits tended to rise. This occurred because most bank liabilities paid relatively low interest rates and they tended to be inflexible when market interest rates were rising. Innovations occurred both because nonfinancial firms were trying to enter and share in the potential profits and because banks were attempting to deter such entrants. With deregulation and the increasing tendency for banks to pay market interest rates on liabilities, this sort of innovation will be less frequent in the future. However, so long as the interest rates banks pay are below the free market rate, it will continue.

A consequence of this erosion of bank monopoly rents was the decline in bank profits shown in Table 8.1. The return to bank stockholders has been low, and bank capital is likely increasingly to consist of subordinated debt, until new profitable lines of activity are developed. Also, as is plainly evident in the composition of new bank services and credit guarantees, bank capital will bear more risks than heretofore. Much of this will not be evident from an examination of conventional bank balance sheets. Effectively leverage will be rising.

A fourth operating principle is to increase central bank surveillance of bank procedures and capital adequacy. There is an unpleasant dilemma for central banks in this, because if capital standards are set too high nonfinancial enterprises will again surreptitiously enter through innovations.[22] If standards are set too low, continuing failures or near-failures are inevitable. While the failures may be equitably distributed between banks and nonfinancial entrants, only the former are the responsibility of the monetary authority. Ultimately, it may be the case that monetary stability requires that banks receive a continuing subsidy either openly or through continuing governmental certification and warranty. Freely competitive markets operating in conditions of uncertainty cannot avoid defaults. Private insurance is unlikely to be able to mobilize sufficient capital resources to avoid an occasional banking collapse. Government insurance of either banks or their private sector insurers seems essential.

As the process of financial innovation continues, it is likely that

---

[22] It might be possible to improve the profitability of banks slightly (and deter entry slightly) by allowing interest to be paid on reserves. In the U.S. required reserves are less than 2 percent of banking assets, and therefore not much to work with. Further, if reserve requirements can be held as government securities, the analytical foundation for the effectiveness of open market operations vanishes in terms of conventional deposit multiplier stories. In a forthcoming Wisconsin Ph.D. dissertation, Rowena A. Pecchenino examines how monetary policy could work in such a system.

new close substitutes for "money" and the services it provides will continue to appear. Unless money is redefined to incorporate them, the income and transactions velocities of M1 and to a lesser extent M2 (because it increasingly is paying market interest rates) will irregularly rise over time. This has been starkly evident for M1 in the U.S. since about 1948. In recent decades, percentage changes in income velocities of M1 and M2 have been considerably more volatile annually in the U.S. than have percentage changes in either monetary aggregate (Hester, 1981, p. 179). Even with redefinitions, the constant dollar value of M1 is lower in 1984 than it was a dozen years earlier and real income is much larger. In short, monetary aggregates are not very useful as policy guides in periods of rapid innovation, when taken in isolation.

I do not wish to be misinterpreted. Almost all financial and economic measures contain information that is useful. My fifth operating principle is that central banks continue to collect information about, redefine, and monitor monetary aggregates and that this information together with other data be used to formulate and justify discretionary policies.

The relationships between interest rates, real or nominal, and percentage changes in GNP also have not been tight. Nevertheless, I shall argue that a sound sixth operating principle is to follow Wicksell and attempt to control the difference between short-term nominal interest rates and the rate of inflation.[23] As I shall also point out, however, there are serious deficiencies with policies that result in wide fluctuations in nominal or real interest rates. These deficiencies put a limit on the potential usefulness of monetary policy as a sole stabilization vehicle; fiscal and monetary policies must be complementary.

The traditional basis for believing that high real interest rates will retard aggregate demand is that individuals will desire to save more, that firms will desire to invest less, and that an appreciating currency will eventually reduce net foreign investment as interest rates rise. In each case the impact will occur with a rather long distributed lag. The traditional complaint against accepting this transmission mechanism is the belief that real interest rates are exogenous and cannot be affected by, say, open market operations. Perhaps the single overwhelming lesson from the Volcker era is that the real federal funds rate can be varied between 1 % and 12 % if a central bank is so inclined. It matters little

---

[23] The choice of a price index to use when measuring inflation is important. I have in mind the GNP implicit price deflator, but other indices may be more appropriate under certain conditions such as an OPEC price rise.

whether one appeals to the laws of supply and demand in securities markets or relies on hoary tales of uncertainty about the stability of banks, future interest rates, or future inflation; the real rate can be moved.

Further, even in the context of financial innovation, arbitrageurs and speculators cause nominal interest rates on different short-term financial assets to move conformingly. This is the major advantage that a policy of controlling nominal or real interest rates has over a strategy of focusing on some monetary aggregate. Within the financial capacity of arbitrageurs, any short-term interest rate reveals the thrust of monetary policy, almost irrespective of the nature of innovations. Monetary aggregates, by contrast, must be repeatedly arbitrarily redefined.

There are two major weaknesses to focusing on real interest rates as a guide to monetary policy, in addition to the lags that I have already mentioned. First, real interest rates are influenced by fiscal policy as the most elementary Hicksian IS-LM analysis predicts. Monetary policy rules to control interest rates cannot be given in terms of open market transactions independently of current and projected future deficits and private sector assets.

Second, the effects of an open market sale are critically sensitive to the nature of contracts outstanding and prospective in an economy. An open market sale of securities will have a different effect depending upon whether or not financial contracts specify interest rates that "float," or are indexed, say, to the treasury bill rate. When interest rate indexation is general and interest rates rise, a transfer of wealth from debtors to creditors occurs which may cause aggregative saving to rise or fall. Depending upon demographic and political considerations, large open market sales may not even be feasible in a democracy when indexation is present or when relatively large amounts of loans must be rolled over at market rates. High real interest rates precipitate high foreclosure and bankruptcy rates, as the recent U.S. experience demonstrates.

The problem with the trend toward growing use of interest rate indexation is not that it causes a redistribution of wealth; restrictive monetary policy has always impaired the welfare of potential borrowers and improved that of some lenders. The problem is that the number of individuals conspicuously and substantially adversely affected by rising interest rates has been considerably increased. Indexation of interest rates has been a consequence of the exceptional volatility of nominal interest rates during the past twenty years in the U.S. and by a declining ratio of capital to assets at financial institutions. It was also a financial innovation.

In the context of a single closed economy, sufficiently high real interest rates eventually will reduce investment demand and the desired stock of capital. It may not be pretty or quick, but it will work. Sufficiently high real interest rates will correspond with a low monetary base, so the issue does not ultimately hang on whether one focuses on real rates or monetary aggregates.

It is no accident that large fiscal deficits and/or increases in government spending have coincided with periods of high nominal interest rates and financial innovation in the four countries studied in Section 2. Expansionary fiscal policy that is accompanied by restrictive monetary policy results in high real interest rates. Unless a general deflation is simultaneously occurring, nominal interest rates and the probability of financial innovation will also be high.

To avoid induced innovations, a seventh operating principle is that central banks should avoid high real interest rates—say, a real federal funds rate of 5% or more. This guideline has the beneficial side effect that it gives firms and individuals time to make a co-ordinated response to a newly restrictive policy and thus reduces the incidence of disruptive insolvencies and bankruptcies. It puts a limit on the contribution that monetary policy can make to anti-inflationary programs, and it should encourage more responsibility on the part of the fiscal authority.

B. Interconnected Economies

In this part I consider the problem of a central bank that is attempting to control an economy in a world which is described by neither a purely fixed nor a purely floating exchange rate system. Therefore, the standard Mundell arguments imply that both fiscal and monetary policies can be effective. The central bank is assumed not to be in a "small" country and thus its actions will affect economies of other countries and may elicit a response from them. I assume that the bank is concerned with the welfare of other economies only to the extent that their progress benefits its economy. To keep the discussion manageable, I assume that countries only aim for a noncooperative equilibrium.

I assume financial institutions exist in all countries and that they are able to do business across borders, both in their own sovereign currency units and in others. Suppose a central bank undertakes a contractionary policy that results in an increase in its country's own real interest rates. Financial capital will flow in because of the newly attractive returns. If capital flows are denominated in the country's own currency units, then its currency will appreciate, its imports rise, and its exports fall. The capital flows themselves will tend to lower the country's domestic interest rates.

An eighth operating principle is that maintaining international capital mobility reduces the magnitude of domestic interest rate fluctuations and thus the probability of financial innovation, if no foreign central bank responds to domestic policy initiatives. Put differently, the decline in net foreign investment means that a *smaller* decline in domestic investment will be required to achieve a target decline in aggregate demand. The country's excess demand has been shifted abroad. Aggregate demand in other countries, of course, increases.

There are three major difficulties raised by the foregoing conventional representation of monetary policy under a floating exchange rate system. First, tautologically the volatility of exchange rates rises relative to a fixed rate system. In practice volatility has been much more severe than under the preceding adjustable peg nonsystem. This volatility has led to some serious losses by sophisticated large banks and to innovations such as a few futures markets in foreign exchange. As in the model of Section 3, institutions' solvency can be compromised by operating with uncovered exchange positions. Exchange rates move unpredictably and hedging opportunities are limited. Many socially valuable plans and projects can fail because of manmade uncertainty in foreign exchange markets.

Second, the argument that a country may shift excess (or deficient) demand through exchange rate movements is fundamentally and seriously incomplete until a recipient of the shift is specified. If all countries are experiencing inflation, a shift of excess demand by allowing one country's currency to appreciate relative to others is unwelcomed by the remaining countries. They may resist by undertaking contractionary monetary policies. Operating autonomously, the central banks of the world could easily ignite a process of interest rate escalation that would be destabilizing, as each attempted to shift burdens to others. As interest rates rose the frequency of innovations would increase and the situation would become increasingly unstable.

Eventually, some country would find the cost of further monetary stringency politically unacceptable and accept an inflationary surge that would make its debt obligations to the rest of the world unbearable and/or use restrictive fiscal policy and exchange controls to reduce aggregate demand. Its citizens would be saddled with the burden of absorbing global excess demand. They would have to default on their debt or forego consumption and investment while their exports satisfied international gluttony.

Third, this representation seems to relieve a country from any obligation to be fiscally responsible. It has become a textbook commonplace to say that, in a floating exchange rate regime, monetary policy is effective and fiscal policy is impotent. Politicians with economic advisors who believe in the validity of this textbook interpretation may well feel little compunction about eliminating budget deficits or raising taxes. It is much more convenient politically to let some other country carry the burden of stabilization than raise taxes or cut expenditures.

I believe my interpretation has a real-world counterpart. Note that inflation rates and nominal interest rates soared in almost all OECD countries (oil exporters excluded) in 1973–74 and in 1979–81 when OPEC price increases occurred. It is not unreasonable that all central banks simultaneously adopted anti-inflationary postures and thereby insured that nominal interest rates rose excessively. As the discussion of the four countries in Section 2 revealed, high rates of innovation often accompanied high nominal interest rates and/or large government deficits. Few OECD governments have resorted to tax increases and almost all continue to have rather large deficits. Newly developing countries expanded output rapidly in response to excess demand from developed countries where unemployment is high and rising. The IMF has forced repressive fiscal policies on debtor nations, particularly those in Latin America. The burden of stabilization has been partly placed on their citizens.[24]

A final operating principle is that central banks worldwide should acknowledge and avoid the fallacy of composition that is inherent in attempting to respond to international shocks only with monetary policy weapons. Central banks and their governments should *collaboratively* seek to absorb such shocks with fiscal restraints that are equitably shared by their citizens and those in other countries.

It is unclear whether the 1973 moves toward a floating exchange rate system have contributed to instability in the international monetary system; that topic will be debated for decades to come. The change in the exchange rate system itself was an innovation that caused numerous new institutions to appear, which have little to do with the processes I have considered in this paper. The dirty floating rate period has been one of highly volatile inflation, interest rates, unemployment, exchange rates, and output when compared to the preceding twenty-seven years. In recent years there were many supply shocks that might have caused

---

[24] It has also been partly borne by the growing numbers of unemployed in all developed nations, by international commerce that has had to bear the increased volatility of exchange rates, and by farmers and mortgage debtors in the United States who were entrapped by record high real interest rates. Only the agile escaped.

even greater chaos in a fixed exchange rate system or, indeed, may even have been promoted by the failures of a collapsing fixed exchange rate system. I would not yet recommend a return to an adjustable peg non-system.

However, central banks should weigh heavily the exchange rate consequences of their actions and avoid imposing costs and causing innovations needlessly. Tariffs, quotas, and much more serious barriers to world commerce are rational responses by elected officials, because costs of adjustment to shocks by workers and firms are enormously high. That is what is ignored when one opts to rely only on freely floating exchange rates to neutralize shocks.

References

Akhtar, M.A. 1983. Financial Innovations and their Implications for Monetary Policy: An International Perspective," *BIS Economic Papers*, No. 9.

Bank for International Settlements. 1984. *Financial Innovation and Monetary Policy*, March.

Bhatt, V.V. 1978. "Interest Rate, Transaction Costs and Financial Innovations, *World Bank Domestic Finance Study No. 47*, January.

Brainard, William C. and James Tobin. 1963. "Financial Intermediaries and the Effectiveness of Monetary Controls," *American Economic Review*, Proceedings, 53, May, pp. 383–400.

Caranza, Cesare and Antonio Fazio. 1983. "Methods of Monetary Control in Italy," in *The Political Economy of Monetary Policy: National and International Aspects*, ed. by Donald R. Hodgman, Boston: Federal Reserve Bank of Boston, pp. 65–92.

Coats, Warren L. Jr. 1981. "The Weekend Dollar Game," *The Journal of Finance*, XXXVI, No. 3 (June), pp. 649–659.

Dean, Marjorie and Robert Pringle. 1984. *Economic Cooperation from the Inside*, New York: Group of Thirty.

de Cecco, Marcello and Marcus Miller. 1984. "Monetary Targeting in Europe," in *The Global Repercussions of U.S. Monetary and Fiscal Policy*, edited by Sylvia Ann Hewlett, Henry Kaufman, and Peter B. Kenen. New York: Economic Policy Council of the UNA-USA, pp. 123–150.

de Roover, Raymond. 1974. *Business, Banking, and Economic Thought*. Chicago: The University of Chicago Press, Ch. 4.

Fellner, William J. 1956. *Trends and Cycles in Economic Activity*. New York: Henry Holt and Co.

Foley, Duncan K. and Martin F. Hellwig. 1975. "A Note on the Budget Constraint in a Model of Borrowing," *Journal of Economic Theory*, October, pp. 305–314.

Friedman, Milton. 1959. "The Demand for Money: Some Theoretical and Empirical Results," *Journal of Political Economy*, 67, pp. 327–351.

Gale, Douglas. 1982. *Money: In Equilibrium*. London: Nisbet/Cambridge, pp. 128–134.

Goldfeld, Stephen M. 1973. "The Demand for Money Revisited," *Brookings Papers on Economic Activity*, pp. 577–638.

———. 1976. "The Case of the Missing Money," *Brookings Papers on Economic Activity*, No. 3, pp. 683–730.

Grossman, Sanford J. and Joseph E. Stiglitz. 1976. "Information and Competitive Price Systems," *American Economic Review*, Supplement, Vol. LXVI, (May), pp. 246–153.

Hakansson, Nils H. 1982. "Changes in the Financial Market: Welfare and Price Effects and the Basic Theorems of Value Conservation," *Journal of Finance*, XXXVII, September, pp. 977–1004.

Hester, Donald D. 1972. "Monetary Policy in the 'Checkless' Economy," *The Journal of Finance*, Vol. XXV, No. 2 (May), pp. 279–93.

———. 1981. "Innovations and Monetary Control," *Brookings Papers on Economic Activity*, I, pp. 141–189.

———. 1982. 'The Effects of Euro-dollar and Domestic Money Market Innovations on the Interpretation and Control of Monetary Aggregates," in *The Political Economy of Domestic and International Monetary Relations*, ed. Raymond E. Lombra and Willard E. Witte. Ames, Iowa: Iowa State University Press, pp. 506–542.

Hodgman, Donald R. 1983. *The Political Economy of Monetary Policy: National and International Aspects*. Boston: Federal Reserve Bank of Boston.

Holbik, Karel. 1973. *Monetary Policy in Twelve Industrial Countries*. Boston: Federal Reserve Bank of Boston.

Keeton, William R. 1984. "Deposit Insurance and the Deregulation of Deposit Rates," *Federal Reserve Bank of Kansas City Economic Review*, April, pp. 28–46.

Krohn, Gregory A. 1984. "Interest Rate Volatility and the Size of the Financial Sector," unpublished dissertation submitted to the University of Wisconsin-Madison.

Magee, Stephen P. and William A. Brock. 1984. "The Rise in the Third World's External Debt/Equity Ratio as a Redistributive Game and the Political Regressivity of Adverse States of Nature." Processed paper delivered at Middlebury, Vermont Conference on the World Debt Crisis.

Poole, William. 1970. "Optimal Choice of Monetary Policy Instruments in a Simple Stochastic Macro Model," *Quarterly Journal of Economics*, LXXXIV, No. 2 (May), pp. 197–216.

Projector, Dorothy and Gertrude S. Weiss. 1966. *Survey of Financial Characteristics of Consumers*. Washington: Board of Governors of the Federal Reserve System.

Saloner, Garth. 1982. "Dynamic Equilibrium Limit-Pricing in an Uncertain Environment," processed, November.

Sargent, Thomas and Neil Wallace. 1981. "Some Unpleasant Monetarist

Arithmetic," *Federal Reserve Bank of Minneapolis Quarterly Review*, Fall.

Simpson, Thomas D. and Patrick M. Parkinson. 1984. "Some Implications of Financial Innovations in the United States," *Federal Reserve Board Staff Studies*, Number 139.

Solomon, Anthony M. 1984. "Some Problems and Prospects for Monetary Policy in 1985." Talk at New York University, November.

Stevens, Edward J., III. 1984. "Risk on Large-Dollar Transfer Systems," processed, November.

Suzuki, Yoshio. 1980. *Money and Banking in Contemporary Japan*. New Haven: Yale University Press.

———. 1984. "Financial Innovation and Monetary Policy in Japan," *Bank of Japan Monetary and Economic Studies*, 2 (June), pp. 1–47.

Vaciago, Giacomo. 1977. "Monetary Policy in Italy: The Limited Role of Monetarism," *Review of Banca Nazionale del Lavoro*, December, pp. 333–348.

Wenninger, John. 1984. "Finnancial Innovation—A Complex Problem Even in a Simple Framework," *Federal Reserve Bank of New York Quarterly Review*, Summer, pp. 1–9.

Zawadzki, K.K.F. 1980. *Competition and Credit Control*. Oxford: Basil Blackwell.

Comments

John S. Flemming

I found both these papers stimulating and congenial: Hester in his interpretative and electic approach to monetary policy and Hall's approach to policy when underlying velocity is stochastic.

Donald Hester highlights the role of innovation as response to controls, which, with a few exceptions, have been weaker in the U.K. than in the U.S. as our regulations are typically less legalistic. The main exception in much of the period was Exchange Control, which, though not mentioned, is certainly subject to a number of the processes described. The importance of the international dimension is certainly not ignored in the U.K. but we would, as he suggests, be rather skeptical of the particular proposal to enforce reserve ratios on U.K. institutions' foreign currency business laid down by the authorities of the country whose currency was involved. The work we do, and have encouraged others to follow, by way of consolidation of international activities of banking groups for supervision purposes may be an alternative viable approach, as Warren McClam suggested, to the problems of gaps in the regulatory system applied to non-residents' foreign currency business.

The international dimension also raises definitional questions for monetary policy. Should the Bank of England seek to control the money holdings of U.K. residents regardless of currency? or the quantity of £ wherever held? In practice data problems push us towards £ holdings of U.K. residents with banks in Britain—£M3. I do not, myself, find this definition satisfactory because it is not comprehensive, and would not scan across countries to world money, but data are available on non-residents' £ holdings in the U.K. as well as residents' foreign currency holdings.

Hester's summary of change in the U.K. does not quite correspond to the way things looked in London. It is certainly true that the "Corset" to which he refers did lead to disintermediation, but until late 1979 the scope for doing this through the Euro-markets was limited by Exchange Control. The reason for the decision (before I joined the Bank) to retain the Corset for several months after the abolition of Exchange Control is obscure. It is true that the 35% fall in £ EER between 1971 and 1976 is not easily explained by relative monetary growth, and its 25% rise to 1980 is even more difficult to explain in these terms. Oil undoubtedly played a role but hardly that of "immunizing" £ from the consequences of "domestic monetary turmoil." The timing of the suggested oil effect is hard to rationalize. There was no relevant oil "news" in 1976—the output growth then occurring having been long expected. I would also question the emphasis on U.K. M1 in Hester's brief but highly colored survey of U.K. developments since 1980. It has, as he says, been particularly subject to institutional developments.

Many of Hester's arguments about the consequences for monetary policy of the erosion of the position of banks repeat those developed over 20 years ago in earlier discussion of the effects of non-bank financial intermediaries. The question, raised earlier in the Conference, of whether the reduced demand for base money will reduce stability depends on whether shocks are additive or multiplicative—i.e., proportional to the reduced base—and whether their variance changes.

Hester's account of the process of erosion suggests a "ratchet." Does this point to the long-run elimination of banks as we know them? Or will the regulatory framework be extended from time to time to embrace many of the previous nonbanks? There is some evidence for the latter view in the U.K. The Banking Act of 1979 for example widened the range of banking institutions brought within the scope of prudential supervision. As mentioned, I have no quarrel with Hester's pragmatic operating proposals.

Hall addresses the problem of control of nominal GNP, or—as it now figures in the U.K. Government's Medium-Term Financial Strategy—nominal GDP. Both Hester and Hall imply that underlying velocity may have stochastic properties in part attributable to the process of innovation. Martin Feldstein has recently suggested that velocity in the U.S. follows a random walk with a drift of 3% p.a. Given an estimate of the variance of the process, an appropriate degree of accommodation of monetary shocks can be computed, as Hall shows. Similarly, more complex formulae can be developed to deal with evolution in the drift parameter or in the variance of the process.

I would suggest that the development of monetary policy in the U.K. since 1979 is entirely consistent with this statistical decision-theoretic approach. It was not, of course, formulated in these terms, which might give rise to some presentational problems. Attempts were more-over made—which are not required by the purely statistical approach, but should contribute to the achievement of ultimate goals—to relate movements in velocity to known institutional developments.

Artis and Currie have presented a somewhat similar model emphasizing not the impact of innovation but the choice between monetary aggregates and the exchange rate as intermediate targets. Although the increasing openness of the economy plays an important role in shifting the parameters of Hall's model, he presents a reduced form from which the exchange rate itself has been eliminated. This prevents him from considering the role assigned to it by Artis, Currie, Hester, or the U.K. authorities.

I turn now to Bob Hall's proposal for interest-paying reserves to contribute a large part of the backing for transaction accounts, an idea which has some similarity with Jim Tobin's and Jim Pierce's proposals.

It is not entirely clear whether Hall's proposal relates to *required reserves* or not. If not it would not differ much from the U.K. situation of virtually no required reserves but banks, for prudential reasons, holding substantial liquid interest-bearing reserves.

It is not our experience that this gives us much greater stability than applies in the U.S. If the interest-bearing reserves are not *required* the reserve-to-deposit ratio may fluctuate, destabilizing the velocity of base money. If the larger reserves *are* required then a bank can meet a deposit withdrawal by selling (in effect) to the depositor a liquid asset. Its reserves will still be inadequate but the multiple contraction will indeed be smaller.

Hall looks only at one side of the banks' balance sheet. If they hold larger quantities of liquid government debt they must, for a given level of deposits, lend less to commercial companies. In the U.K. this is met by regarding some commercial bills as reserve assets. Is this Hall's proposal for the U.S., or would he expect the corporate sector to rely more heavily on the capital market? What would be the cost of diverting companies to this less preferred source of finance? Might banks offset the income-stabilizing effect of large interest-bearing liquid reserves by indulging in much riskier commercial lending?

If the reserves are *required* is it base, or the supply of reserve assets, that he sees as the key to monetary control? Is there a danger of over-supply or of government reducing the return on reserve assets to the point at which people hold what are in fact transaction balances in the form of claims on less liquid assets, reintroducing all the problems met 50 years ago by deposit insurance?

Indeed I am not as sure that the essence of the problem is the security of transaction balances as other participants have suggested. Jim Pierce referred to the objective of avoiding "runs." It is arguable that you cannot have a run on mutual funds invested in marketable assets. The problem of runs is associated with the non-marketability of bank *loans*. The price of a claim on a mutual fund making loans depends on the directors' arbitrary subjective valuations. If the risks associated with this are met by "guaranteeing" the value of most of the claims in terms of currency, or any other objective indicator, we have a potential for runs in response to rumor about the value of the underlying loans. Deposit insurance may be an answer—reserves, including those bearing market interest, would seem merely to shift the problem a little way but not at all clearly to reduce its significance.

Comments

John Wenninger

In many ways these two papers were good complements: Professor Hester provided some history as well as some institutional and international perspective, while Bob Hall presented a much more theoretical approach. There are, however, two substantive policy issues on which the authors seem to disagree even though they more or less agree on the nature of the problems that innovations cause for monetary policy.

First, both authors seem to agree that central banks today should be concerned about the stability of the financial system. Professor Hester takes the conventional approach and says central banks should increase their surveillance of financial markets and make sure that intermediaries have adequate capital. He would also like to see reforms for clearing transactions. And he believes central banks should be ready to play their role as lender of last resort. And while Professor Hall does not explicitly exclude these types of actions, his primary recommendation is that the Federal Reserve should accommodate the large increase in the monetary base that would result from paying interest on reserves. A large monetary base, he argues, would make the financial system more stable. He does not argue for higher reserve requirements on transactions deposits, so one is left to believe the larger monetary base would be held as excess reserves.

It seems, however, that as long as the Federal Reserve makes the discount window available during a crisis, the monetary base would be sufficiently elastic without the Federal Reserve paying interest on reserves or buying a large volume of government debt. Moreover, it is not clear that during a financial crisis, an individual bank or group of banks could obtain funding without help from the central bank even if a larger monetary base was provided. Other banks still would not be willing to lend those additional excess reserves if they felt the borrowing institutions were not solvent. In other words, there would be no mechanism to ensure that the additional excess reserves would end up where they would be needed during a crisis, and hence the crisis could become more widespread. It is not always a question of how many reserves there are in the banking system overall, but rather whether a small quantity of those reserves can be directed to the right place at the right time until confidence is restored.

Therefore, the central bank would still be in the same position with a larger reserve base that it is in currently, that is, it would need to act as lender of last resort to institutions that were having funding problems. As a result, as long as the central bank stands ready to make a large volume of loans backed by government debt, or even other assets, during a crisis, it does not appear that paying interest on reserves and buying a large volume of government debt would help the stability of the financial system. Paying interest on reserves might make sense for other reasons, but as far as the stability of the financial system goes, it is difficult to see where the benefit would be.

The two authors also seem to agree on the other basic issue: that is, innovations have made financial shocks a more important source of instability for the economy and the central bank should use a flexible approach to policy as a result—flexible in the sense that whatever the central bank's instrument might be, it must be reset in response to shifts in the IS and/or LM functions.

But then after agreeing on the basic premise, they again emphasize different conclusions on how the central bank should proceed. Professor Hester seems to argue that if innovations cause severe problems in using monetary targets, then there is little choice but to use interest rates—an answer one would have expected from earlier work by William Poole, James Tobin, John Hicks, and others.[1] But he is also quick to make the distinction between real and nominal rates so that central banks would be responsive to changes in inflation. But here again Professor Hall seems to have a different point of view. He argues that if the relationship between the monetary base and GNP is not stable, then the central bank should adjust its monetary base instrument whenever the LM curve shifts or is expected to shift—in essence what James Tobin calls a velocity adjusted monetary target.[2]

---

[1] William Poole, "Optimal Choice of Monetary Policy Instruments in a Simple Stochastic Model," *Quarterly Journal of Economics* (May 1970); James Tobin, "Monetary Policy: Rules, Targets and Shocks," *Journal of Money Credit and Banking*, Volume 15, Number 4, (November 1983); John Hicks, "The Foundations of Monetary Theory," *Money Interest and Wages—Collected Essays on Economic Theory*, Volume 2, Harvard University Press (1983).

[2] James Tobin, "Monetarism: an Ebbing Tide," *The Economist*, April 27, 1985.

Here again, it is not clear that Professor Hall's solution is the best one, at least at first glance. If he believes that the LM curve will be the primary source of instability in the future, why does he argue for a velocity adjusted monetary base approach when an interest rate target would automatically offset the impact on GNP of all LM shifts? In other words, why go through the relatively more difficult task of forecasting and offsetting financial shocks with the monetary base when it is possible to use an interest rate target in the short run and face the relatively easier task of responding to less severe shifts in the IS function to keep GNP on some desired path?

The problem, of course, is that many people are skeptical about whether central banks would be willing to vary interest rates enough to get the job done. Interest rates are politically sensitive, and hence the central bank might need to operate under political constraints that it might not have under velocity adjusted monetary targets. Perhaps monetary targets are still useful in practice, even with innovations, as long as the central bank is required to justify any adjustments or misses in terms of unexpected velocity movements.

Therefore, the practical question of what approach to take in implementing monetary policy is more complicated than just the relative stability of the IS and LM curves. Even if the public does not like high interest rates, the public might be more willing to accept high real interest rates if it was believed that the high rates were a by product of pursuing a sensible monetary target than if the public believed the central bank was in some sense directly responsible for setting the level of rates. As a result, the best way to achieve Professor Hester's goal of having real interest rates respond in a meaningful way to economic developments might be to adopt Professor Hall's velocity adjusted monetary target approach.[3]

[3] For more on this topic, see Henry C. Wallich, "Recent Techniques of Monetary Policy," *Economic Review*, Federal Reserve Bank of Kansas City, May 1984, p. 23 and 24.

Comments

Robert Raymond

The two papers on which I have to comment are very different. A first family of papers, typical of those which are provided in a conference such as this, is made up of detailed descriptions of what has happened, what is happening, and what could possibly happen. They can be compared to those large paintings which represent landscapes with hills, valleys, rivers, trees, and a few silhouettes, made by prominent artists during the eighteenth century. Professer Hester's paper belongs to this family.

Professer Hall's paper could rather be compared to a modern abstract painting. I could not read it without remembering how one of my professors opened his course on Don Patinkin. He told us: Don Patinkin tremendously improved monetary analysis by describing a world which does not exist.

Each of the two authors follows a different approach.

Hester explains the observed changes and then considers innovations as mainly endogenous, while in Hall's model they are exogenous.

In fact, reactions to monetary policy measures can be considered as endogenous. In this respect Hester accurately describes the dialectic interaction between monetary policy and the behavior of financial intermediaries and their customers.

But in other cases, innovations can be treated as exogenous, especially in a small or less developed country, when they come from external incentives.

The two authors also have different views about how innovation affects the efficiency of monetary policy: monetary policy is improved according to Hall and weakened according to Hester.

I myself nurtured the hope that monetary authorities would be placed in a position to perform their task better, thanks to financial innovation. May I recall that until recently my country had a financial structure which submitted its economy to the credit paradigm, making it what we call an overdraft economy. It had some similarities with the financial structure of Japan. This has been undergoing changes in the last few years. Both a deliberate policy and the increase of PSBR have led to a strong development of the financial market and to subsequent innovations.

We found that it was difficult to run an overdraft economy. Because of the size of corporate sector debt vis-à-vis the banking sector, the central bank does not feel free to raise interest rates suddenly and sizeably, because of the immediate impact on firms' profitability. So we welcome the development of a larger and more flexible capital market. Of course, the central bank itself has to adapt, but it will have more opportunities for intervention.

Professors Hall and Hester reach an identical conclusion on one point: the banks should pay the market price on transaction deposits. Of course, this would imply that banks charge their customers for any kind of operation (especially transaction payments) they conduct for them. This being admitted, the authors' proposal is not a revolutionary one. It is closer to a tautology. It is as if a Roman said: if Jupiter removes the clouds, we will have sunny weather.

The two authors present two different sets of recommendations.

The operating principles espoused by Prof. Hester are classical, pragmatic, and very sweet to the ears of a central banker:

—real interest rates positive enough, but not too much, carefully geared by the central bank, but not used for targeting;

—a central bank better informed and active on all markets;

—commercial banks with a high capital ratio.

All right, this medicine is good in any set of circumstances.

Professor Hall's proposals are more peculiar. They consist in targeting nominal GNP rather than the money supply and in paying a market interest rate on compulsory reserves.

Let me start with Prof. Hall's model.

I have some difficulty in fully understanding the logic of the model. Using the IS-LM curve implies that there is a monetary policy and that the supply of money can be modified. Thus, the monetary base should be exogenous. I am afraid that if a market interest rate is paid on reserves, the base becomes either endogenous or a random item.

If you consider, in addition, that in a deregulated open economy interest rates are under heavy external pressure, I do not see clearly who will control nominal GNP and how. May I add that the model applies to a country which practices clean floating, which is not so frequent outside the United States and especially in Europe, where we have a regional fixed exchange rate system.

I also have a few question marks in mind about the impact of velocity. According to Figure 2, it seems that V has not been neutral recently in the U.S. and that it has become less predictable or not predictable at all. Professor Hall tells us that up to 24% of the variance can be explained by the use of a simple regression. According to our calculations, this leaves room for an uncertainty of 2% of GNP until 1980 and twice as much after that. How then could it be possible to target GNP in the U.S. economy?

The comment of the same graph links the sudden volatility of velocity to the recession. But the model is based on the assumption that the LM curve is not very sensitive to real shocks. Does this mean that the U.S. financial system is not yet deregulated enough?

I now come to some more general issues. Would it be convenient to target nominal GNP instead of any money stock aggregate, as Prof. Hall suggests? I suppose that such a method would also be qualified by Prof. Hester as relying upon "a very primitive information set."

I shall not analyze this matter in depth, as it has been discussed at length in the OECD. Mr. Volcker expressed a negative opinion on this point at a hearing in Congress.

We now all use sophisticated models. If they are good enough, they provide us not only with nominal GNP, but also with real growth, various measurements of prices, the level of interest rates, and several monetary aggregates. The question is, at which of these variables should we look?

For a central bank, some practical reasons make it preferable to target the money stock, when it is possible. GNP figures come late and/ or are subject to significant revisions. Besides that, the transmission mechanism between M and GNP is very complex; the lag with which the latter reacts to a move in monetary policy is important.

A GNP target is more appropriate for a medium-term strategy. Unfortunately, it seems to me that in the long run it would not be sufficient: policy-makers are concerned not only with nominal GNP, but also—and even more—with each of its components separately; they strive to increase real growth and to reduce the level of inflation. In the long run, we all would like to become Japanese.

Professor Hall tells us that the central bank should pay interest on reserve deposits made by commercial banks. This would allow—as a counterpart—for larger reserves.

I have some sympathy for this idea. It is true that increasing the total amount of compulsory reserves would reduce the impact of monetary shocks on money market interest rates.

In France, for instance, the level of compulsory reserves is very low. If French monetary policy were to rely exclusively upon open market operations and if the monetary base were exclusively made of reserves in proportion to some kind of deposits, then it would be wise to raise the reserve requirements significantly. Otherwise, a sudden change in the foreign assets of the central bank or a large cash operation by the Treasury would upset the interbank money market rate, unless the central bank would automatically sterilize the effects of such a shock. If the decision is made, let us say, to increase the volume of reserves fivefold, and if at the same time the central bank is not willing to let the prime rate move upwards, then it is necessary to balance the cost of this decision for banks by paying interest on compulsory reserves.

Of course, in my opinion, this interest should be well below the market rate, in order to maintain the monetary base exogenous and to keep an efficient brake on money creation, as I have already explained.

Last, but not least, comes the recommendation that any kind of "Regulation Q" should be removed, so as to make it possible for banks to pay interest even on transaction accounts.

The aim being to avoid transfers from money to financial assets that are close substitutes for money, the proposed solution is nothing but converting money into a close substitute for financial assets. Then monetary aggregates will either vanish or become meaningless.

Fortunately enough, banks still use accounting systems and publish balance-sheets, so that, by carefully looking at their accounts, it remains possible to interpret the figures. Even where "Regulation Q" is still in force, I hope no central bank blindly follows its money stock target as Hester suggest early in his paper.

In addition, innovation is not always exogenous—there I agree with Hester—and is not always that sudden. In France we had lost our demand for money equation, but more sophisticated studies helped us to rediscover it, slightly modified, and even to better understand how the parameters change year after year. It is fair to say that this can be done "ex post," but that it does not enable us to calculate a precise formula for the coming year.

As a consequnce of these considerations, it is comfortable for the central bank to have a thorough knowledge of the various elements which are included in banks' liabilities, some of which only can be used as means of payment. I would be only too glad to keep the good old M1 in order and to be able to identify it to working ablances closely related to nominal GNP, or to domestic spending, or, even better, to prices. I have no hope of seeing a perfect correlation between M1 and these other aggregates, but it would help to keep this correlation as it is, or, possibly, to improve it.

I cannot say I like Regulation Q, even if I consider that there is no justification to pay high interest on working balances, because a sudden depreciation of the exchange rate, for instance, leads the authorities to raise the whole structure of interest rates dramatically. Working balances in domestic currency are not supposed—by definition—to be converted into foreign currencies and to feed outflows of capital.

I still consider that reserve requirements should preferably apply to sight or check deposits or closely connected accounts, in order to maintain a sufficient spread between liquid working balances and more stable elements of the assets of economic agents.

So the question is still in my mind: by assimilating transaction accounts to any other kind of accounts, would the central bank simplify or complicate monetary policy?

Comments

Teh Kok Peng

I have no comments on Prof. Hall's paper except to note that his suggestion of the central bank paying near-market interest rates on reserves and saturating the economy with reserves, if implemented by a central bank and successful in dampening financial shocks, would be an example of a desirable financial innovation—desirable from point of view of improving the effectiveness of monetary policy—introduced by a non-enterpreneurial public agency. I shall concentrate on Prof. Hester's paper, not so much to comment on it as to draw strands from it to make two general points which I think are largely implicit in his paper.*

The first point is the public good nature of financial services and the very costly externalities imposed on the real economy if there are instabilities in the financial sector. Thus, in Prof. Hester's view, monopoly rents, created by regulations and barriers to entry, are tolerated and often welcomed by government officials because they serve to enhance the solvency and stability of depository institutions. As economists, we all favor competition that results in improved cost and allocative efficiency. However, there does appear to be a tendency in the financial sector for competition to result in excessive risk-taking. Within the financial sector then, there is a trade-off between efficiency and stability. However, as Prof. Hall pointed out in his comments on the first day, financial services typically account for a small part of an economy's output; he cited his own example of spending more on dry cleaning than on financial services. The overriding importance of the financial sector therefore lies in its stability, to facilitate the implementation of monetary policy for achieving stable output growth of

*The views expressed here are my own, and do not reflect the views of the Monetary Authority of Singapore.

the real economy. I should add that monopoly rents in a regulated financial industry can be controlled, as in the case of utilities, and that it is possible to do away with the worst aspects of regulations, such as Regulation Q on interest rates, to avoid negative real interest rates. Further, a regulated industry does not necessarily impede innovations, as the example of American Telephone & Telegraph's Bell Laboratories has shown.

The second point is the importance of fiscal policy. Both keynote speakers, Prof. Friedman and Prof. Tobin, as well as other discussants, have referred to it. Generally, countries which do not have fiscal deficits or whose fiscal deficits are small in relation to their domestic savings do not appear to have problems in setting and achieving their monetary targets, despite financial innovations. It would seem that many destabilizing financial innovations—those that impede the implementation of monetary policy—occur in countries which have fiscal problems. Such innovations are a response to actual inflation or to expectations of an inflation tax, which is feared when sustained monetary stringency and overcoming the fiscal problem both become politically unacceptable. It has been pointed out that in a world of international capital mobility, monetary stringency is sufficient to maintain price stability for quite a while. I wonder whether we may not be over-generalizing from the recent U.S. experience. The U.S. is in many ways a special case. It is the key reserve currency country and the ultimate political safe haven in the eyes of investors worldwide. I wonder how long such capital inflows could have lasted for some other countries with the same monetary-fiscal mix as the U.S., especially if the country were a less developed one.

Let me now recount Singapore's experience in order to show the importance of fiscal policy and savings (forced or otherwise) for effective monetary policy (or, more properly since 1981, exchange rate policy) and price stability. The Central Provident Fund (CPF), a compulsory fully funded savings scheme for old age, which was considered in Mr. Greenwood's paper to be responsible for starving the banking sector of funds, was actually highly instrumental in providing long-term funds to finance the development budget for infrastructural investment during the early years of Singapore's rapid economic development. Without the CPF funds, taxes or external borrowings would have had to be increased. In more recent years, increases in the rate of CPF contribution to 50% of an employee's salary (25% contribution from the employee and the other 25% from the employer) and the shift of the budget to a situation of surplus have caused public sector savings in Singapore to be one of the highest in the world. It is this phenomenon that is responsible for price stability in Singapore, and for the need of monetary policy, conducted through foreign exchange intervention, to be expansionary.

To elaborate, the CPF and fiscal surpluses are continually having a deflationary effect on the economy by draining liquidity from the banking system when such deposits are transferred to the Monetary Authority of Singapore (MAS). MAS therefore has to re-inject this liquidity into the financial system and does so primarily through exchange intervention, leading to accumulation of foreign reserves. Such intervention also is the way we manage the trade-weighted index of the Singapore dollar with the objective of dampening imported inflation, and thus we manage trade-weighted exchange rates rather than target monetary aggregates.

Nevertheless, we do monitor the monetary aggregates as well. As is the case in the U.S., though to a less extreme degree, financial innovations have posed problems to defining an appropriate measure of money. The introduction of autosave accounts, daily interest rates on savings accounts by finance companies and banks, Automatic Teller Machines (ATMs), and credit cards in the past few years have provided disincentives to maintaining large transaction balances on current accounts with banks. This trend would be accentuated by more recent innovations planned to usher in a cashless society—the introduction of Electronic Fund Transfer at Point-of-Sale (EFTPOS) and Inter-bank Giro. Savings deposits with the Post Office Savings Bank, which are tax-free and with which ATM facilities can be used, have also increasingly become important at the expense of deposits with banks. Thus, M1 is becoming less appropriate as an indicator of money than the broader measures of money.

Professor Cargill mentioned on the first day that Singapore (and Hong Kong) should be distinguished from the other Asian countries in that these two cities have sought to develop as financial centers.

However, Singapore has mainly sought here to develop offshore financial services for the region and beyond in areas like offshore banking, financial futures, offshore fund management. Obviously, being a financial center and traditionally a free port, Singapore has hardly any control over the pricing and allocation of credit except for supervisory and prudential reasons. However, there is strict control aimed at preventing the use of the Singapore dollar for international transactions. It reflects our policy-makers' concern that such internationalization of the Singapore dollar would hamper our effectiveness in responding to financial shocks.

Finally, I would like to look at the issue of financial innovation and

304 TEH KOK PENG

liberalization from the perspective of a less developed country. In a stabler and simpler time, at least on the monetary front, long-term capital flowed from the developed to less developed countries, where its marginal product was considered to be higher. I still believe that the marginal product of capital is usually higher in a less developed country. But in a world of volatile interest and exchange rates, there is an increasing preference for more liquid, safer financial assets by residents in developed countries and a more ready supply of such assets brought about by financial liberalization and innovations in these same countries. We now have the phenomenon of international competition for savings by our developed countries. This is one competition in which, for the less developed countries, if you can't beat them, it is even more difficult to join them, at least in the short to medium run.

For many less developed countries, liberalizing capital flows would result in loss of their scarce savings. The lack of financial liberalization did not prevent the rapid growth of the northeast Asian countries, and it could be argued that at least in one case, that of Japan, it was a very important means of mobilizing domestic savings to finance the high investments required during the rapid growth years of the 1950s and 1960s. Therefore, I suspect that talk of the desirability of breaking down the segmentation of capital markets on an international basis to achieve the optimum international distribution of capital is not likely to impress the policy-makers in the less developed countries unless it can be shown to be a Pareto superior move and the gainers do actually compensate the losers.

Summaries

Concluding Remarks

Niels Thygesen

So much has been said and particularly written by our main contributors at this Conference that time is needed to absorb it and put it into shape. I cannot offer conclusions, but I at least hope to remind you of some of the main issues we have been discussing, raising questions rather than giving answers. I shall do so under three headings. First, I will make some remarks about what seems to me a striking feature: that we have been dominated in our discussions by U.S. experience and prescriptions based thereon, rather than by those of other participating countries. Second, I want to address some issues of monetary control that have come up in the papers; and, third, I want to address the issues of financial innovation and the balance between financial innovation and monetary control.

Specific Features of the U.S. Financial System

Turning to the first point, I find it striking that we have been discussing to a very large extent U.S. financial markets and monetary experience. Six of our eight speakers were from the United States. We all enjoyed that, not only because they are excellent economists with good papers, but also because most of us have been trained in economics or finance on the basis of U.S. literature, and we are—or think we are—sufficiently familiar with the U.S. financial scene to at least participate in an exchange of views about it. There is also the justification for focusing so strongly on the subject that the United States remains overwhelmingly important in the world, and its policies and financial events have repercussions on the rest of us directly through interest rates and movements in the dollar. Still, the discussion at the conference has been somewhat biased, in my view, as regards both monetary control and financial reform or deregulation, because of the specific and extreme nature of the U.S. experience.

The U.S. financial system has, at least until very recently, basically been marked by the dramatic experience of the 1930s and the legislation then enacted to regulate financial institutions in order to prevent a repetition of financial crises and bank failures. The main instruments were the Federal deposit insurance scheme and ceilings on demand and time deposit rates—measures that we are now told by leading American observers must be regarded as inadequate to the environment of the 1980s, and that are in the process of being dismantled as a result of the legislation passed by the U.S. Congress in 1980 and 1982. Another special U.S. feature is the fragmented supervision system which has added to the complexity of financial regulation—and, recently, de-regulation.

Relative to any other major industrial country, the United States clearly has an excessive number of deposit-taking institutions, because U.S. legislators have shown far more concern than those in other countries over the concentration of financial power. In Japan, in Western Europe, in the countries in the Pacific area, the monetary authorities and the supervisors are used to dealing regularly with very large institutions. They have a more positive attitude to mergers; and they conduct monetary policy by applying moral suasion to the "leading" institutions directly or through their associations. In the United States the ban on interstate banking, now also eroding fast, has even prevented an effective national payments mechanism from arising. When you add to all these institutional complications the unsafe lending to some domestic sectors, and overseas to sovereign borrowers in developing countries, and a series of in themselves minor, but very widely reported, runs on small savings institutions, it is no wonder that U.S. financial markets have become nervous, and that the rapidly unfolding process of deregulation or decontrol of the 1980s has been subjected to second thoughts by the U.S. public, by foreign observers, and by several speakers at this conference. What are the proper inferences for reconciling the requirement for an efficient yet safe financial system on the one hand and the need for monetary control in the U.S. environment of the 1980s on the other hand? And what are their relevance for other countries with well developed but rather different financial structures?

One major concern for U.S. economists, raised most clearly in the contributions by Tobin and Pierce, is that for the safety of transactions balances. Waves of withdrawals of deposits in small institutions in several states and difficulties for some large banks, most dramatically in the case of Continental Illinois, have drawn attention to the fragility of depository institutions in the U.S. environment of increasingly competitive financial markets and geographically fragmented retail banking. In particular, the observed events have raised doubts about the adequacy of the insurance provisions for bank deposits through the FDIC and comparable arrangements for the savings banks which appear even more vulnerable, because the very solvency of the S & Ls has been eroded by fixed-rate lending in a period of rising market interest rates. For these reasons the view that deregulation has proceeded too fast has gained ground. One possible prescription is to revive the idea of Henry Simons of 100 percent reserves against transactions balances (i.e., demand deposits) to inspire maximum confidence in the payments mechanism, as suggested by Tobin.

There are, as his paper and the discussion recognize, serious practical problems in delimiting that part of the banking system's liabilities which should be subjected to this strict regime from the rest, where a principle of *caveat emptor* could apply. But one may also ask whether there are not alternative and preferable routes to avoiding the problem of depositor loss of confidence which rightly preoccupies the critics. One such alternative would start from the premise that many of the current U.S. problems arise not from too much, but from too little and too timid a dose of deregulation. The geographical constraints on depository institutions remain too severe and the policy towards mergers too restrictive to permit a consolidation of U.S. depository institutions. Another possibility, largely neglected in the discussions at this conference, is to take a critical look at the capital requirements of the financial institutions. This is one major instrument for preserving confidence in the financial system—though one that can have the desired effect only over a long time horizon. The main effort in my view must therefore lie in the direction of going still further into deregulation by permitting the better consolidated depository institutions to spread their activities geographically through mergers and acquisitions while preventing nonbanks from nibbling away at the more profitable activities related to the payments mechanism.

However justified the concerns of our U.S. colleagues over the stability of their increasingly competitive short-term financial markets, the U.S. experience is of limited relevance to most other countries represented at this conference. Depositors have less reason to feel nervous and to feel the need to evaluate when the readiness of their central bank—or, ultimately, the taxpayers—to help out may come to an end. The depository institutions are relatively larger and more consolidated; some are nationalized—the postal giro and banking systems and many of the largest commercial banks in continental Europe—and the very large market share of the banking system makes it less vulnerable to intrusion from new competitors. In most countries deposit rates have been unregulated longer than in the United States, and banks are more confident of their competitive position. The rescue operations required to save a small number of exposed institutions have largely been within the private banking sector with no more than approval from the authorities required. There is to my knowledge no example of a rescue operation of such proportions that a conflict between monetary policy objectives and financial stability has emerged, as one might argue has been the case on some occasions in the United States, notably in the restructuring of Continental Illinois.

In conclusion, as non-U.S. observers watch the debate on financial stability in the United States, the main relevance of that debate to their domestic debate seems limited. There are some features to avoid: excessive specialization and rigid regulation of interest rates—and their subsequent rapid removal.

Monetary Control

The implication of financial innovation and deregulation—if we want to retain that term for a policy that tries to foster an efficient and competitive financial sector—is that the design of monetary policy has to be evaluated anew, particularly the targetting on intermediate monetary objectives which has been practiced in many countries over the past decade.

In post-war monetary policy we seem to have come through three broad phases. In the first phase, lasting in the United States only until the Treasury-Federal Reserve Accord of 1952, in Europe until some time in the 1960s, and in Japan well into the 1970s, most interest rates were effectively pegged: bank deposit and lending rates through linkage to the discount rate, bond rates through open market operations. That period came to an end as the implications of interest-rate stabilization for money creation and ultimately inflation came to be more clearly perceived.

A second phase followed, with a dual interest rate structure: fairly rigid in the banking sector, due either to direct public controls or to acceptance of administrative rate setting—in some cases outright cartel arrangements—among the depository institutions; and more variable, market-determined rates in bond markets. This phase ended in the United States as aggressive liability management by banks and others spread and administrative regulations, notably Regulation Q, were gradually phased out, in the 1970s for large deposits and more recently for smaller deposits. In most European countries this phase has also come to an end at different points in time over the past decade; in Japan it may be said still to persist, since bank deposit and lending rates continue to exhibit less influence of market forces than in Europe and North America. The second phase prompted the formulation of monetary policy in terms of targets for one or more of the main monetary aggregates. Since the authorities were to some extent able to control relative interest rates—the differential between the rates on deposits which were a major part of the money stock and rates in other financial markets, represented by e.g. the government bond rate—they could exert influence over the money stock through the demand for money— assuming, obviously, that the money demand function was well understood, i.e., related in a predictable way to relative interest rates. Some degree of control over the latter was also essential when budget deficits rose in the 1970s and governments wanted to prevent a rapid acceleration in the money stock through the sale of bonds to the nonbank sector without driving all interest rates up. The supply of bonds could be absorbed for a time without steep rises in interest rates, as long as bank deposit rates did not rise correspondingly.

The tactic of exerting monetary control by changing relative interest rates on bank deposits and money was never very reliable, as both academic research into the properties of the demand for financial assets and the failure to hit announced monetary targets over periods of a year or less have demonstrated. And the degree of control attainable a decade ago, when monetary targets became widely used, has been eroded by a process which may be labelled "financial innovation" or "marketization," confronting monetary policy-makers with a situation where most rates observed on financial markets are closely correlated. In this third phase it is no longer possible to bring about major (not to speak of longer-lasting) differentials between interest rates on those financial instruments which have traditionally been included in the definition of the monetary aggregates and those which have not. As the discussion of the second phase has suggested, any precise dating of the start of the third phase is arbitrary; one may watch an indicator, e.g. the share of one or more monetary aggregates that bears a variable, market-related interest rate (see Akhtar 1983), but no particular significance can be attached to an arbitrary value of this or other indicators of marketization. Difficulties of measurement cannot conceal that in a more qualitative sense most European countries and North America entered this third phase in recent years, while Japan and most Asian countries have retained sufficient control over reltive interest rates to classify them as still in the second phase.

The higher degree of substitutability between various catgories of financial assets and the lower interest elasticity of the demand for money, which this implies, is not necessarily a cause for concern for monetary policy-makers. In principle it implies a more vertical LM-curve, a tighter relationship between money and nominal income. Unfortunately, however, the increasing steepness of the LM-curve appears to have been accompanied by increasing volatility of the relation of money to income, so that control of a monetary aggregate implies less in terms of control of many income than was thought some years ago. This instability affects all definitions of money, though in different degree. The traditional distinction between transactions and investment balances in bank deposits has become blurred; now even transaction balances are not stably related to income. With a more market-oriented yield on money the willingness to hold financial assets in monetary form has become more linked to total wealth than to income. This is another reason why the money-to-income link is not as close as it was thought to be, an observation which strengthens the case for a nominal income target along the lines suggested by Robert Hall.

Quite apart from the increased instability of velocity the rising volatility of interest rates is a source of concern. It is a tradition in economic theory going back to the Swedish economist Knut Wicksell that business cycles and cycles of inflation and deflation can often be related historically to tensions between relatively sluggish interest rates in financial markets and rapidly shifting expected real rates of return on physical assets—an idea taken further by Keynes. With the volatility of financial interest rates in recent years it is difficult to maintain this basic concept of a difference between the stability of returns on real and financial assets. There must be a strong suspicion that financial rates today move to reflect much more closely than in the past the return on real assets. If that is so, the power to influence demand through monetary policy has not improved. But we may be overstating the degree of interest-rate volatility to be expected in the future; the instability of financial markets in the early 1980s could have been a transitory phenomenon, resulting from the dramatic efforts to disinflate in the United States and elsewhere and to adjust monetary policy procedures to achieve that aim more efficiently. However, I still suggest that increased interest rate instability has come to stay, regardless of the level of inflation.

We have had a discussion of the appropriateness of monetary base control as a method of conducting monetary policy. The monetary base, consisting largely of currency in the hands of the public and reserves bearing a low interest rate, are not subject to the strictures of having become close substitutes for other financial assets, and they might still offer some handle in monetary policy. The problem with the monetary base is not that it is unreliably related to income—most studies show it to be closely related—but that it is not easily controllable by the monetary authorities over the short run. As one would expect, we are offered somewhat different recommendations on how to design a monetary base regime by our two keynote speakers, James Tobin and Milton Friedman. Tobin would accommodate pressures in financial markets by leaning against interest rate changes, increasing the monetary base as interest rates were rising and vice versa. Friedman would be less accommodating, presumably because he basically believes the LM-curve to be relatively more stable than does Tobin.

It is not clear to me that it would make a great difference whether interests were paid on required reserves, as suggested by Hall, or not. If the rate on reserves were still somewhat below the market interest rates I do not see why banks should necessarily want to hold more than minimum required reserves as they do now, but that, of course, could be discovered through the mechanism proposed by Robert Hall. Monetary base control will still provide some anchor for the longer-term evolution of the financial system, and despite its defects it may be the best that the monetary authorities can aim for in the fluid environment of the 1980s. The experience of the Bundesbank in conducting monetary policy in Germany along those lines suggests that it is not without useful longer-run effects.

I shall not take up the ultimate in financial innovation, the permitting by the national monetary authorities of the issue of private currency. I agree with James Tobin that it is hardly feasible, and in any case nobody has tried it for more than one hundred years. We do, however, have in Europe a not uninfluential school of economists advocating competition among national currencies within Europe; the idea is that one would make it possible for the stronger national currencies to extend their currency domain by allowing them to be used in normal transactions in other countries. Gradually one would end up with a monopoly situation for the soundest currency, but the interesting aspect of the suggestion really lies in the process of currency competition that leads to that result and which is designed to achieve the same objectives as Friederich von Hayek's proposed denationalization of money (for a good survey see Vaubel 1977).

Financial Innovation and Reform

I propose to move from these issues of monetary control to financial innovation and to do so via the international aspect of financial reform of increasing integration through capital movements. This topic has played a surprisingly modest role in this conference, since it is referred to primarily in Bryant's paper. Surprisingly, U.S. economists seem to have lost interest in the issue of capital liberalization, though it is only 11 years ago that the United States removed its last restrictions on capital flows.

It was thought when the world moved to flexible exchange rates that this would check financial integration, but today it is clear that the trend over the past decade has unmistakably been towards greater financial integration despite the high degree of flexibility of exchange rates. Obviously nominal interest rates in the main countries are far from fully aligned; and some countries, in particular Japan, have succeeded in a high degree of decoupling from the U.S. markets, a step which has only been possible because of floating exchange rates. Germany and other low-inflation countries in Europe have also to a considerable degree managed to decouple themselves from the United States, so integration is not perfect. Yet in the short run interest rate shocks are transmitted with considerable force largely from the United States to other financial markets; autonomy in interest-rate policy is something for the somewhat longer run, and it depends, of course, greatly on the climate in each particular country, resulting from the mixture of fiscal policy and inflationary trends.

What should concern us, and clearly did concern Bryant, is the package of very liberal attitudes to capital movements, limited coordination of macro-economic policies, strong differences in tax regimes—sometimes even developing into competition in laxity, as we saw with the changes in withholding tax on government securities first initiated in the United States and then elsewhere. This package can be an explosive mixture under a flexible exchange regime. One important difference in outlook between views in the United States, both official and academic, and in Japan and Western Europe on the other hand, is in the readiness of U.S. observers to accept that the exchange rate is a price determined largely in financial markets, and hence one that must be expected to fluctuate widely. It is little consolation that it may not fluctuate quite as much as other financial market prices, an observation made by some U.S. financial economists. As Dr. Teh and other Asian speakers have reminded us in the discussion, exchange rates are seen as too important in many Asian countries to be left to be determined as an asset market price; there are exchange-rate targets and there are sometimes capital restrictions to make them more attainable. It is certainly also the case in Europe that exchange-rate objectives have considerable importance and that there is less enthusiasm about completely free capital movements. I take it that the attitude is much the same in Japan—only more so.

The question I really want to raise is whether the traditional textbook view that a high degree of capital mobility is primarily incompatible with fixed exchange rates is tenable. It seems in the light of the experience of the last decade to be easier to have a high degree of capital mobility when you have exchange-rate targets than when rates are as flexible as they have been for the dollar and for some other currencies, e.g. Sterling. The effects of liberalizing capital movements are not always easily predictable in a framework of flexible rates. If one recalls the agreement concluded in May 1984 between the Treasuries of the United States and Japan on liberalization of Japanese capital movements, that agreement was presumably intended over time to lead to some upward pressure on the yen as a result of internationalization and substantial inflows of capital into Japan. What we have seen instead is that the liberalization of outward capital movements from Japan has led to massive investments by Japanese financial institutions in U.S. markets, to a tune even exceeding the very considerable current account surplus of Japan. This outflow of funds has kept the yen low, causing some surprise to those who had seen the 1984 agreement as a step towards some realignment between the yen and the dollar. As we come to the point where the dollar begins to show weakness, many Europeans are asking themselves what will happen as the dollar actually starts to depreciate; the massive outflows of funds from Japan might then turn in the direction of Europe and cause a sharp appreciation of the European currencies which will be difficult to manage. There are in other words costs and benefits which must be calculated carefully before liberalizing capital movements fully in a regime of floating exchange rates, and we have to take particularly seriously improvements in the mechanisms of international policy coordination to take the risks that they entail. The proposals for managed disintegration through some use of the price mechanism in the form of a tax on foreign exchange transactions, originally proposed by Tobin and taken up by Bryant, would hardly appear to be feasible, given that such a mechanism would also affect real transactions which we do not want to impede. In the longer term a better solution would be to move to a system of sufficiently stable exchange rates in order to prevent capital movements from throwing exchange rates as far from equilibrium as we have seen in the early 1980s.

From this background on international trends toward financial integration let me turn to the subject of deregulation or financial reform in a more national context. We are interested in these issues of financial reform, not only because of their implications for monetary control as discussed above, but also because the financial sector is a very important industry in itself in terms of output, employment, etc. Robert Hall compared the financial sector to the dry-cleaning industry, but such a comparison is clearly facetious, considering the size and value added of our financial institutions; they are very interesting from the viewpoint of industrial organization, and efficiency gains should be sought, even if there may be some loss of monetary control. The problem is that efficiency in the financial sector is extremely difficult to assess, and multi-country studies may not help us much as long as a conceptual framework for evaluating efficiency gains is not developed.

Let me state briefly some of my early impressions of listening to the conference and reading the papers and returning as a starting point to the distinction between two types of financial reform mentioned in Dr. Yumoto's and his colleagues' interesting survey paper. The least controversial type of innovation is clearly that of Type 2, related to technical progress which reduces costs and improves risk allocation among financial institutions. These improvements are reflected largely in greater efficiency in the payments mechanism. I want to address the rest of my remarks to what Dr. Yumoto calls Type 1 reforms, which may be either constructive or harmful. Let me look at four types of such responses to monetary or regulatory policies, in order of decreasing desirability.

The first category of Type 1 changes are those that are in a sense responses to policy actions of an excessively restrictive kind. For example, in Europe banks and other financial institutions have reacted to credit ceilings on direct lending by creating off-balance activities, notably direct lending from savers to investors through parallel markets with some guarantee from the bank. The efforts to innovate through circumvention of excessively restrictive monetary policies and regulations may be regarded as a healthy signal to the authorities in the long run to use more market-oriented methods of conducting their policies. They also serve as a means of restoring market share to the more efficient institutions in the financial sector who are most affected by disintermediation.

The second kind of financial innovation, which could also be viewed in a favorable light, is that introduced by the government itself through the management of the public debt. Several governments have shown considerable innovative capacity in both their domestic and foreign financing. Some of the sophistication of the Eurobond market and of some national bond markets has been due to government experiments with variable-rate issues, indexed bonds, and other less traditional instruments. This has been all to the good, as long as it has not entailed any special tax favors for the purchasers of these instruments.

In a third category, which is clearly less desirable, I would classify those innovations which are designed largely to avoid taxes. A major task in limiting excessive capital movements or domestic financial inventiveness is to close the existing tax loopholes and, in particular, to create a unified tax treatment of capital gains and coupon yields and to do it across all financial instruments. There is also a need for harmonizing the taxation of the yield on financial assets across borders and not to engage in granting competitive tax favors to attract foreign capital.

The fourth and most questionable type of financial reform includes in my view those that involve an outright transgression of traditional, well-established divisions of labor between the major institutions in the financial markets. It is difficult to see the welfare gains of letting banks sell insurance policies or letting insurance companies lend directly, or—to take another example—of letting brokerage houses or department stores become heavily involved in the evolution of the payments systems. There are no economies of scale involved in such transgressions, and the evolution towards comprehensive financial services through one institution may tend to bind the individual customer, whether corporate or private, more closely to a single source than is desirable.

This brings me, Mr. Chairman, to my basic conclusion, which is that innovation is a basically helpful and probably irrepressible element in our financial environment in the 1980s. It does entail some efficiency gains for the important financial sector, sometimes bought at the cost of a loss of monetary control. It also creates new opportunities for more constructive monetary policies than we have seen in the past, and effectively restrains policies that rely on direct intervention in financial markets. But financial innovation and reform need to be reviewed very carefully in the institutional context of each particular country, and in this sense the present conference has been most useful, though it may have focussed, as I argued initially, to an excessive extent on the somewhat discouraging experience in the United States. Financial innovations and reform become dangerous primarily when they happen within a constraining and outdated framework of regulation, or in a situation of unstable monetary policies. They may also have harmful effects if they take international capital liberalization to the point where the instability of the last few years is perpetuated. But on the whole financial innovation and reform create opportunities rather than problems for the monetary authorities as well as for the general public.

References

Akhtar, M.A. 1983. Financial Innovations and Their Implications for Monetary Policy: An International Perspective, *BIS Economic Papers* No. 9, Bank for International Settlements, Basel.

Vaubel, R. 1977. Free Currency Competition, *Weltwirtschaftliches Archiv*, Band 113, pp. 435–461.

Summing-Up: Three Issues of Financial Reform and Innovation

Maxwell J. Fry

This conference provided a potential opportunity for a comparative evaluation of financial innovation and monetary policy in Asia and the West. In fact, the discussion concentrated rather heavily on the U.S. experience. My concluding note therefore elaborates on three issues that perhaps could have been covered more fully from the viewpoint of the developing Asian countries represented at the conference.

In comparing the financial systems of most Asian developing countries with those of the developed countries, four structural differences should be borne in mend. First, financial markets are oligopolistic in most Asian developing countries, whereas they are generally competitive in the industrialized countries, particularly so in the United States. Second, although detailed regulations concerning financial transactions exist in all countries, they are generally enforced much more consistently and effectively in the developed than in the developing countries. Regulations that appear the same on paper may be quite different in practice. Third, disintermediation in the developed economies implies substitution from indirect to direct financial claims. In most developing countries it implies substitution from deposits into tangible assets used as inflation hedges. Finally, the driving force behind the recent financial innovations and reforms in the industrialized countries may well have been market forces. In the developing countries, however, the ideas of McKinnon (1973) and Shaw (1973) have had substantial impact, perhaps most obviously in the policy recommendations of the International Monetary Fund and the World Bank.

When similar changes such as monetary reform take place in many countries, a comparative analysis may be particularly fruitful in identifying common causes and effects. An examination of those countries that did not swim with the tide may be equally useful in understanding the phenomenon at hand. Most developing countries of Asia did not

implement the kind of financial reforms undertaken by many industrialized countries over the past decade. The main reasons appear to
be the oligopolistic structure of their financial markets, the concomitant political power of the large banks, and government manipulation
of the financial system to finance investment in priority sectors of the
economy.

Compared with changes that have taken place in the financial sectors
of most developed countries over the past decade, those that have taken
place in the Asian developing countries have been minor and hardly
constitute reform. For example, monetary reforms have been instigated
with considerable fanfare in the Philippines but, due largely to increasing concentration within the financial system, most observers feel:
"Plus ça change, plus c'est la même chose." Specifically, the interest
rate ceilings that were abolished under the interest rate reform appear
to have been replaced by a cartel agreement linke dto the Manila Reference Rate, which is supposed to be determined competitively in the
free market. It is not. Removal of many balance sheet restrictions has
produced increased concentration in the Philippine financial system
rather than the intended increased competition. Interest rate deregulation had unanticipated consequences in Thailand too because of its
oligopolistic banking system. Bearing this in mind, I turn to three specific issues of monetary reform and financial innovation that are particularly relevant to the Asian developing countries.

1. Monetary Reform, Financial Innovation, and Macroeconomic Stability

This section covers two points arising out of Milton Friedman's keynote address at the beginning of this conference. Friedman emphasized
the importance of inflation as the underlying cause of monetary reform
and financial innovation.

a. Disintermediation

Interest rate ceilings on deposit liabilities of financial intermediaries
were endemic in both the developing countries of Asia as well as in the
industrialized countries between the mid-1930s and the mid-1960s.
Unlike the industrialized countries, in particular Britain and the United
States, most Asian developing countries did not and still do not possess
active markets in direct financial claims. Accelerating worldwide inflation that started in the 1960s was accompanied in a predictable manner by rising nominal free-market interest rates. This produced disintermediation in the industrialized countries when deposit rate ceilings

became binding. Savings that formerly flowed through financial intermediaries were diverted to unrestricted markets in direct financial claims. This created considerable difficulties for the financial intermediaries that were drained of funds, but had little impact on aggregate saving and investment.

In the Asian developing countries, however, disintermediation involves in the main substitution of tangible assets for indirect financial claims. As inflation accelerates, real deposit rates fall and turn negative. Non-income-earning tangible assets become an increasingly attractive substitute for financial assets whose interest income no longer compensates for the erosion in purchasing power. The concomitant reduction in money demand (defining money broadly to include virtually all indirect financial claims) puts upward pressure on the price level and so compounds the inflationary pressures that caused disintermediation in the first place.

The accumulation of inflation hedges may or may not be recorded as investment in the national income accounts. To the extent that it is, the incremental output/capital ratio falls. To the extent that it is not, the volume of saving and investment declines. Both recorded effects have the same influence on the rate of economic growth. The rate of growth necessarily declines as a result of this kind of disintermediation.

Given the far more disruptive effects of disintermediation in the Asian developing countries than in the industrialized countries, I conclude that financial reforms or financial innovations that remove or circumvent interestate ceilings in these countries are bound to exert a strong stabilizing effect on their economies. In particular, such reforms and innovations reduce the growth-reducing and demand-increasing effects of inflation.

b. Interest on Reserves

The second point here springs from the considerable discussion that took place during the conference on the payment of interest on bank reserves. Robert Hall advocates interest payment on all bank reserves, while James Tobin is willing to leave the reserve requirement tax in place and advocates payment of interest only on excess reserves. Required reserves impose a tax on financial intermediation. This tax rises with both the level of nominal interest rates and the required reserve ratio and can be sizable. Half the Asian developing countries for which I have data imposed required reserve ratios against sight deposits at or above 10 percent in 1981. In the Philippines, the required reserve ratio against both sight and time deposits was 20 percent in that year, while in Taiwan it was 25 percent against sight deposits. In Korea, the required reserve ratio against sight deposits reached 35 percent in 1966. With a rate of interest on loans of 26 percent at that time and no interest paid on required reserves, the maximum average deposit rate that Korean banks could have paid was 16.9 percent, assuming deposits equalled the sum of loans plus required reserves, banking incurred no resource costs, and there were no government subsidies. In fact the Korean government did subsidize deposit rates of interest.

I find it difficult to accept that there could exist an optimal positive discriminatory tax on financial intermediation. It is even harder to see how this optimal tax could move exactly in step with nominal interest rates. A number of industrialized and developing countries do pay interest on banks' required reserves. In India, Korea, and the Philippines, for example, interest is or has been paid on required but not excess reserves precisely for the purpose of reducing the reserve requirement tax.

I know of no country in which interest is paid only on excess reserves or even on total reserves. The main reason for not paying interest on excess reserves is to keep the opportunity cost of holding such reserves as high as possible. Excess reserves are then held at minimal levels and the money supply multiplier is more predictable. This can be of particular importance in some of the Asian developing countries in which there are long lags in data collection and compilation. A lag of up to six months before money stock estimates are available is atypical but not unknown.

2. Intermediation between Savers and Investors

Early in the conference, Hall suggested that the only important reason for analyzing financial innovations is to examine their effects on monetary control. Friedman proposed that a second reason is to examine their effects on the transmission mechanism from money to income. A third crucial reason for analyzing monetary reforms and financial innovations springs from the financial sector's role in intermediating between savers and investors.

The Anglo-Saxon industrialized countries have deep and broad markets in direct financial claims. Continental Europe, Japan, and to the greatest extent most Asian developing countries do not. Particularly in the Asian developing countries, this means that a large proportion of investment is financed by bank credit. Monetary reform and financial innovation can have and have had enormous impact on the efficiency with which financial intermediaries allocate investible funds.

With fixed and binding deposit and loan rate ceilings, real institutional interest rates move inversely with the inflation rate. Over the period 1960–1983 the Asian developing countries experienced huge fluctuations in real rates of interest—far greater than the fluctuations in free-market rates in the United States that worry Donald Hester. Recent econometric analysis of 14 Asian developing countries reveals significant and positive correlations between on the one hand the investment rate, the incremental output/capital ratio, and hence the rate of economic growth, and on the other hand real institutional rates of interest (Fry 1981; 1984). As real institutional interest rates are pushed further below free-market equilibrium levels, the greater becomes the inefficiency with which investible funds are allocated. Therefore any monetary reforms or innovations that effectively free nominal interest rates on more financial assets and so prevent real interest rates from being pushed down well below free-market equilibrium levels tend to improve allocative efficiency.

The gang of four—Hong Kong, Korea, Singapore, and Taiwan—is considered jointly as an amazing success story in terms of high rates of economic growth. However, the cost of Singapore's real GNP growth rate of 8 percent (continuously compounded) a year over the period 1972–1983 was an investment rate that averaged 42 percent of GNP annually. Hong Kong achieved a growth rate of 8.2 percent a year over the same period with an average annual investment rate of 29 percent of GNP. Given the much greater extent of government involvement in the direction of investible funds through the financial markets of Singapore than of Hong Kong, I suggest that part of the explanation for this sizable difference lies in differences in the efficiency with which investible funds are allocated by the financial sectors in these two economies (Fry 1986a).

3. International Capital Mobility

Ralph Bryant suggested that the world is beyond the halfway mark on the scale between no international capital mobility and perfect international capital mobility. This view is challenged by Feldstein and Horioka (1980), Feldstein (1983), and Penati and Dooley (1984). Recent empirical work that I have conducted on 14 Asian developing countries [Fry 1986b] supports the position taken by Bryant, Caprio and Howard (1984), and Harberger (1980). I estimate a life-cycle saving function and a flexible accelerator investment function on pooled time series data for 1961–1983. The saving estimate is

$$Sn/Y = 0.375(\hat{g}) + 0.188(TT) + 0.041(d - \pi^e)$$
$$(7.174) \qquad (4.386) \qquad (3.182)$$

$$- 2.489(DEP) + 0.664(Sn/Y)_{t-1}, \qquad\qquad (1)$$
$$(-5.341) \qquad (18.148)$$

$$\bar{R}^2 = 0.913$$

where Sn/Y is the ratio of national saving to GNP (both expressed in current prices), g is the rate of growth in real GNP, TT is the rate of growth in income attributable to terms-of-trade changes, d is the continuously compounded nominal rate of interest on 12-month time deposits, π^e is the continuously compounded expected rate of inflation (estimated in money demand functions for each country using polynomial distributed lags on actual inflation rates), and DEP is the population dependency ratio (rescaled to equal 0 for zero population growth and 0.03 for 3 percent population growth). The instruments used in the first stage in addition to all the exogenous right-hand side variables are the rate of growth in the labor force, the rate of growth in agricultural output divided by the lagged ratio of agricultural output to GNP, the rate of growth in the industrialized countries' output, the rate of growth in exports, and the rate of growth in exports divided by the lagged ratio of exports to GNP.

Equation (1) indicates that the rate of growth in income exerts a significantly positive effect on the saving rate, as posited by the life-cycle model. Income growth attributable to terms-of-trade changes produces a smaller effect on the saving rate than income growth attributable to output changes, a finding consistent with terms-of-trade induced income changes being regarded as less permanent than output induced changes. The real deposit rate of interest also exerts a significantly positive effect on the saving rate. As expected the dependency ratio has a significantly negative effect on the saving rate.

The investment function is estimated over the period 1962–1983 rather than over the period 1961–1983 because terms-of-trade data start in 1960 and lagged terms-of-trade changes are included in the function

$$I/Y = 0.304(\hat{g}) - 0.108(TT) + 0.100(TT)_{t-1}$$
$$(5.469) \qquad (-2.205) \qquad (2.121)$$

$$+ 0.063(DCp/Y) - 0.200(rw) + 0.784(I/Y)_{t-1} \qquad (2)$$
$$(2.525) \qquad\qquad (-2.640) \quad (19.135)$$

$$\bar{R}^2 = 0.907$$

where I/Y is the ratio of domestic investment to GNP, DCp/Y is the ratio of private sector domestic credit to GNP, and rw is the real world rate of interest proxied by the real U.S. treasury bill yield.

Current changes in the terms of trade exert a negative effect on the investment ratio, while lagged changes produce a positive effect. A temporary improvement in the terms of trade that raises temporarily home goods' prices also raises the domestic real interest rate (Persson and Svensson 1985, p. 54). Temporarily higher home goods' prices raise the opportunity cost of using home goods to add to the capital stock, e.g. in the form of inventories. Thus the higher domestic interest rate this year lowers the optimal capital stock and investment declines. Next year the optimal capital stock rises again as the domestic interest rate declines to the world rate and investment increases. In terms of inventory investment, stocks are run down while prices are temporarily high and built up again later.

The private sector domestic credit ratio exerts a significantly positive influence on the investment rate. If the real deposit rate is held below its free-market equilibrium level, the effective (albeit unobservable) real loan rate would move in the opposite direction to the real deposit rate (Fry 1982). The lower the real deposit rate, the smaller the volume of saving and hence the higher the market-clearing loan rate of interest. In such case, the real deposit rate should have a positive impact on the investment rate. When the real deposit rate of interest is substituted for the domestic credit variables in equation (2), its coefficient is indeed positive and significant. In contrast the market-determined U.S. real interest rate has a significantly negative impact on the domestic investment rate. By deterring investment, higher real U.S. interest rates *improve* the balance of payments in this sample of LDCs.

I test the ability of this model to explain changes in the current account over the period 1962–1983 in two ways. The first involves subtracting the investment rates estimated by equation (2) from the saving rates estimated by equation (1). This gives the current account position estimated implicitly by the structural equations of this model. Regressing the actual current account $(Sn/Y - I/Y)$ on the estimated current account, both expressed as ratios to GNP, gives a correlation coefficient of 0.65. The second approach is to estimate the reduced-form equation from the model directly. This produces a correlation coefficient of 0.63. All significant coefficients have signs corresponding to those in the structural model. In particular, the coefficient of the world real interest rate is positive in the reduced-form current account estimate.

All the explanatory variables in the saving and investment functions reported above, with the exception of the growth rate, have been treated as exogenous. However, were the current account itself exogenous, e.g. determined solely by large politically motivated flows of foreign aid, other explanatory variables would have to adjust to equate national saving with domestic investment plus the current account surplus. Specifically, an exogenous increase in capital inflows could reduce the domestic interest rate, so reducing national saving and increasing domestic investment. Except for Singapore since 1978, however, domestic interest rates have not been determined competitively in this sample of countries. Unless some other right-hand side or instrumental variable used in equations (1) or (2) is in fact endogenous, an exogenous current account would ensure that this saving-investment model had virtually no explanatory power in predicting movements in the current account.

In fact the structural estimates of national saving and domestic investment rates presented here explain 65 percent of the variance in current account ratios for this sample of countries over the past two decades. Furthermore, domestic investment is affected negatively by a rise in the world real rate of interest. Hence these results challenge the view that world capital markets are highly imperfect. On the other hand they are consistent with the hypothesis that fluctuations in these current accounts have been endogenous during the regression period.

The evidence that saving and investment rates are highly correlated can be explained not by world capital market imperfections but rather by the facts that saving and investment rates are both determined by the rate of economic growth when international labor mobility is highly imperfect. With perfect international labor mobility, regions with high investment would attract labor inflows. In such case, high investment would not be associated with relatively high rates of growth in per capita incomes. When labor is immobile between nations, however, per capita incomes will grow faster in high-investment than in low-investment countries, at least in the medium run. High per capita income growth causes high saving rates according to the life-cycle saving model. Hence when labor is immobile, high investment rates cause high growth rates in per capita income that in turn cause high saving rates.

References

Caprio, Gerard, Jr. and David H. Howard. 1984. "Domestic Saving, Current Accounts, and International Capital Mobility." Washington, D.C.: Board of Governors of the Federal Reserve System, International Finance Discussion Paper No. 244, June.

Feldstein, Martin. 1983. "Domestic Saving and International Capital Movements in the Long Run and the Short Run," *European Economic Review*, 21(1/2), March/April, pp. 129–151.

Feldstein, Martin and Charles Horioka. 1980. "Domestic Saving and International Capital Flows," *Economic Journal*, 90(358), June, pp. 314–329.

Fry, Maxwell J. 1981. "Interest Rates in Asia: An Examination of Interest Rate Policies in Burma, India, Indonesia, Korea, Malaysia, Nepal, Pakistan, the Philippines, Singapore, Sri Lanka, Taiwan and Thailand." Honolulu: University of Hawaii, Department of Economics. Paper prepared for the Asian Department of the International Monetary Fund, mimeo, June.

Fry, Maxwell J. 1982. "Analysing Disequilibrium Interest-Rate Systems in Developing Countries," *World Development*, 10(12), December, pp. 1049–1057.

Fry, Maxwell J. 1984. "Financial Saving, Financial Intermediation and Economic Growth" in *Domestic Resource Mobilization through Financial Development, Volume II: Appendixes*. Manila: Asian Development Bank, Economics Office, pp. 21–53.

Fry, Maxwell J. 1986a. "Financial Structure, Monetary Policy, and Economic Growth in Hong Kong, Singapore, Taiwan, and South Korea, 1960–1981" in *Export-Oriented Development Strategies: The Success of Five Industrializing Countries* edited by Anne O. Krueger, Vittorio Corbo and Fernando Osso. Boulder, CO: Westview Press, forthcoming.

Fry, Maxwell J. 1986b. "Terms-of-Trade Dynamics in Asia: An Analysis of National Saving and Domestic Investment Responses to Terms-of-Trade Changes in 14 Asian LDCs," *Journal of International Money and Finance*, 5(1), March, pp. 57–73.

Harberger, Arnold C. 1980. "Vignettes on the World Capital Market," *American Economic Review*, 70(2), May, pp. 331–337.

McKinnon, Ronald I. 1973. *Money and Capital in Economic Development*. Washington, D.C.: Brookings Institution.

Penati, Alessandro and Michael Dooley. 1984. "Current Account Imbalances and Capital Formation in Industrial Countries, 1949–81," *International Monetary Fund Staff Papers*, 31(1), March, pp. 1–24.

Persson, Torsten and Lars O.E. Svensson. 1985. "Current Account Dynamics and the Terms of Trade: Harberger-Laursen-Metzler Two Generations Later," *Journal of Political Economy*, 93(1), February, pp. 43–65.

Shaw, Edward S. 1973. *Financial Deepening in Economic Development*. New York: Oxford Univeristy Press.

Program of the Conference

Institute for Monetary and Economic Studies
Bank of Japan

Second International Conference
"Financial Innovation and Monetary Policy: Asia and the West"

May 29–31, 1985
International Conference Hall, Keidanren Kaikan,
1–9–4 Otemachi, Chiyoda-ku, Tokyo, Japan

Aim of the Conference

For many countries, the last ten years were a decade of dramatic progress in innovation, deregulation, and reform of the financial system. These structural changes have momentous implications for the implementation and effectiveness of monetary policy.

While many factors have contributed to this development, several seem to have been of overriding importance. First, the increasing interdependence among economies and financial markets under the floating regime has been a strong impetus to structural changes in individual financial systems. Second, as a result of the world-wide acceleration of inflation and economic instability following the first oil shock, both the level and volatility of interest rates increased. This, in turn, created further incentives for innovation. Third, the growth of deficit finance has accelerated both the development of open securities markets and governmental dependence upon them. The growth of these markets has naturally stimulated competition among different types of financial institutions and has been an important factor of disintermediation. Finally, there has been rapid progress in the computer and telecommunication technologies which drastically reduced transaction costs in and between financial markets. These factors also helped to induce a wave of deregulation, which has further promoted structural changes of the financial system in the direction of market innovations.

Such changes are inevitably accompanied by shifts in the demand for various financial assets and in the transmission channels of monetary policy. These shifts have generated serious concern among central bankers about the effectiveness of their monetary policy instruments. Prominent among such concerns are the appropriateness and feasibility of monetary targeting due to the instability of money demand in the transition phase. It is a challenge for the theorists to provide the necessary tools and methods for analysing and solving these problems.

The Conference seeks to examine these phenomena which are present in many countries in differing proportions. Discussion by economists from academia, central banks, and various international organizations should contribute to a better understanding of the monetary system in the future— both in the national and international contexts—and to the effectiveness of monetary policy.

Wednesday, May 29

Session I (morning)

Chairman
Yoshio Suzuki (Bank of Japan)

Opening Address
Satoshi Sumita (Governor, Bank of Japan)

Keynote Speeches
Milton Friedman (Hoover Institution), "Monetary Policy in a Fiat World"
James Tobin (Yale University), "Financial Innovation and Deregulation in Perspective"

Session II (afternoon)

Backgrounds and Causes of Financial Innovation: An International Comparison

Chairmen
James L. Kichline (Federal Reserve System)
R. Lindsay Knight (Reserve Bank of New Zealand)

Papers:
Masashi Yumoto, Kinzo Shima, Hajime Koike, and Hiroo Taguchi (Bank of Japan), "Financial Innovation in Major Industrial Countries"
John G. Greenwood (G.T. Management Ltd., Hong Kong), "Financial Liberalization and Innovation in Seven East Asian Economies"

Comments:
  Thomas F. Cargill (University of Nevada, Reno)
  Warren D. McClam (Bank for International Settlements)
  Norbert Bub (Deutsche Bundesbank)

Free discussion

Thursday, May 30

Session III (morning)

The Process of Financial Deregulation, Monetary Reform, and the Financial System of the Future

Chairmen
  Frank E. Morris (Federal Reserve Bank of Boston)
  Si-Dam Kim (Bank of Korea)

Papers:
  Ralph C. Bryant (Brookings Institution), "International Financial Intermediation: Underlying Trends and Implications for Government Policies"
  James L. Pierce (University of California at Berkeley), "Financial Reform in the United States and the Financial System of the Future"

Comments:
  Jim S. Mallyon (Reserve Bank of Australia)
  Joseph Bisignano (Federal Reserve Bank of San Francisco)
  Shōichi Rōyama (Osaka University)
  Stephen Potter (Organisation for Economic Cooperation and Development)

Free discussion

Friday, May 31

Session IV (morning)

Implications for Monetary Policy

Chairmen
  Gordon G. Thiessen (Bank of Canada)
  Syahril Sabirin (Bank Indonesia)

Papers:
  Robert E. Hall (Stanford University), "Monetary Policy under Financial Innovation and Deregulation"

Donald D. Hester (University of Wisconsin), "Monetary Policy in an Evolutionary Disequilibrium"

Comments:
John S. Flemming (Bank of England)
John Wenninger (Federal Reserve Bank of New York)
Robert Raymond (Banque de France)
Teh Kok Peng (Monetary Authority of Singapore)

Free discussion

Session V (afternoon)

Summing-up and General Discussion

Chairmen
Sho C. Tsiang (Cornell University)
Hugh T. Patrick (Columbia University)

Summing-up:
Niels Thygesen (University of Copenhagen)
Maxwell J. Fry (University of California at Irvine)

Free discussion

Participants

Kazumi Asako
Yokohama National University

Jean-Pierre Beguelin
Swiss National Bank

Bruno Bianchi
Banca d'Italia

Joseph Bisignano
Federal Reserve Bank of San Francisco

Ralph C. Bryant
Brookings Institution

Norbert Bub
Deutsche Bundesbank

Albert E. Burger
Federal Reserve Bank of St. Louis

Thomas F. Cargill
University of Nevada, Reno

Andrew Crockett
International Monetary Fund

John S. Flemming
Bank of England

Milton Friedman
Hoover Institution

Maxwell J. Fry
University of California, Irvine

Siri Ganjarerndee
Bank of Thailand

John G. Greenwood
G. T. Management Ltd.

Robert E. Hall
Stanford University

He Qi
People's Bank of China

Donald D. Hester
University of Wisconsin

James L. Kichline
Division of Research and Statistics, Federal Reserve System

Si-Dam Kim
Bank of Korea

R. Lindsay Knight
Reserve Bank of New Zealand

Gerard Korteweg
De Nederlansche Bank

Marie-H. Lambert
Bank National de Belgique

Warren D. McClam
Bank for International Settlements

Jim S. Mallyon
Reserve Bank of Australia

Frank E. Morris
Federal Reserve Bank of Boston

Purita F. Neri
Central Bank of the Philippines

Jae-Yoon Park
Seoul National University

Hugh T. Patrick
Columbia University

Rinaldo Pecchioli
Organisation for Economic Cooperation and Development

James L. Pierce
University of California, Berkeley

Stephen J. Potter
Organisation for Economic Cooperation and Development

Robert Raymond
Banque de France

Shōichi Rōyama
Osaka University

Syahril Sabirin
Bank Indonesia

Karl A. Scheld
Federal Reserve Bank of Chicago

Andrew Sheng
Bank Negara Malaysia

Kinzo Shima
Bank of Japan

Yoshio Suzuki
Bank of Japan

Ryuichiro Tachi
Bank of Japan

Gordon G. Thiessen
Bank of Canada

Niels Thygesen
University of Copenhagen

James Tobin
Yale University

Sho C. Tsiang
Cornell University

Kazuo Ueda
Osaka University

Hirofumi Uzawa
University of Tokyo

John Wenninger
Federal Reserve Bank of New York

Tan Kong Yam
Monetary Authority of Singapore

Teh Kok Peng
Monetary Authority of Singapore

Hiroshi Yomo
Bank of Japan

Masashi Yumoto
Bank of Japan

Zhou Lin
People's Bank of China

Index